P9-CEZ-909

ASSESSMENT FOR EARLY INTERVENTION
Best Practices for Professionals

The Guilford School Practitioner Series

EDITORS

STEPHEN N. ELLIOTT, Ph.D.
University of Wisconsin—Madison

JOSEPH C. WITT, Ph.D.
Louisiana State University, Baton Rouge

ASSESSMENT FOR EARLY INTERVENTION
Best Practices for Professionals

Stephen J. Bagnato
John T. Neisworth

THE GUILFORD PRESS
London   New York

© 1991 The Guilford Press
A Division of Guilford Publications, Inc.
72 Spring Street, New York, NY 10012

All rights reserved

No part of this book may be reproduced, stored in a retrieval system, or transmitted, in any form or by any means, electronic, mechanical, photocopying, microfilming, recording or otherwise, without written permission from the Publisher.

Printed in the United States of America

This book is printed on acid-free paper

Last digit is print number: 9 8 7 6 5 4 3 2

Library of Congress Cataloging-in-Publication Data

Bagnato, Stephen J.
  Assessment for early intervention : best practices for
professionals / Stephen J. Bagnato, John T. Neisworth.
    p. cm. — (The Guilford school practitioner series)
  Includes bibliographical references.
  Includes index.
  ISBN 0-89862-359-6 (hardcover). — ISBN 0-89862-238-7 (pbk.)
  1. Developmental disabilities—Diagnosis. 2. Preschool children-
-Psychological testing. 3. Behavioral assessment of children.
4. Parent and children. I. Neisworth, John T. II. Title.
III. Series.
  [DNLM: 1. Child Development Disorders—diagnosis. 2. Child.
Preschool. 3. Family. WS 360.6 B147a]
  RJ135.B34 1991
DNLM/DLC   91-6540
for Library of Congress   CIP

Foreword

This book is overdue! From the Parents Association for Retarded Citizens (PARC) decision in the Eastern District Court (1971) and generalizations from that ruling enacted in the Education for all Handicapped Children Act (PL 94-142), it has become clear that we need more effective educational and psychological provisions for children who exhibit delays in development. Noting that, on their own, school leaders were slow to react to the special needs of infants, toddlers, and early school-age children, Congress mandated (through PL 99-457) additional attention to the educational needs of the youngest members of our society who seem to be starting life behind, or who are having difficulty keeping up with, most of their (preschool) peers. This mandate affects many psychologists.

Most child or school psychologists are unprepared to deal with referrals of very young children, partly because, until the advent of recent court and legislative action, school laws had prohibited enrollment of children with delayed development at the usual age in public schools. Today, we recognize that young handicapped children are in great need of formal educational programming.

That young children, i.e., those of preschool age, need special treatment by psychologists can be inferred from the characteristics of some of the most widely used psychological tests. Early editions of the Stanford Binet presented quite different tasks for children in the preschool years than for those eligible for and progressing in school. The current (4th) edition has some subtests for younger children exclusively. Weschler's first children's scale has different instructions and activities for 5- to 8-year-olds than for those aged 8 and above. Later he offered a preschool and primary school scale which had different items from those used in the children's scale, but even those items were not designed for infants or toddlers.

University programs in child and school psychology emphasize the instruments mentioned above far more than those that would be helpful in assessing the problems of, and developing interventions for, preschool-age children. Most supervised training of graduate students interested in youngsters emphasizes work with school-age children—generations of child/school psychologists have not been prepared to work with infants and toddlers and only marginally prepared for working with children four and five years of age. Not only have psychologists been poorly prepared to treat young children, but there has been a dearth of texts to assist them. The authors offer this book as a remedy to fill that gap.

Drs. Bagnato and Neisworth have collaborated since the mid-1970s on programs to meet the needs of at-risk infants and preschool-age children. Much of this book is based on their clinical and research experiences with children and their parents in family settings and in clinics and agencies serving very young children with delayed development. In these settings the authors have focused not only on the children but also on their surroundings and not just on diagnosis or classification but on interventions to improve the quality of their lives.

Assessment for Early Intervention is based on principles of child development and psychological assessment. Those who read the book, and who translate the words to action, will need a strong background in the various aspects of developmental psychology for the young. Also, they will need to be skilled in working with individuals from different lay and professional backgrounds, and be able to listen carefully to the child and significant persons in the environment, to observe obvious and subtle events, and to interact effectively in groups of people concerned about the child in question. The authors present principles and, with many specific suggestions, make them meaningful. Guidepoints are presented several times in each chapter as advanced organizers and each chapter concludes with suggested activities to improve practice. Tables listing recommended instruments appear in several places as do "checkpoints" for good practice.

The authors believe a "completed assessment requires several sessions, occurs across multiple settings, uses the judgments of several people, and focuses on competencies to meet current and expected environmental demands" (p. 8). In most instances, parts of the assessment will be performed by individuals from more than one professional discipline and will include judgments by parents. The authors illustrate how assessments, which include more than data from standardized tests, can be ecologically and socially valid, have immediate treatment utility, and fit into Individual Family Service Plans (required by PL 99-457).

The authors, believing that other books focus sufficiently on psychometric properties of standardized tests, direct the reader to those features of assessment that are neglected, i.e., developmental/curriculum-based assessment and involvement of parents and/or other adults who figure prominently in the life of the child in question. The authors put great emphasis on obtaining information from multiple sources, instruments, and settings; actively involving parents (and others) in the process; and in developing plans of action. Many of the suggestions offered, particularly those involving establishing relationships, staging assessments, and parent interactions, will be helpful to psychologists and others dealing even with older children.

Assessment of young children is a slow process—frequently more time-consuming than for older children. To be effective it requires a combination of norm, curriculum, and judgment-based scales including observations (i.e., use of scales) in several situations to generate a broad useful profile of the child to guide selection of program objectives and interventions.

This book will be helpful to all psychologists working with, or preparing to work with, very young children. Early attention to disabling conditions is essential. Waiting until children are of school age is often too late for either prevention of further damage or for remediation of that which has occurred. Although the questions at the end of each chapter appear to be developed for professionals already in practice, I believe this book will have a wide audience in graduate students concerned with the development of young children and their education.

JOSEPH L. FRENCH
Professor of Educational Psychology and
  Special Education
Chairman, Program in School Psychology
The Pennsylvania State University

About the Authors

STEPHEN J. BAGNATO, Ed.D., N.C.S.P., is a developmental school psychologist and Assistant Professor of Pediatrics and School Psychology at the University of Pittsburgh School of Medicine. He is also Coordinator of the Toddler/Preschool Program of the Child Development Unit, Children's Hospital of Pittsburgh and Co-Principal Investigator of Developmental Support for Medically Handicapped Children and Families, a federally funded model early intervention demonstration project. Honored nationally for his applied brain injury research, Dr. Bagnato has published over 50 clinical research studies in early intervention, school psychology, and developmental disabilities, a unique and practical team decision-making system, *System to Plan Early Childhood Services (SPECS)*, and co-authored five books including *Linking Developmental Assessment and Early Intervention: Curriculum-based Prescriptions* and *The Young Exceptional Child: Early Development and Education*. Dr. Bagnato is an editorial board member of *The School Psychology Review, The Journal of Psychoeducataional Assessment*, and *Topics in Early Childhood Education*, and is a member of the School Psychology, Pediatric Psychology, Clinical Child, and Clinical Neuropsychology subdivisions of the American Psychological Association, and was recently elected as a Distinguished Fellow of APA in Division 16.

JOHN T. NEISWORTH, Ph.D., is Professor and Senior Graduate Faculty Member and Director of the Early Childhood Special Education, Division of Educational and School Psychology and Special Education, at The Pennsylvania State University. He is co-author of the well-regarded *HICOMP Preschool Curriculum*, the team-decision-making battery, *System to Plan Early Childhood Service (SPECS)*, and twelve textbooks in special education, including *Linking Developmental Assessment and Early Intervention: Curriculum-based Prescriptions, The Young Exceptional Child*, and *The Exceptional Child: A Functional Approach*. Dr. Neisworth is a founding co-editor of the journal *Topics in Early Childhood Special Education* and an editorial board member of *The Journal for Early Intervention, Child and Family Behavior Therapy, Child Care Quarterly*, and *Journal of Psychoeducational Assessment*, and is currently Director of the federally funded Empirical Preschool Teacher Education Program at Penn State, designed to provide graduate training and certification in Special Education.

Contents

Introduction

Psychologists are becoming pivotal members of early intervention teams. This book is dedicated to psychologists who work in preschool settings. It builds upon and expands their expertise to focus on handicapped infants, preschoolers, and families. Their skills in assessment, consultation, direct intervention, program evaluation, and research can increase the quality of early intervention services. But the beliefs and practices of traditionally trained psychologists, particularly school psychologists, do not align with the central mandate of Public Law 99-457—expanding the eligibility requirements for earlier developmental and family support services. This aim requires a different outlook and different ways of assessing and making decisions about young children with special needs. Applying school-aged perspectives and practices with preschool children is ineffective, unethical, and legally questionable. The mission of *Assessment for Early Intervention* is the planning and delivery of family-centered early childhood developmental intervention.

Assessment for early intervention is not a test-based process. *Early childhood assessment is a flexible, collaborative process in which teams of parents and professionals formatively revise their collective judgments and decisions about the changing developmental, educational, mental health, and medical needs of young children and their families.*

Assessment for Early Intervention is a book about the competencies of the psychologist as assessor and decision-maker, not about the adequacies or inadequacies of various assessment measures. In essence, the competent psychologist is a competent assessment instrument.

As you read this guidebook, be aware of the following ten prominent themes. Assessment for early intervention:

- is team-based
- includes parents as partners
- focuses on family needs
- emphasizes collaborative decision-making
- is multidimensional
- relies on convergent information
- stresses social validity
- employs informal and formal methods equally
- is ecological, and, most importantly
- has treatment validity—it prescribes and evaluates early intervention.

Rather than be an obstacle to children and families who need early intervention services, the contemporary psychologist can be one of the strongest and most effective professionals in the exciting field of early intervention.

1

What Is Unique about Preschool Psychology?

ISSUES IN PRACTICE

- How do preschool and school-age psychological services differ?
- Is intelligence testing useful with preschoolers?
- Is the child or family the focus of early intervention sevices?
- What makes "teamwork" critical to early intervention?
- Can we predict and measure a child's developmental progress?

Psychologists are challenged to be creative in providing services to young developmentally disabled children and their families. Public Law 99-457 presents these challenges as "new directions" in service delivery (Meisels & Shonkoff, 1990). All early intervention disciplines are redefining and refocusing their practices to align them with the new mandates. Psychologists are pivotal members of early intervention teams and should be especially current in their outlook and ways of offering services. Movement toward subspecialization in psychology emphasizes the importance of new roles for psychologists in early intervention. Trends toward subspecialization in "applied developmental psychology" (Wertlieb, 1979) and "developmental school psychology" (Bagnato, Neisworth, Paget, & Kovaleski, 1987) are especially noteworthy.

**TABLE 1.1. NASP Early Intervention
Position Statement (1987)**

1. Target development needs
2. Assess and treat multidomains
3. Promote valid early identification
4. Foster flexible "team" procedures
5. Stress parent–child approaches
6. Ensure noncategorical service delivery
7. Establish broad intervention options
8. Support specialty credentials (DSP)
9. Guide interagency collaboration
10. Advocate government funding

Applied developmental psychology has been described as a hybrid discipline that includes the examination of the child's developmental competencies in social, school, and family contexts, assuming a much more ecological view of child development. The applied developmental psychologist integrates and applies knowledge from developmental, medical, and mental health fields.

A subspecialty with a similar applied developmental emphasis is *developmental school psychology,* defined as

> that early childhood subspecialty that emphasizes team decision-making, curriculum-based assessment and goal-planning, ecological interventions, family-centered strategies, and staff consultation in diverse settings for infants, preschoolers, and families with special needs. (Bagnato, Neisworth, Paget, & Kovaleski, 1987, p. 2)

The two national school psychology organizations (National Association of School Psychologists [NASP] and American Psychological Association [APA]—Division 16) have been the most proactive psychology subspecialties in creating guidelines for personnel preparation and the provision of early intervention services. The NASP Early Intervention Position Statement (Schakel, 1987) and Early Childhood Assessment Position Statement (Bracken, Bagnato, & Barnett, 1990) provide the clearest definitions of "best practices." Tables 1.1 and 1.2 summarize these early intervention practices. These professional statements emphasize a developmental "whole-child" perspective, a family-centered approach, the flexible use of teams in making decisions, noncategorical service delivery, broader intervention options, curriculum-based assessment procedures, and specialized credentialing for early intervention specialists.

The Carolina Institute on Infant Personnel Preparation (Bailey & Simeonsson, 1988a), through surveys and interdisciplinary conferences, has offered guidelines for psychologists and others working with young children and families. The primary mission of psychology is viewed as

TABLE 1.2. PL 99-457: Implications for Assessment

- Assessment tools should assist in the decision-making of early educators (i.e., have treatment utility).
- Measures should have documented reliability and validity for the purposes intended.
- Assessment information must come from more than a single instrument and occasion. Information should come from multiple sources, instruments, and settings.
- Parents must be actively involved in the assessment of their children.
- The focus should be on functional rather than categorical (diagnostic) assessment. Traditional diagnostic classification at the preschool level is usually premature and indefensible.
- Assessment should examine the whole child and not just a fragment of development.
- Team evaluation, involving the parent, should be the cornerstone for program planning based on multidisciplinary assessment.
- The child's program plan and evaluation should include a specification of the extent or intensity of prescribed special services.
- Assessment should provide information to assist in developing the IFSP; the child's plan must be seen in the context of the family.

"deriving a comprehensive picture of child and family functioning and to identify, implement, and evaluate interventions" (Bailey & Simeonsson, 1988a). Major roles of the psychologist who works with preschoolers include

- assessing behavioral characteristics
- identifying the coping strategies and resources of families
- planning and providing psychological and developmental interventions
- coordinating interdisciplinary efforts
- collaborating with families and professionals
- case management
- increasing the precision of diagnostic criteria in terms of need for services
- prevention
- evaluating intervention effectiveness

No matter what the subspecialty, psychology within early intervention must assume a broader developmental and ecological view of the child, use more functional team assessment and treatment approaches, and focus services on the child in the family context. Note that the job descriptions of the early intervention psychologist meet the mandates and spirit of PL 99-457 (see Table 1.2). As a way to present best practices in assessment for early intervention, this chapter describes the orientation and responsibilities of the "developmental school psychologist."

PROFESSIONAL ORIENTATION

The developmental school psychologist accepts and practices six approaches or viewpoints that are consistent with contemporary early intervention services.

Interdisciplinary Orientation

Teamwork is critical within early intervention. The complexity of the young child's needs and the central influence of family factors on development demand the collaboration of multiple professionals with the parents. An interdisciplinary approach is required at a minimum; a transdisciplinary approach, however, may be most effective wherein team members share roles and responsibilities in a flexible manner. With young children, medical needs often complicate assessment and program planning. Valuable competencies are needed in blending the views of educational, medical, and mental health professionals and the parents. Skills in team dynamics and consensus-building are needed to enable the coordination of team decision-making among pediatricians; teachers; physical, occupational, and speech/language therapists; social workers; and related personnel. The developmental school psychologist guides teamwork so that the family has a central role and an equitable voice in decision-making.

Developmental–Behavioral Perspective

Strict and traditional psychometric views and approaches are inappropriate with young children and their families. Rather, a comprehensive developmental perspective should be employed that allows the planning of sequential instructional objectives and the monitoring of progress and program impact. Further, child status must be appraised in several developmental and behavioral domains. With young children, competencies in play and socialization may be much more relevant and important than the traditional preoccupation with cognitive skills.

Developmental principles provide the goals and content for instruction and therapy while behavioral methods offer the strategies for building and maintaining those competencies. This combined developmental–behavioral outlook has practical implications for issues including curriculum-based assessment and progress evaluation, program accountability, classroom grouping patterns, structured versus play-based learning, parent–child interaction, and readiness to use response-contingent toys and other electromechanical and computer-based learning technologies.

GUIDEPOINTS

- Rely on an interdisciplinary team approach for assessment and intervention.
- Emphasize assessment of social, communication, and play skills rather than "intelligence."
- Link assessment to intervention using adaptive, curriculum-based methods.

Functional, Handicap-Sensitive Approach

Professionals are steadily moving toward assessment of childrens' functioning and away from a categorical approach to diagnosing and classifying children. A child's special needs and eligibility for services are appraised in terms of stage of developmental competence and level of functional ability or disability. The traditional categories of mental (e.g., mental retardation), neuropsychological (e.g., autism), and physical disabilities (e.g., cerebral palsy; Down syndrome) have little relevance and few practical implications for planning instruction and therapy. In contrast, functional assessment enables professionals and parents to talk on common terms and to convert estimates of severity of disability into estimates of the scope and intensity of services needed (see Chapter 2). Similarly, this functional developmental perspective allows professionals to work with children in a longitudinal manner throughout the early childhood period of birth to 8 years whether disability is mild or severe. Professionals attempt to identify the child's strengths and employ relevant adaptive strategies, such as augmentative communication systems, computer aids, and electromechanical toys, that will offer compensatory ways for a child to explore and learn from the environment. Linking assessment to intervention is the primary outcome of this perspective, best exemplified by curriculum-based and judgment-based methods. Both of these methods foster team decision-making and identify intervention goals and options.

Family Focus

The child is not the exclusive focus for assessment and intervention. Instead, services are family-centered with the parents cooperating as partners in the process of designing an Individualized Family Service Plan (IFSP). The IFSP includes the team's appraisal of and goals for the child as well as the family's "self-inventory" of their own strengths and service needs for supporting their special child. Working to understand and improve the parent–child interaction is central and requires a combination of applied behavior and family systems techniques to promote change.

Treatment-Based Practices

Early intervention specialists understand that they must be accountable for their work with children and families. The effectiveness of instruction and therapy must be monitored and documented. Thus, the efforts of the psychologist and all team members are focused on planning curricular goals and using methods that work. Within early intervention, all services have a developmental focus: assessment, curriculum goal-planning, and Individualized Educational Plan (IEP)/IFSP content. Child progress and program evaluation are *linked* by this common developmental foundation. Assessment and instruction cover the same multiple domains of functioning (e.g., cognitive, language, motor, social, self-care, behavioral) for diagnosis, identification of skills and deficits, and evaluation of curricular gains. Carrying out curriculum-based assessments over time is the most sensitive method for evaluating child progress and program impact. In this way, assessment never loses its treatment-based focus. *The purpose of assessment is to guide and gauge intervention.* This is assessment for instruction and therapy—assessment *for* early intervention.

Ecological Perspective

Professionals in early childhood recognize the crucial role of the child's social and physical context. Observations, ratings, direct testing, as well as interventions must be conducted across people and settings. Multiple assessment instruments, occasions, and settings provide a solid basis for describing child status. Having parents and others provide their estimates of child performance adds social validity to the assessment process and findings. Is a child's language "improved" when a test says it is or when parents and others indicate it is improved? Both assessments are valuable and contribute to the "truth."

Throughout the United States, different agencies are responsible for infant and preschool services. Some regular early childhood programs and settings may emphasize socialization experiences, self-concept development, and free play discovery learning; in contrast, programs operated by public school special education units and mental health/mental retardation agencies often emphasize structured classroom settings, applied behavior analysis, and precision teaching to promote skill development. Each program or approach should match the child's developmental/learning characteristics and needs. The psychologist must be aware of available services or other options and help select the best circumstance for the child and family.

GUIDEPOINTS

- Use a functional, noncategorical framework to determine special needs and program eligibility.
- Focus on the family as the client.
- Monitor child progress longitudinally.
- Broadly consider the impact of child/family's social and physical environment at home and in preschool.

ROLES AND RESPONSIBILITIES

The developmental school psychologist has nine major roles as described in this section. Psychologists working in early intervention settings have a broader outlook on development, service delivery, and collaboration with parents and other professionals. The importance of the family, assessment/curriculum linkage, accountability, and the use of handicap-adaptations, alternative services, and team decision-making are prominent considerations that must be translated into practice.

Family Consultant

It is clear that early intervention is most effective when parents are partners in the program, both giving and receiving information and help. Psychologists and other mental health specialists must view consultation with the parent and family members as an essential responsibility. Knowing that the entire family environment (i.e., physical and social) or family *system* influences the child's adjustment and development, the psychologist can work with family members regularly. Also, "family" must be viewed in broad terms to include foster families, extended families, and friends who may have responsibilities and concerns for the child.

Through consultation, the psychologist can help the family to understand the services and methods of the early intervention program, foster trust, show the family that collaboration is welcome and crucial for success, and ensure that the entire team is working toward the same goals for the child. Supportive counseling techniques are used to help the family understand and adjust to their child's disabilities. Interactive therapy sessions with the child and parent in the home or preschool can use modeling strategies and simulations to help the parent read and respond to the child's cues. Parents can learn effective management techniques and promote the maintenance of learning from preschool to home.

Parents can provide accurate and valuable information about their child's strengths and needs as well as their own needs. The IFSP relies on the family to set the priorities for themselves and their child with the expert collaboration and advice of professionals. Services and goals must be tailored to these family priorities. The psychologist helps the parent clarify objectives and feelings so that the program's efforts and resources can be directed most effectively.

Adaptive Assessment Specialist

As emphasized previously, young children, especially those with neurodevelopmental disabilities, cannot be accurately assessed using conventional cognitive and conceptual measures. In fact, traditional intellectual assessment is arguably the least relevant assessment with special infants and preschoolers; observations and appraisals of social competence, self-regulation, communication, and symbolic play are more sensitive indicators of learning and more functional targets for instruction and therapy. Psychologists in preschool settings are particularly skilled in the assessment of children with complex affective, behavioral, sensory, communication, and neuromotor dysfunctions. They recognize that such assessments must be flexible and include a battery of informal as well as formal scales and procedures. Accommodations for sensory and neuromotor deficits are made, including the use of switch toys, textured objects, light wands, and alternate communication aids. *A completed assessment requires several sessions, occurs across multiple settings, uses the judgments of several people, and focuses on competencies to meet current and expected environmental demands* (see Chapters 4 and 6). Psychologists must learn to be good playmates, astute observers of preschool behavior, persistent "detectives," and comfortable with ambiguity; they must be willing to leave behind the security of their Binet kits, Wechsler scales, and time-worn biases. Early childhood assessment requires a broad outlook, flexible procedures, familiarity with child development, and a spontaneous and natural style of interaction.

Program Evaluator

Ongoing or *formative* evaluation enables the staff to document gains and to determine effective and ineffective program elements. Ongoing curriculum-based assessment and behavior analysis of instruction allow the team to be accountable. The psychologist's expertise in research methodology is important to the accountability effort—the documentation of change required on the IEP/IFSP. Numerous benefits flow from program evaluation: quality control, staff feedback and morale, parent satisfaction, support for continued funding, and research evidence for the field. Fortunately, program evaluation need not be an arduous, time-consuming task. Procedures and instruments used for child assessment can also serve as a basis for program evaluation (see Chapter 10).

Intervention Consultant

Consultation with instructional and therapeutic staff is perhaps the most visible way the preschool psychologist can help the program. Behavioral consultation takes the form of organized "brain-storming" in which problems are identified and solutions are suggested. Through direct observation, interviews, and trial solutions in the preschool setting, the psychologist can help professionals and aides develop strategies that work. Examples include "good behavior" games, activity-imbedded reinforcement, and peer-pairing versus larger groupings; computers to increase motivation and the pace of learning; planned ignoring and differential reinforcement of alternative behavior to decrease inappropriate behaviors; use of sound and visual signals (e.g., timers and recorded special music) for starting and stopping events to ease activity transitions; and encouraging friendships between handicapped and nonhandicapped peers.

GUIDEPOINTS

- Work with the parent to foster trust and model collaborative behavior.
- Guide team decision-making.
- Adapt assessment to the child's special needs.
- Stress the importance of program accountability.
- Help the team "brain-storm" about behavior management and instruction.

Team Assessment Coordinator

The complexity of the special needs of young handicapped children necessitates the contributions of multiple professionals and the family. Team appraisals and collaborative decision-making are fundamentals for effective early intervention. Serial assessments based on the program's curriculum are shared among several team members (e.g., parent and professionals in early education, physical and occupational therapy, speech/language therapy, social work, and psychology) who survey several developmental and behavioral domains. Within early intervention, the psychologist's role must not be restricted to individual assessment. Indeed, as an assessment specialist with expertise in group processes, the psychologist can be most effective as the coordinator of team appraisals and decision-making. The psychologist can help the team select a core developmental curriculum, choose complementary assessment measures, design a workable progress evaluation format, and guide meetings and collaborative decision-making (see Chapter 2).

Clinical Research Coordinator

Psychologists can help design and conduct research that answers important practical questions. Single-case or small group studies instead of large group research should be the emphasis in early intervention. Multiple baseline, reversal, and changing criterion designs are especially applicable for many questions posed. Typical concerns in preschool programs include the effectiveness of various instructional strategies, documenting the efficacy of Ritalin trials for 5-year-old children with Attention-Deficit Hyperactivity Disorder (ADHD), comparisons between peer-paring and small group instruction for children with language disorders, and measuring the social interactions of young exceptional children. Larger administrative questions may concern the efficiency and participation of team members during child study team meetings and the overall progress of children with various disabilities enrolled in the early intervention program.

Systems Facilitator

Early intervention does not involve just the public schools. Special efforts must be devoted to understanding and promoting relations among staff working for different agencies with varying missions. The psychologist can help the several agencies to maintain a mutual focus on the child and family and to smooth transitions between one agency's program and another. Interagency collaboration is needed at each transition point; for example, from an infant intervention program operated by Mental Health (e.g., Association for Retarded Children) to a specialized public school preschool program to a regular kindergarten program in a different elementary school. Time spent ensuring that preschool and school-age child study teams are "talking the same language" is time well spent.

Inservice Educator

Continuing professional development must be one of the central administrative concerns of any early intervention program. The diverse levels of training of staff and aides and the credentialing mandates of the new law require inservice education and training on a regular basis. The psychologist can be instrumental in organizing inservice events that foster continuing professional development and specialty credentialing. Inservice training should stress such areas as infant and preschool assessment, use of curricula for monitoring child progress, typical and atypical child development, family counseling, conferencing with parents, behavior management, and medical issues.

Primary Prevention Advocate

The developmental school psychologist should advocate primary prevention; this means helping a program and community foster the mental and physical health of children and families. Examples include working with physicians and other agencies and disciplines to organize community health fairs and developmental screening efforts, conducting public service radio and TV spots on child development issues, and organizing parent support groups.

GUIDEPOINTS

- Demonstrate the immediate practical value of clinical research to the program.
- Promote interagency collaboration.
- Stress the team's continuing professional development.
- Spearhead community efforts that prevent child/family problems.

IMPLICATIONS OF ASSESSMENT FOR EARLY INTERVENTION

PL 99-457 has redefined the scope and process of assessment for early intervention. The following seven principles summarize the hallmarks of assessment for early intervention:

1. *Assessment in early intervention must be interdisciplinary.* Use several team members and the parents to share assessment duties and to reach collaborative decisions about the child's needs.

2. *Assessment must be ecological and socially valid.* Describe how the child behaves with different people, settings, and materials at home and at school to increase the comprehensiveness and validity of assessment.

3. *Parent's judgments are essential for comprehensive early childhood assessment.* Use parent's ratings to gather information about typical moods and behavior patterns, and to challenge other limited testing results.

4. *Family "self-assessment" is the basis for IFSP development.* Help parents identify their needs and resources to improve the child's "life space."

5. *Assessment must be noncategorical and have immediate treatment utility.* Appraise the child's skills on a curriculum sequence that prescribes goals for individual instruction and therapy across several functional areas; assess for instruction.

6. *Assessment must be handicap-sensitive.* Modify assessment procedures to accommodate the child's sensory and response capabilities.

7. *Assessment, intervention, and evaluation are linked and inseparable activities.* Use a developmental approach to ensure that the competencies assessed, taught, and monitored over time are similar.

SUGGESTED READINGS

Bagnato, S. J., Neisworth, J. T., Paget, K. D., & Kovaleski, J. (1987). The developmental school psychologist: Professional profile of an emerging early childhood specialist. *Topics in Early Childhood Special Education, 7*(3), 75–89.

Barnett, D. W. (1986). School psychology in preschool settings: A review of training and practice issues. *Professional Psychology, Research and Practices, 17*(1), 58–64.

Mowder, B. A., Widerstrom, A. H., & Sandall, S. (1989). School psychologists serving at-risk and handicapped infants, toddlers, and their families. *Professional School Psychology, 4*(3), 159–171.

Wertlieb, D. (1979, June). Applied developmental psychology: New directions? *APA Monitor,* 10–14.

Widerstrom, A. H., Mowder, B. A., & Willis, W. G. (1989). The school psychologist's role in the early childhood special education program. *Journal of Early Intervention, 13*(3), 239–248.

BEST PRACTICE SUMMARY CHECKLIST

Chapter 1

What Is Unique about Preschool Psychology?

[ ] 1. Persuade your supervisor at the next department meeting to begin an examination of the differences between psychological services in school versus early childhood settings and review the NASP Position Statements on Early Intervention Services and Early Childhood Assessment.

[ ] 2. Follow this meeting with a series of planning and work sessions devoted to establishing professional guidelines in your setting for the following issues: parent involvement, eligibility determination, teaming, serial developmental assessments, curriculum linkages, increased time for staff consultation, direct intervention, progress evaluation procedures, and applied research.

[ ] 3. Organize a monthly program of inservice activities regarding early intervention practices that include other educational and therapy staff and "take home" applied work assignments.

[ ] 4. Develop a personal liaison network with other community professionals who provide nonschool-based services to preschoolers and families: pediatricians, MH/MR base service units, children and youth services, hospitals, private schools (e.g., Easter Seals, pediatric rehabilitation centers).

[ ] 5. Collaborate with other community professionals to create a resource guide that lists and details agencies and their contacts who provide specialized services to infants, preschoolers, and families.

[ ] 6. Cooperate with school-based child study teams to develop a flexible set of procedures to smoothly transition preschool and kindergarten age children who need specialized or mainstreamed services.

[ ] 7. Join the several interdisciplinary professional organizations that focus on early intervention practices and receive the following major journals:

> Division for Early Childhood: *Journal of Early Intervention;*
> NASP/APA Preschool Interests Subgroup: *Preschool Interests;*
> National Association for the Education of Young Children;
> *Young Children, Topics in Early Childhood Special Education, Infants and Young Children,* and *Early Education and Development.*

2

How Can Teamwork Be Effective?

ISSUES IN PRACTICE

- Why are multidisciplinary teams not recommended in early intervention?
- What is "collaborative goal-setting"?
- Does clinical judgment have a valid role in child assessment?
- Can program or intervention "intensity" be measured?
- How can parent and professional assessment of children be equated?

Working as a team has become synonymous with early intervention. Professionals recognize that serving young handicapped children and families is a complex venture that demands a multispecialist approach. No one professional or discipline "owns" a developmental domain or disorder. Development is interactive and so is effective early intervention. Neuromotor dysfunctions, for example, distort progress in several interrelated developmental domains: play, motor, socialization, self-care. The several team members (e.g., physical therapist, communication specialist, early educator, psychologist) must coordinate their goals and methods to assess and promote progress for children with neuromotor impairments. Public Law 99-457 recognizes the need for cross-disciplinary work and so mandates a multidimensional and multidisciplinary approach to evaluation and intervention. It targets both broad and narrow needs in physical, cognitive, speech/language, psychosocial, and self-help domains for the child. The law also emphasizes the family's needs for information, financial resources, help in coping with stress, and the need for services matched to child and family circumstances. The law specifies that the professionals involved be available for assessment and intervention; these include educators, language specialists, physical and occupational therapists, vision and hearing specialists, psychologists, social workers, physicians, nurses, and nutritionists. The parent, however, is a *crucial* member of the team who provides and gains information to help the child thrive. In short, PL 99-457 institutionalizes the team approach.

The federal initiative will have a special impact upon the provision of psychological services to young at-risk and handicapped children. (See Chapter 1 for a discussion regarding the broader, more creative roles and responsibilities of the applied developmental psychologist.) For the school psychologist, the National Association of School Psychologists (NASP) Position Statement (Schakel, 1987) provides an important guideline about effective team procedures; that is, those procedures that "encourage the use of flexible team assessment approaches which take into account the unique attributes and variability of young children and the influence of home and family factors on their development" (p. 5).

This chapter offers guidelines on how to implement a flexible and effective team approach. The discussion begins with a review of the prevalent models of team functioning and the roles of various professionals on the team, and then illustrates how a team approach can be organized and "synchronized" through the System to Plan Early Childhood Services (SPECS) (Bagnato & Neisworth, 1990a,b).

GUIDEPOINTS

- Use comprehensive assessment to capture the scope and interrelatedness of developmental domains.
- Include family appraisal to augment child assessment and to meet federal mandates.
- Collaborate with allied professionals to plan and deliver the multiple and related services needed for early intervention.

THREE TEAM MODELS

The very existence of teaming as a service technique underscores that a child's problems are the result of complex biological and environmental interactions and that collaboration among specialists is necessary. "Teamwork," however, is a buzzword often used to give the illusion of collaboration in the absence of any team identity or coordinated efforts. Teams evolve their own styles based upon shared purposes, aims, and methods; yet, the social chemistry between every person on the team is the true measure of team identity or "groupness." To be effective as a team, team specialists must trust one another, respect each other's legitimate roles and expertise, be ready to freely share judgments in a problem-solving process, allow others to assume and share part of their typical role responsibilities, and accept structuring from a permanent or rotating team coordinator. Numerous resources have explored the team concept in early intervention (Fewell, 1983; Golin & Duncanis, 1981; Holm & McCartin, 1978; Woodruff & McGonigel, 1988). Three major forms of team functioning are described in the literature; each form of teaming affects the manner and style in which psychological services are delivered.

Multidisciplinary Model

The most widely used but, frankly, inadequate model is the multidisciplinary team (MDT). MDTs use several professionals who emphasize their own disciplinary perspectives in assessing particular developmental domains in an independent manner. Collaboration between the several specialists is infrequent. Thus, the diagnostic picture of child and family functioning that emerges is most often fragmented and often faulty. The MDT model does not promote a "whole-child," interactive view. The most tangible evidence of this fragmentation is the diagnostic report that is completed at the end of an MDT evaluation. This report is usually an unintegrated collection of the separate reports of each professional, merely stapled together. The recommendations offered are typically redundant, contain confusing goals and directives for the parent, and worse, may actually be conflicting. For the program, MDT evaluations perpetuate interventions that are discipline-specific and unorchestrated. One is reminded of the parable about the several blind men who each examined a different part of an elephant and then provided very different descriptions of the beast. Actually, the MDT model masquerades as a team approach and thus is not recommended.

Interdisciplinary Model

Interdisciplinary teams (IDT) share unifying views and practices. IDTs assume a whole-child perspective and stress the integral involvement of parents as partners on the team by a process of collaborative goal-setting. They enable team members and parents to integrate their assessment/intervention efforts by organizing services around functional skills or developmental domains (e.g., cognitive, language, perceptual/fine motor, social–emotional, gross motor, self-care) rather than by the discipline that provides those services. Curriculum-based systems are most often used by IDTs as common tools to focus services and to link assessment, program goal-planning, and progress evaluation (Bagnato & Murphy, 1989). While IDTs rarely "release" role responsibilities, team members place a high premium on frequent consultation so that a unified view about child/family needs is created. Intervention goals are designed so that common goals are integrated into each discipline's therapy. For example, language goals are included as central features of the communication-disordered child's activities within the early childhood special education classroom. Opportunities for social and object play are integrated into physical therapy routines. The IDT model exemplifies a real team approach, but members must constantly work at reducing conflict and ensuring coordination of services. Reports produced by IDTs are integrated and seldom contain conflicting views. The cross talk among members and their familiarity with each other and with each discipline's role help to yield comprehensive, coordinated assessment and reporting.

Transdisciplinary Model

Procedures that enable team members to share or "release" assessment and therapeutic expertise with each other characterize the transdisciplinary team model (TDT). TDT models are built upon an interactive approach to service delivery. TDT formats minimize disciplinary boundaries and promote team consensus. Team members and parents work actively together in dyads or triads with the child. The emphasis is upon arena-style assessments and consultation with designated team members who deliver instruction and therapy based on plans that integrate goals from all disciplines. The parent and family are central partners who eventually learn and assume primary responsibilities as collaborative decision-makers and cotherapists for their child. TDT models are most successful when team members have worked together for a long period and have perfected a give-and-take chemistry that encourages each team member to feel valued, even though consultation rather than direct service delivery becomes their primary model of operation.

GUIDEPOINT

- Promote an inter- or transdisciplinary team approach to produce a unified, practical program plan.

PROMINENT TEAM MEMBERS

Psychologists who work in the schools are familiar with a multidisciplinary approach for children with special learning, behavioral, and emotional needs. However, the team approach in early childhood settings is distinctive in three ways: (a) greater numbers of professionals involved, (b) the style of team collaboration, and (c) the central role of parents as partners. Interdisciplinary and transdisciplinary (especially with infants) team approaches are the most frequently employed structures for delivering early childhood services. Team specialists thrive upon conjoint interactions for assessment and instruction/therapy. Common goals and methods in the form of curriculum-based procedures are the benchmarks of preschool "teaming." Finally, parents do more than merely attend Individualized Educational Program (IEP) meetings during the preschool years. Rather, parents are integral team members who have a central voice in designing and implementing child and family plans that fit their particular life circumstances. Psychologists in early childhood settings must be familiar with the other professionals common to the field. The following discussion identifies and portrays these "core" team members.

Early Childhood Special Educator

An early childhood special educator is the primary interventionist on the team. He or she combines developmental content and behavioral methods to help young handicapped children learn in both individual and group settings, whether home- or center-based. In many programs, the educator, parent, and speech/language specialist comprise the interdisciplinary team. The teacher works to integrate team member goals into the classroom instructional and therapeutic plan and to balance efforts across developmental domains. *The educator requires assessments and reports that have immediate and practical use in child program planning.*

Speech/Language Specialist

Speech/language difficulties are the most frequently observed problems in early childhood. Thus, the speech/language specialist is an essential member of the early intervention team. The professional guides the team in understanding the child's ability to use language pragmatically for social communication, and helps integrate language goals into ongoing classroom routines. As needed, the language specialist also helps the team to use signing and assistive communication devices.

Occupational and Physical Therapist

For preschoolers with neuromotor dysfunctions, the services of occupational and physical therapists are invaluable on the interdisciplinary team.

For example, proper positioning by neuromotor therapists enables psychologists to obtain more accurate assessments of young cerebral-palsied children. Occupational therapists and physical therapists help the team and parents understand the impact of motor impairments on other areas of competence. Often, the neuromotor therapist is the member most likely to be selected to implement the team's intervention plan for children who have neurological and multiple impairments.

Family Service Worker

The family service specialist, usually a social worker, enables the team to appraise and incorporate family issues as a central concern in early intervention programming and service delivery. The family service worker is a parent advocate who emphasizes the characteristics of the family and home environment to facilitate quality care and stimulation for the young child with special needs. These characteristics include level of stress within the family, economic concerns, the home environment, need for information, social support, and parenting skills. The family service worker helps the parent to become an integral partner and collaborative decision-maker on the interdisciplinary team.

Developmental Pediatrician

With the inception of PL 99-457, developmental pediatricians will become more active consultants collaborators on child service teams. The developmental pediatrician helps clarify relationships between the young child's medical needs, developmental competencies, and endurance for program participation. Issues such as seizure monitoring, use of portable respirators, care of gastrostomy tubes, and diagnosis of attention disorders are some central concerns. Also, many pediatricians are parent advocates and can contribute judgments on mother–infant interaction and family history and coping style (Bagnato & Hofkosh, 1990).

GUIDEPOINTS

- Become familiar with other primary specialists, such as the early childhood special educator and speech/language therapist.
- Depend on occupational and physical therapy specialists when working with children with neuromotor difficulties.
- Recognize the crucial role of the family service provider or social worker in family appraisal and participation.

A MODEL FOR ASSESSMENT-BASED TEAM DECISIONS

With the mandates of PL 99-457, early intervention programs will be challenged to address more broadly the complex needs of at-risk and handicapped infants and preschoolers, and their families. Interdisciplinary team procedures are the key to the effectiveness of preschool service delivery efforts. Team procedures are mandated by the new law and must synchronize the work of developmental, educational, medical, and mental health professionals, and parents and paraprofessionals.

Despite advancements in child tests, curricula, and methods, programs are typically without an organizing structure for interdisciplinary team appraisal which can synthesize multisource assessment information about children and families, translate data into a blueprint for service delivery, and gauge child progress as a function of planned intervention. Early interventionists as well as program administrators repeatedly declare that instead of more tests and more curricula they need to have some sort of organizational format that allows them to coordinate team decision-making; they need a streamlined way to reach consensus about child/family needs and program components.

Research on team functioning identifies three important issues: (a) team activities rarely reflect the use of a "planned, systematic and functional decision-making process" (Kabler & Genshaft, 1983, p. 150); (b) structured team decision-making models are much more effective than unstructured ones (Kaiser & Woodman, 1985; and (c) teacher (team member) judgments are often just as effective for diagnostic and program planning purposes as standardized test-based criteria (Gresham, Reschly, & Carey, 1987). Effectiveness should be judged in practical and tangible terms: broader coverage of developmental, behavioral, and family needs; numbers of team members actively participating in group decision-making; increased involvement of parents in team negotiations; increased options for service delivery; wider consideration of program features; and relationship between scope of child/family needs and program "intensity." Tables 2.1 and 2.2 offer a brief outline of problems and solutions for teamwork.

GUIDEPOINTS

- Avoid an ad lib, haphazard approach to team meetings that often result in a "tower of babble."
- Use some unifying format to orchestrate and speed team assessment and reporting.

TABLE 2.1. Team Work Problems

- Inexperience in group dynamics
- Lack of structure and mission
- Absent leadership or facilitation
- Strong professional boundaries and jargon
- Unequal member influence
- Perfunctory parent participation
- Little collaboration
- Decisions by fiat not consensus
- Preconceived views about child and family
- Disparate data unresolved
- No common assessment tools
- No ecological data
- Limited exposure to child and family
- Emphasis on diagnosis/IQ versus service delivery

TABLE 2.2. Team Work Solutions

- Training in group processes
- Collaborative decision-making model
- Common team assessment tools (CBA, SPECS)
- Facilitative leadership style
- Natural cross talk among members
- Discussion by domain not discipline
- Tolerant discussion of discrepancies
- Build consensus and team views
- In-depth discussions of service needs vs diagnosis
- Emphasis on single-case progress data

System to Plan Early Childhood Services (SPECS) (Bagnato & Neisworth, 1990) is a field-derived, team decision-making format that links interdisciplinary assessment and intervention. This section of the chapter details the purposes and features of SPECS, describes its components, demonstrates how it influences team operations, presents a short case study to illustrate its use, and then summarizes how SPECS meets the mandates of the new law.

Purposes and Features of SPECS

SPECS offers common tools for team decision-making to generate a consensus about child and family needs. This consensus offers the team a method for translating assessment data directly into plans for education and therapy. Finally, SPECS offers an economical method for evaluating child progress and program effectiveness. Thus, SPECS serves clinical purposes—assessment, service delivery planning, progress/program evaluation—as well as administrative purposes—team organization, case coordination, staff allocation, and program impact.

SPECS uses structured clinical judgment ratings to appraise the functional competencies of children 24–72 months of age in six domains and 19 developmental and behavioral subdomains. Judgment-based assessment provides the most natural vehicle for team collaboration if the rating scales are structured. Based upon a functional, noncategorical approach, SPECS incorporates data from multiple sources (e.g., tests, curricula, interviews, observation, parents, team members, several settings) so that team members can cross talk through consistent and readily understood language and ratings about child needs. SPECS uses a consensus rating system to help the team determine the type and extent of therapy services that will be provided for each child and family. This consensus also enables team members to pose specific questions about needed program requirements that are scored to generate a "program intensity profile" encompassing 10 separate dimensions.

SPECS Components

SPECS consists of three interrelated components that link team assessment and intervention. *Developmental Specs* (D-Specs) is the primary child appraisal instrument in the system. It uses numerous 5-point Likert rating scales to record the judgments of parents and team members about the child's developmental and behavioral capabilities and needs across 19 developmental areas. Traditional areas are surveyed, for example, gross motor skills and receptive language abilities; in addition, emphasis is placed upon several important characteristics that are difficult to assess but which are crucial in program planning: attention, normalcy, temperament, self-control, social competence, and motivation.

The second SPECS component, *Team Specs* (T-Specs), organizes team and parent judgments to enable the team to determine "consensus" ratings of each developmental area that can be profiled. This consensus is then cross-referenced with 10 therapy options (e.g., speech/language therapy, behavior therapy, transition services, physical therapy) and scored to generate decisions regarding the type of services needed (e.g., consult, direct therapy).

Program Specs (P-Specs), the third component, translates the T-Specs consensus data about type of therapy into specific decisions about the content, methods, and strategies that should comprise the child's service plan. Specific questions organized and weighted by the "intensity" of the intervention option selected by the team give the 10 service areas more detail. These questions are summed to determine subarea and overall "program intensity ratings" by quartiles (25th = low intensity, 50th = medium, 100th = high) in each of the 10 areas which include Adaptive Services, Early Education, Physical Therapy, Transition Needs, and Medical Needs. P-Specs enables the team and administrative personnel to compare beginning-of-the-year and end-of-the-year intensity ratings to determine progress. Data from the D-Specs, T-Specs, and the P-Specs are used to chart child progress and program impact.

GUIDEPOINTS

- Advocate use of SPECS or a similar system to standardize and speed the missions of the child service team.
- View the three major jobs of the team—assessment, identification of needed services, and program planning—as a continuum of related collaborative decisions.

Use of SPECS for Team Meetings

Figure 2.1 illustrates the flow of activities for team decision-making using SPECS. The psychologist often assumes the role of interdisciplinary team coordinator and can promote and model "best practices" through cross talk and collaboration among team members and parents by virtue of special expertise in group processes. Following the five steps described below can facilitate more collaborative efforts among professionals and parents.

Step 1: Have all team members contribute to the assessment. A child is referred to your program initially for possible identification of special needs and enrollment for intervention. After an observation or actual assessment by team member(s) and an interview with the parent, each professional and the parent can contribute ratings or observational and test data. The D-Specs is a common tool that translates the results of any assessment (whether formal or informal) onto a 5-point continuum that facilitates cross talk among the parent and other team members. Ideally, D-Specs is completed by the teacher, speech therapist, psychologist, parent, social worker, and any other member to profile judgments of the preschooler's capabilities and needs in 19 developmental and behavioral areas. No one team member "owns" a particular developmental domain. The D-Specs enables each team member to contribute judgments in all functional areas.

Step 2: Determine team consensus. Convene the team to discuss the child's status and service delivery/therapy needs. Use a natural give-and-

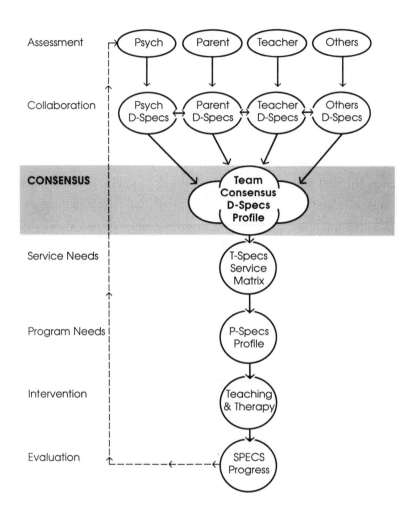

FIGURE 2.1. SPECS cycle.

take style of negotiation. This style encourages the parent, paraprofessionals, and professionals to present their judgments and the reasons for
them. The team coordinator helps the team reconcile discrepancies in
perceptions. Then, the coordinator guides the team to establish a consensus rating of the child's status in each developmental domain; this is
graphed on the T-Specs.

   Step 3: Establish the level of service needed. Using these consensus ratings,
the team coordinator completes the T-Specs which enables the team to
cross-reference the team ratings with the therapies and service delivery

options that are indicated. For example, speech/language services are cross-referenced with the developmental areas of expressive language, receptive language, and basic concepts. Thus, the team can determine if the child's problems warrant a consultation (closer look by the therapist) or whether the child should be placed in therapy immediately.

Step 4: Determine the needed "program intensity" on the P-Specs. After establishing a team consensus and determining the extent of individual therapy needs, your team coordinator uses the P-Specs to guide the members to answer questions regarding the type and intensity of programming for your child in such areas as behavior therapy, adaptive services, speech/language therapy, and medical services. Answers to these questions are weighted by scores that reflect the effort, intrusiveness, and restrictiveness of the decision option chosen. Then, an overall Program Intensity Score is calculated to reflect the team's perception about the extent of services that will be needed in this child's individualized program.

Step 5: Repeat SPECS to monitor progress. The psychologist on the early intervention team is perhaps in the best position to advocate economical ways to monitor child progress and program impact. Your team must recognize that progress evaluation is not only best practice but also mandated by federal law. A progress/program evaluation system helps the team gauge effective and ineffective intervention goals and methods, inform parents of their child's gains, and ensure accountability to administrative groups and funding agencies. SPECS is a synchronized or "linked" system in which assessment, intervention, and evaluation are interrelated operations.

You can reconvene the team at regular intervals (e.g., semiannually) to reevaluate the child and parent/family using the SPECS components. Particularly, the P-Specs can be rescored at the end of the year in each of the 10 intervention areas to determine decreases in amount of services needed and thus program intensity. Increases in developmental competence (higher D-Specs levels) correspond to decreases in program intensity (lower P-Specs percentages). When this judgment-based team data is congruent with the child's actual progress on the program's developmental curriculum and norm-based measures, the preschool program will have powerful evidence of learning and behavior change that has generalized

---

GUIDEPOINT

- Remember that a child's program must be reviewed and reevaluated at least semiannually.

across people, settings, and materials. You can document and validate the program's instructional and therapeutic effectiveness.

A CASE VIGNETTE OF TEAM COLLABORATION

Larry Potter is 4¹/₂ years old but may not be ready for kindergarten. His parents are concerned about his attention skills and ability to work independently and to get along with friends. In addition, they report weaknesses in language and motor skills. Despite these problems, they think he is smart but cannot seem to "put his knowledge together." They are worried that his premature birth and its complications are finally "catching up with him."

At Mrs. Potter's request, the school psychologist, Terry Shaw, began to assess Larry's development using a battery of measures including the McCarthy Scales of Children's Abilities (McCarthy, 1972) and the Battelle Developmental Inventory (Newborg, Stock, Wnek, Guidubaldi, & Svinicki, 1984). Once this was completed, he wanted to report the results and impressions to the other members of the interdisciplinary early intervention team. First, he translated his findings, observations, and judgments onto the D-Specs rating scales (see Figure 2.2) and profiled these ratings on the profile sheet (see Figure 2.3).

As Figure 2.3 reveals, the psychologist (based on both direct assessment and observation) rated Larry as having mild developmental deficits overall. Nevertheless, important variations are apparent, such as near average problem-solving abilities but significant difficulties in basic readiness concepts. Similarly, significant problems in self-regulation, particularly attention, exist. Finally, mild neuromotor and communication problems are indicated. Using these ratings, Mr. Shaw conveys his perceptions of the extent of Larry's problems to other team members at the meeting.

At this point, the team decides that other members will complete assessments in various ways before the next meeting. For example, the teacher and speech therapist will work together to evaluate Larry's adjustment to classroom activities and routines. The occupational therapist will appraise motor capabilities in a needs assessment session. The social worker, the team's parent advocate, will visit Mrs. Potter at home and conduct an interview and observation of Larry. In addition, the mother will provide her insights into Larry's strengths and weaknesses. The results of all their appraisals by whatever formal or informal methods will be translated onto the D-Specs rating scale. Mr. Shaw encourages all team members to attempt to rate Larry in all areas.

In the next stage, the team meets again to compare and discuss their individual assessments through the common language of the D-Specs rating scale. Figure 2.4 presents the T-Specs team summary form which con-

RECEPTIVE LANGUAGE

Understanding information as shown in various ways, such as the following directions and identifying objects and pictures.

5 Typically understands information, especially speech and gestures, as well as or better than most children of the same age.

4 Usually understands most information expected of a child about the same age.

③ Sometimes comprehends speech and gestures, but shows observable problems in understanding.

2 Only occasionally understands; generally fails to comprehend most speech and gestures.

1 Rarely shows any understanding of surrounding events.

ATTENTION

Skill in directing, sustaining, and shifting attention (looking and listening), especially when required for specific events.

5 Typically pays and shifts attention as well as or better than most children of the same age.

4 Usually pays and shifts attention, but is inconsistent.

3 Sometimes pays attention to sights and sounds appropriately, but shows noticeable problems in attention.

② Only occasionally pays and shifts attention appropriately; is generally distractable and difficult to teach.

1 Rarely pays attention except briefly to loud or sudden events.

SELF-CONTROL

Skill in managing own behavior, including doing what is needed in situations with others, following rules and directions, and eventually starting and stopping behavior without constant control by adults.

5 Typically controls own behavior as well as or better than other children of the same age.

4 Usually, but inconsistently, shows the self-control of same-age children.

③ Sometimes controls own behavior, but shows observable problems with others, following rules, and controlling self without guidance.

2 Only occasionally controls own behavior; others must frequently supervise and manage the child.

1 Rarely shows any self-control; constant supervision and control is necessary.

FIGURE 2.2. Three scales from D-Specs.

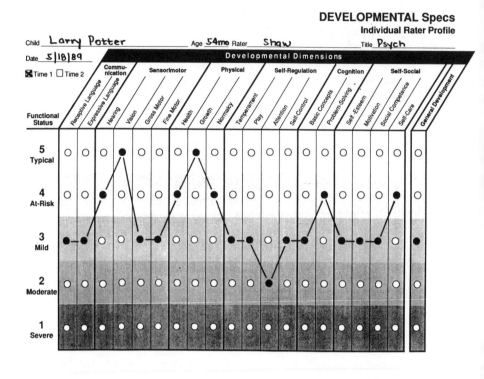

FIGURE 2.3. D-Specs profile of a psychologist's rating of Larry.

trasts team member ratings. Note the generally high agreement among them. Major discrepancies are evident only in Mrs. Potter's lower ratings of Larry in self-regulatory areas such as self-control and temperament, but higher rating in play skills. Mr. Shaw, the psychologist, finally guides the team in negotiating a consensus about Larry's developmental and behavioral capabilities (see Figure 2.3). Note that team consensus ratings are arrived at through discussion and shared perceptions; they are not merely the sum or arithmetic average of individual ratings. "Interdisciplinary decisions are more than the sum of thinking of professionals and parents; shared perspectives lead to more accurate observations and evaluations, and more appropriate and thoughtful recommendations" (Healy, Keese, & Smith, 1989, p. 73).

Figure 2.5 shows how use of the T-Specs consensus ratings enables the team to complete the T-Specs service matrix. Observe in Behavior Therapy, for example, the sum of the team's ratings indicates that Larry needs direct services immediately in order to manage his attention and self-control difficulties.

TEAM Specs
Team Summary

Child **Larry Potter**   Age **54 mo.**   Date **5/18/89**   ☒ Time 1   ☐ Time 2

Developmental Dimensions

Team Member	Receptive Language	Expressive Language	Hearing	Vision	Gross Motor	Fine Motor	Health	Growth	Normalcy	Temperament	Play	Attention	Self-Control	Basic Concepts	Problem-Solving	Self-Esteem	Motivation	Social Competence	Self-Care
Parent	4	3	3	5	4	3	4	5	5	2	4	2	1	4	5	3	2	4	3
Early Childhood Special Educator	3	3	4	5	3	3	5	5	4	3	3	2	3	3	4	3	3	2	4
Paraprofessional Aide																			
Speech/Language Therapist	3	3	4	5	4	4	5	5	3	3	3	2	2	3	3	2	3	3	3
Developmental School Psychologist	3	3	4	5	3	3	4	5	4	3	3	2	3	3	4	3	3	3	4
Physical Therapist																			
Occupational Therapist	4	3	4	5	3	3	4	4	3	3	3	2	3	3	3	3	3	4	3
Pediatrician																			
Social Worker																			
Vision Specialist																			
Hearing Specialist																			
Preschool Program Supervisor																			
Other																			
Range	3-4	0	3-4	0	3-4	3-4	4-5	4-5	3-4	2-3	3-4	0	1-3	3-4	3-5	2-3	2-3	2-4	3-4
TEAM CONSENSUS	3	3	4	5	3	3	4	5	3	3	3	2	3	3	4	3	3	3	3

Team Ratings

Record each member's ratings Service Options, determine the range, and discuss discrepant ratings to reach a consensus.

FIGURE 2.4. Display of D-Specs ratings by several team members.

Finally, the P-Specs poses a series of specific questions that the team completes in each of the 10 intervention/service areas guided by Mr. Shaw. For instance, the high level of need in the area of behavior therapy (Figure 2.6) results in the decision to create an individualized behavior management plan; use a behavior contract with strong social rewards; provide discipline through a combination of planned ignoring and differential reinforcement of other behavior (DRO) procedures; focus upon inattention, impulsivity, and social withdrawal; and accomplish this through consultation by the psychologist to the early childhood special educator.

Similar needs are shown in the area of transition services (Figure 2.7). Mr. Shaw graphs these ratings on the SPECS Program Intensity Ratings Profile (Figure 2.8). Medium intensity services at the 47% level are needed overall. The most intense services are observed in the areas of Early Education (55%), Speech/Language Therapy (50%), Occupational Therapy (65%), and Transition Services (55%). The team with Mrs. Pot-

Service Matrix

Enter Team Consensus ratings in the unshaded squares, sum across, and divide by number for average.

Service Options	Receptive Language	Expressive Language	Hearing	Vision	Gross Motor	Fine Motor	Health	Growth	Normalcy	Temperament	Play	Attention	Self-Control	Basic Concepts	Problem-Solving	Self-Esteem	Motivation	Social Competence	Self-care	Total	Service Average	Service Decision	
1.0 Special Early Education	3	3					3		3		3	3	3	2	3	3	4	3	3	3	42 +14	3	DSR
2.0 Adaptive Arrangements	3	3			4	5	3	3				3								3	27 +8	3	DSR
3.0 Behavior Therapy	3	3									3	3	3	2	3			3	3		20 +7	3	DSR
4.0 Speech/Language Therapy	3	3													3						9 +3	3	DSR
5.0 Physical Therapy						3			3											3	6 +2	3	DSR
6.0 Occupational Therapy								3												3	6 +2	3	DSR
7.0 Vision Services				5																	5 +1	5	NS
8.0 Hearing Services			4						5												4 +1	4	CR
9.0 Medical Services	3	3	4	5	3		3	3	5												24 +6	4	CR
10.0 Transition Services (optional)	3	3	4	5	4	5	3	3	4	5	3	3	3	2	3	4	3	3	3	3	63 +19	3	DSR

Developmental Dimensions — Communication: Receptive Language, Expressive Language; Sensorimotor: Hearing, Vision; Physical: Gross Motor, Fine Motor, Health, Growth, Normalcy; Self-Regulation: Temperament, Play; Cognition: Attention, Self-Control, Basic Concepts, Problem-Solving; Self-Social: Self-Esteem, Motivation, Social Competence, Self-care

Service Decision Criteria
(Compare each Service Average to the scale below. Round to the lowest whole number.)
5 – No service indicated
4 – Consult recommended
3 – Direct Services recommended
2> Direct Services needed
1> Direct Services needed

FIGURE 2.5. Conversion of team ratings to needed service options.

3.0 BEHAVIOR THERAPY

From Team SPECS: Service Average ___3___
Service Division __DSR__

3.1 Is an individual behavior management plan needed for this child?

Time 1 Time 2
- ☐ ☐ No (0)
- ☑ ☐ Yes (1)

3.1 — Time 1 Time 2: [1] [ ]

3.2 What special reinforcement strategies are needed? (Check each that applies.)

Time 1 Time 2
- ☐ ☐ None (0)
- ☑ ☐ Strong social reward (1)
- ☑ ☐ Behavior contract (2)
- ☐ ☐ Token economy (3)
- ☐ ☐ Primary reinforcement (4)

3.2 — (Sum values of all options checked under 3.2) [3] [ ]

3.3 What special disciplinary techniques are necessary? (Check each that applies.)

Time 1 Time 2
- ☐ ☐ None (0)
- ☐ ☐ Planned ignoring (1)
- ☑ ☐ Ignoring with reinforcement of alternate behavior (2)
- ☐ ☐ Time out (3)
- ☐ ☐ Supervised physical restraint (4)

3.3 — (Sum values of all options checked under 3.3) [2] [ ]

3.4 What types of behavior management needs are most notable for this child? (Check each that applies.)

Time 1 Time 2
- ☐ ☐ None (0)
- ☑ ☐ Inattention (1)
- ☑ ☐ Impulsivity (1)
- ☐ ☐ Overactivity (1)
- ☑ ☐ Social withdrawal (2)
- ☐ ☐ Aggression (2)
- ☐ ☐ Self-stimulation (3)
- ☐ ☐ Self-injury (3)
- ☐ ☐ Other (3): _____

3.4 — (Sum values of all options checked under 3.4) [4] [ ]

3.5 How much behavioral/psychological service (e.g., school psychologist, counselor, social worker) is needed?

Time 1 Time 2
- ☐ ☐ None (0)
- ☑ ☐ Consultation (1)
- ☐ ☐ Direct Service sessions per week:

    Time 1 Time 2
    - ☐ ☐ One (1)
    - ☐ ☐ Two (2)
    - ☐ ☐ Three (3)
    - ☐ ☐ Four (4)
    - ☐ ☐ Five (5)

3.5 — [1] [ ]

Briefly describe any additional behavior therapy concerns or needs.
Psychologist will work directly with parents, also.

3.0 BEHAVIOR THERAPY
Intensity Ratings Sum (IRS)

(Sum scores for items 3.1–3.5) [11] [ ]

FIGURE 2.6. Selected behavior therapy options from P-Specs.

3.0 Transition Readiness Checklist

10.10 Which behavior/learning problems or needs listed below must be considered in team decision-making for this child at transition? (Check each that applies.)

Time 1	Time 2		INTENSITY RATINGS
			Time 1 Time 2
☑	☐	Inattentive (1)	
☑	☐	Impulsive (1)	
☑	☐	Distractible (1)	
☑	☐	Needs adult guidance to complete tasks (1)	
☑	☐	Has trouble following classroom routines (1)	
☑	☐	Lacks self-directed behavior (1)	
☑	☐	Fails to follow 2- or 3-step directions (1)	
☑	☐	Has trouble recognizing numbers/letters (1)	
☐	☐	Has trouble writing numbers/letters (1)	
☑	☐	Lasks effective peer/adult communication skills (1)	
☑	☐	Has trouble interacting with peers (1)	
☑	☐	Lacks sharing, waiting, and turn-taking skills (1)	
☑	☐	Lasks listening comprehension skills (1)	
☐	☐	Lacks self-care skills (1)	
☐	☐	Lacks mobility skills to move about independently (1)	(Sum values of all options checked under 10.10)
☐	☐	Other: (1) _____	
			12 ☐

FIGURE 2.7. Transition needs selected by the team on P-Specs.

ter's consent has decided to provide these services in a diagnostic kindergarten setting; Larry's IEP will now be written based on the SPECS team assessment and service delivery program results.

We emphasize that arriving at a consensus in assessment and deciding on service options and a program plan are jobs that must be accomplished by the team. Some system must be employed to arrive at and record team consensus regarding child status and program design. It is likely that other models and materials will be developed to meet team needs as interdisciplinary services for youngsters expand. SPECS is a way to standardize, simplify, and speed the necessary decision-making.

Team procedures are mandated by federal legislation in early intervention. SPECS complies with PL 99-457 in design, content, and use. Table 2.3 provides a short-hand summary of the essentials of the new law and how SPECS matches those mandates.

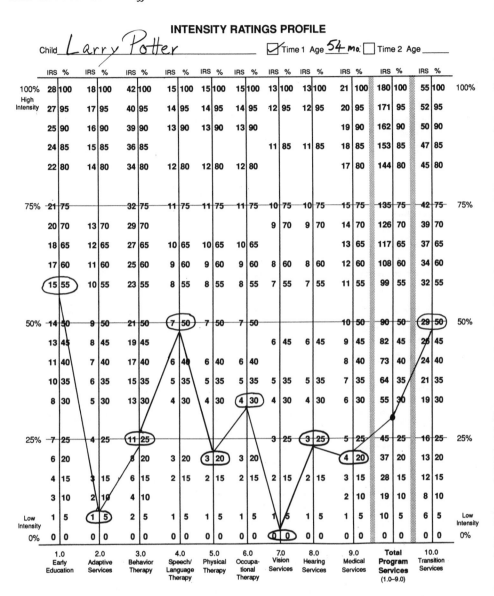

FIGURE 2.8. Program intensity profile for Larry.

TABLE 2.3. SPECS Features Corresponding to PL 99-457 Provisions

PL 99-457 Mandate	SPECS Feature	SPECS Component
Noncategorical diagnosis	5-Point functional ratings	D-Specs, T-Specs
Developmental delay definitions	Five classification levels	D-Specs [a]
Objective criteria	Operational definitions and scoring	D-Specs, T-Specs, P-Specs
Team evaluation	Team consensus ratings and collaborative program decisions	T-Specs, P-Specs
Developmental whole-child focus	Six domains, 19 developmental dimensions	D-Specs, T-Specs
Individual child/family plan	45 Instruction and therapy questions	P-Specs [b]
Case management	Case coordination	P-Specs
Explicit service linkages	10 Service options	T-Specs,[c] P-Specs[c]
Service delivery intensity	Intensity ratings	P-Specs
Child plan with family focus	Child and family program needs	P-Specs [d]
Parent participation	Integrated parent judgments and goals	D-Specs, T-Specs, P-Specs
Program/progress evaluations	Time 1/time 2 child/program monitoring	D-Specs, T-Specs, P-Specs
Interagency coordination	Interdisciplinary case management decisions	T-Specs, P-Specs
Program transitions	Transition competencies and needs	P-Specs [e]

[a] Individual Rater Profile, Team Consensus Profile. [b] Program Options. [c] Service Matrix. [d] Family Needs Checklist. [e] Transition Services Questionnaire.

SUGGESTED READINGS

Allen, K. E., Holm, V. A., & Schiefelbusch, R. L. (1979). *Early intervention: A team approach.* Baltimore, MD: University Park Press.

Gibbs, B., & Teti, D. (1989). *Interdisciplinary assessment of infants: A guide for early intervention professionals.* Baltimore, MD: Paul Brookes.

Golin, A. K., & Ducanis, A. J. (1981). *The interdisciplinary team.* Rockville, MD: Aspen.

Moore, K. J., Fifield, M. B., Spira, D. A., & Scarlato, M. (1989). Child study team decision-making in special education: Improving the process. *Remedial and Special Education,* 10(4), 50–57.

Spencer, P. E., & Coye, R. W. (1988). Project BRIDGE: A team approach to decision-making for early services. *Infants and Young Children,* 11(1), 82–92.

BEST PRACTICE SUMMARY CHECKLIST

Chapter 2

How Can Teamwork Be Effective?

[ ] 1. Encourage your team to use an interdisciplinary rather than a multi-disciplinary approach to assessment and program planning.

[ ] 2. Consider the use of "arena" assessments and a transdisciplinary style when working with infants and severely impaired preschoolers.

[ ] 3. Conduct inservice sessions for your team that emphasize "team-building" exercises to foster shared purposes, collaborative problem-solving, and role sharing.

[ ] 4. Hold team discussions regarding creative ways to integrate the parent and family issues into team decision-making.

[ ] 5. Conduct a quality-control and time-efficiency study of your team's typical method of operation to highlight needed improvements.

[ ] 6. Use common assessment instruments and a structured format for team deliberations that focus and speed team decision-making.

3

How Does the Preschool Psychologist Stage an Assessment?

ISSUES IN PRACTICE

- Is it appropriate to prompt and reward a preschooler's behavior during assessment?
- Is body position an important assessment consideration?
- Must psychologists vary the words and phrases they use to communicate with young children?
- Can special adaptive toys be used in an assessment?
- Are autistic preschoolers "testable"?

Traditional styles of evaluation require children to sit at a table, respond on demand, and perform without rewards, and require psychologists to impassively follow standardized procedures. Teachers, psychologists, and others who work with preschoolers sense that they must use different arrangements and styles of interaction when assessing preschool children. We must recognize the emotional needs and behavioral styles of toddlers and preschoolers and adjust interactions accordingly or our efforts will fail. Generally, the aims and methods for assessing preschoolers are quite different from those for school-age children. Psychologists require keen observational skills, creative flexibility in procedures, and, most of all, the sensitivity to detect and respond to the young child's interests, moods, and needs. These attributes are magnified in importance and "put to the test" when assessing young developmentally disabled children. *The preschool psychologist must not only be a good playmate but a good manager of behavior.* Simply, the psychologist must be skilled in *staging* a preschool assessment. Staging refers to arranging the environment, selecting materials, and adjusting language and style to sustain the preschooler's attention and social interactions in order to ensure *optimal* child performance during assessment.

This chapter discusses style and methods for staging preschool assessments. Three topics are covered: developmentally appropriate preschool behaviors that influence performance; general guidelines for staging assessment for at-risk and mildly handicapped preschoolers; and specific staging guidelines for children with low-incidence handicaps (moderate to severe disabilities).

TYPICAL PRESCHOOLER CHARACTERISTICS AND ASSESSMENT PERFORMANCE

Often, behavior that we consider troublesome in school-age children is developmentally appropriate for the preschool child. For example, inattention, distractibility, impulsiveness, overactivity, noncompliance, and some degree of aggressiveness are worrisome when observed in a fourth-grade child, but are to be expected with preschool children. The task of diagnosing attention disorder and hyperactivity during the preschool years is thus a particularly difficult one. Often, however, this diagnosis is more a reflection of the adult's lack of tolerance rather than of the child's intrinsic problem. Ulrey and Rogers (1982) provide a description (summarized below) of four behavior patterns that are developmentally appropriate for preschoolers and offer general suggestions for reducing their impact on performance during assessment.

Fear of New Situations

Typically, preschool children may be fearful or wary of new situations. This can include difficulties separating from the parent, fear of unfamiliar people, and reactions to failure on new activities. For this reason, a quick systematic desensitization procedure is usually effective. This involves a positive, gradual, low-demand approach to allow the young child time to adjust to the new situation. Have the parent present, initially, in the classroom or "testing room" to reassure the preschooler that you, your toys, and the situation are safe. Talk to the parent first while allowing the child to explore the room freely to give time for this reassurance to occur naturally. The presence of novel toys placed selectively about the room encourages the child's discovery and provides you with the opportunity to make contact in a nonthreatening way, and to set the occasion for a rewarding play interaction that will encourage the child to play apart from the parent.

Encourage the child to play with the assessment materials in a more structured place and manner. As you begin, be certain to choose assessment items that will maintain the child's interest and task orientation. Despite the standardization of most measures, it is nevertheless crucial to intersperse easy and difficult tasks—particularly with young children who have motor, behavior, language, and social-interaction problems. The child will give up on tasks easily if they are viewed as too hard and if failure is probable. For example, gross motor tasks and verbal reasoning tasks must be interspersed and alternated to maintain interest. If the child is unable to complete a task after two to three attempts, switch to an activity the child has completed successfully before and allow the child to gain some success at something familiar. Completion of a task is often more reinforcing than social praise alone, especially from a stranger.

GUIDEPOINT

- Reduce the preschooler's fear of the unfamiliar through basic desensitization procedures.

Overactivity and Distractibility

Psychologists must remember that only a few preschoolers have learned a "set" for paying attention, answering questions, and doing tabletop activities on demand. Their testing failures are often the result not of their deficiency but of our assuming that they have these prerequisite readiness behaviors. For this reason, redoing tasks at a later time and observing spontaneous play behavior are necessary to discover if the child really has acquired a particular skill or concept. Attention span may be fine for familiar tasks, but may vary markedly with other demands including the use of two-step directions, increases in item difficulty, directions to look, listen, and draw at the same time, and an emphasis on the child's least well-developed skill area. Be vigilant about reducing competing stimuli, choose naturally exciting tasks, give frequent praise, and separate the steps for doing auditory, visual, and verbal tasks.

GUIDEPOINTS

- Don't expect sustained attention.
- Reduce distractions.
- Reduce the complexity of demands.
- Provide motivating toys and tasks.

Negativism and Oppositional Behavior

Preschoolers have little experience in staying with an activity just because someone says so. Moreover, their natural push toward independence and autonomy will inevitably lead to conflict if one fails to understand these dual factors of lack of experience and natural noncompliance. In assessment situations for which time is limited, psychologists should rather establish an atmosphere of cooperative turn-taking—"working and playing together." Start with games or active toys that permit turn-taking. This models the behaviors appropriate for the preschooler and also allows them the opportunity to be rewarded for (unwitting) compliance! Once again, it is important to intersperse structured tasks, such as table-top activities, with more free play opportunities as a reward. For example, formal puzzle tasks can be followed by drawing activities or picture identification tasks followed by free play with puppets. Most importantly, we must agree that *no child is untestable.* More than one and often several assessment sessions in different situations are necessary to move beyond situational opposition and noncompliance to achieve an optimal survey of the preschooler's competencies.

GUIDEPOINTS

- Encourage working and playing together.
- Alternate preferred and nonpreferred tasks.
- Use several situations and sessions.

Perseveration

Repetition of behavior is a common occurrence with preschoolers. Young children may perseverate because they are rewarded for it or, for example, because they know only one way of playing with a toy. Psychologists can reduce perseveration by teaching new responses (e.g., cause–effect play versus banging) and then reinforcing these different, new behaviors. Similarly, with unfamiliar and difficult tasks, they can praise "hard work" and guessing or trying rather than only success. Using the preferred perseverative task to reward work on the more difficult, less desirable task is often effective.

GUIDEPOINTS

- Model, prompt, and reward new behaviors.
- Permit perseverative task to reward work on other items.

STAGING FOR AT-RISK AND MILDLY HANDICAPPED PRESCHOOLERS

Several considerations are important when organizing an assessment for young children with suspected or mild developmental difficulties, including those at high risk for learning disabilities, attention disorders and hyperactivity, communication disorders, and possible mental retardation. These considerations have been arranged into five major clusters: Physical Environment, Body Positioning, Attitude and Interactive Style, Routines and Transitions, and Motivation and Management.

Physical Environment

The condition of a classroom or assessment room greatly affects the behavior and adjustment of young children. Such factors as room lighting, temperature, noise, and even arrangement of furnishings can ruin the best staged setting. Psychologists should strive to reduce distractions by any convenient means such as room dividers or carrels if possible or, more likely, by positioning chairs and tables toward corners, away from distracting noises and movement.

Planning of room layout is critical for many children. This means placing and arranging chairs, tables, and toys strategically about a room so that the child has easy access to the materials, and distance is maintained from doors and windows. In fact, the familiar environment of the preschool setting should be considered the best context in which to evaluate the child's skills. Here the child knows the materials, understands what is expected behavior, feels comfortable, and is likely to be less wary of strangers. When the child is not in a preschool or in the home during assessment, it is important that the arrangement of the room be "homelike."

GUIDEPOINTS

- Use the child's usual setting for testing and observation when feasible.
- Simulate the child's setting when the typical setting is not available.
- Arrange the setting to minimize distractions and attempts to leave.

Body Positioning

One of the most crucial and generally neglected considerations is body positioning for the child. Psychologists must recognize that young children do not have the same skill in trunk control and equilibrium that older children do. Therefore, the importance of the proper choice of child-sized tables and chairs cannot be overemphasized. The child should be seated at a chair that is padded, allows feet to bear weight slightly on the floor, and, preferably, has arm rests or sides to contain and stabilize the young child. Similarly, the table surface should be approximately waist high and allow the child proper position, height, and leverage for such tasks as drawing, assembling, and block building. Some children with neuromotor immaturities are affected quite negatively by improper body positions, presumably because they must concentrate on maintaining balance and position. Thus, they fail to attend and persist on tasks when they are tense and preoccupied. Moreover, the young child should spend no more than 15–20 minutes at the chair and table at any one time, and should be given the opportunity to work and play in other positions.

GUIDEPOINT

- Be certain to provide optimal positioning, seating, and surfaces.

Attitude and Interactive Style of the Psychologist

Infant and preschool evaluations also differ from school-age evaluations in the purpose, attitude, and behavioral style of the psychologist. *The objective of early childhood assessment is to obtain an optimal estimate of the child's functional skills,* in order to plan an individualized program of instruction and therapy so that progress can be monitored. Therefore, the psychologist must alter the environment, materials, and prompts needed to allow the child to do his/her best. (This approach, of course, differs from the rigid adherence to standardized procedures associated with diagnosis.) This interactive style requires that the psychologist be flexible in maintaining a structured play atmosphere that motivates the child while enabling one to gain accurate clinical observations regarding the child's competencies and deficits. The psychologist cannot be afraid of "acting like a fool" to keep the child attentive, aroused, and task-oriented. Keeping the child focused involves responding to his/her interests and preferences to some degree while also imposing structure.

Preschool children respond best when the psychologist identifies the child's behavioral and temperamental needs beforehand and reacts accordingly to signs of anxiousness, fear, or loss of interest. Many children work best with a side-by-side seating arrangement. This may involve seating the child in a chair and at a table tailored to size. Instead of sitting across from the child, the psychologist should sit beside the child (60°–90° angle) with an arm gently about the child's shoulder. This serves to contain the child and cue him/her about the expected behavior of sitting and working at a table for certain tasks. Tasks should be presented from the child's side in a calm, gradual approach with fluid changes from task to task. This also conveys the message that "we are working and playing, together." Often, using a soft, quiet voice models slow, deliberate habits for the child. This also requires him/her to listen more carefully for directions and to attend better. Using this soothing style, the psychologist can also shape the child's behavioral style by a combination of physical prompts and verbal cues as needed, such as "Remember, we look before we point"; "Let's use our little voice"; "Show me quiet hands" (accompanied by a manual prompt). This style illustrates clearly that effective assessment behaviors are the same as effective teaching behaviors.

GUIDEPOINT

- Act as the child's friend and playmate as well as an adult in charge.

Routines and Transitions

Routines and transitions between routines are very important for any preschooler, especially those with language, learning, and behavior problems.

Preparation for transitions will greatly reduce disruptive, off-task behavior. Preschoolers must be told beforehand what changes are coming and what they will be doing so that they know what to expect. This attention to preparatory routines will ease the transition and reduce the possibility of resistance, fear, and tantrums. Similarly, frequent breaks must be taken between tasks and situations to extend the child's endurance and to maintain attention and task performance.

Rapport-building and examiner familiarity is an example of a preparatory routine that has been studied only recently (Fuchs, 1987). Despite the importance of rapport, few test manuals provide guidance on the most effective and specific ways to promote rapport. Fuchs' research (1987) concluded that psychologists must spend considerable time with a child in the preschool program (or home) before the evaluation, or the child's performance will diminish considerably.

In addition, other contextual factors influence test performance. The presence of parents during the assessment is often important for young preschoolers who need reassurance. In addition, parents who observe the assessment share a common base of information with the psychologist who can refer to and explain the meaning of a child's behavior more clearly. However, the assessment situation should be viewed more broadly as a time to appraise the child's capacity to practice separating from parents and adjusting to new circumstances. For example, the psychologist can observe whether the child is interested in novel toys and cooperative games and may not need the parent present.

Cooperative games and high interest toys such as arcade video games and movable, sound-producing cars and trains with microswitches frequently allow the psychologist and young child to become comfortable with each other. Do not expect preschoolers to be excited by and interested in the objects in the test kits. Usually these objects are too small and alien to the child's play experiences. Preschool psychologists must invest in a wide variety of toys that are multisensory, developmentally appropriate, and useful for establishing rapport. In addition, the toys can be used later as reinforcers and preferred activities, which can foster work on less preferred but more challenging assessment tasks.

Psychologists must be careful to change from one task to another with a slow, fluid manner and avoid abrupt transitions. The young child's attachment to particular toys must be respected and new toys offered gradually as replacements. Young children often perseverate with toys and need to learn how to accept new tasks and use more mature play behaviors such as matching forms in a formboard rather than stacking the forms or banging and feeling their texture.

Preschoolers who are overactive, impulsive, inattentive, and inexperienced with table tasks often can be assessed better with two evaluators: one to administer the tasks while the other contains the child, prompts "quiet hands," and verbally cues waiting, sharing, and turn-taking behaviors as well as observes evidence of skill acquisition. A second evaluator (e.g., aide) can model behaviors for the child and help create a "group" that is working and playing together.

GUIDEPOINTS

- Establish rapport by spending time with the child.
- Include parents and/or a favorite toy or object.
- Maintain a calm, easy-going manner.
- Allow breaks when it seems useful for preparation or for a reward.

Motivation and Management

It cannot be overstated that effective assessment procedures are nearly identical to effective teaching methods. Preschool psychologists must maintain a balance between work and play activities. Also, they must be willing to go beyond merely administering tasks and impassively scoring behavior to being an active "manager" and facilitator with young children. The combination of balanced work and play with structure and management increases motivation and fosters optimal performance.

The use of rewards is vital with preschoolers no matter what the test manuals indicate! Preschool psychologists should regularly use stickers, tokens, social praise, and task-imbedded reinforcers such as novel activities to establish and maintain motivation through incentives. A developmental hierarchy of reinforcers can be used that is based on an initial scrutiny of the child's level of development and social competence. Similarly, psychologists must also view their job as evaluating the child's ability to change behavior through discipline and limit-setting. Preschoolers should be given choices as a way of encouraging cooperation while emphasizing that compliance is required ("you can play with either the train or the bear; which do you want?").

Young children need models for behavior. Preschoolers feel more secure and are more compliant when they know what will happen, how they are expected to behave, and how adults will respond to their behavior. Thus, the assessment session is inevitably a controlled situation for observing the young child's competence in adjusting to more structured routines and learning important prerequisite behaviors. Contrary to a psychometric perspective, the preschool assessment session is a miniteaching episode and the psychologist is the teacher-figure. Answering questions, completing puzzles, and drawing designs at a table are strange, new experiences for many preschoolers who have been unaccustomed to following directions and staying seated. We must analyze how quickly they can learn prerequisite skills. Modeling and demonstration of expected behaviors are important as are rewards for effort and compliance. *However, it is just as important to evaluate children's reactions to limit-setting.* Psychologists should feel that not only is it okay to discipline preschoolers, but that it is required and necessary. Planned ignoring of inappropriate behavior and social praise for desired behavior are basic strategies. Also effective are combined verbal and physical prompts that direct the child's eyes to the pictures, encourage pointing at the pictures instead of hitting the cards, and reduce impulsive grabbing of materials. These management strategies must be used to shape appropriate looking, listening, waiting, and sharing. In extreme circumstances, time out in a chair at a corner for tantrum behavior may be required; similarly, we must not be afraid to show an angry face with an angry or displeased voice tone when disciplining a child, thereby heightening the cues that distinguish appropriate from inappropriate behavior for the young inexperienced preschooler. A mild or impassive approach may not provide the contrast needed to stop ongoing inappropriate behavior. Of course, many children may need only a slight sign of displeasure from the adult. The required level of reprimand must be detected by the psychologist.

Finally, word choice and phrasing are important, especially given the young language-disordered child's limited memory skills for long and multiple directions and limited understanding of only the basic words and concepts. Psychologists and teachers must recognize the necessity of using active, concrete directions with young children. "Look with your eyes" is superior to "pay attention." "Listen with your ears" can be accompanied by a manual cue such as holding your ears out. When first entering the room for the assessment, the psychologist can prepare the child sufficiently by simply saying "I have some new toys to show you in my room; we can work and play together with them." Other examples may include "Put your finger on the car" instead of "Show me the car." With some children, it may be necessary to use short telegraphic statements (when there is a severe lack of language) such as "Kermit—sit," "roll ball," or "ball under chair."

In summary, a combination of novel, active, multisensory toys, behavior management strategies, varied room arrangements, and judicious word choices can combine to allow young at-risk or mildly handicapped children to display capabilities in the assessment situation that approximate performance in the "real world," and show their "best" selves.

GUIDEPOINTS

- Use rewards, praise, and favorite activities to maintain motivation.
- Alternate work and play.
- Use active, concrete directions.
- Model needed prerequisite behaviors to facilitate assessment of target tasks.
- When needed, use planned ignoring, a stern tone of voice, limits, and a brief time out.

STAGING FOR CHILDREN WITH LOW-INCIDENCE DISABILITIES

Psychologists are challenged and often frustrated when called upon to assess young children with serious impairments. Aside from temperamental and behavioral considerations, accommodations must also be made for the child's sensory, neuromotor, cognitive/linguistic and affective/behavioral limitations. Special arrangements are necessary in these circumstances to circumvent disabilities and to maximize performance by using both environmental and, often, prosthetic adaptations to the usual assessment context. Young children with prominent disabilities include those with visual impairments, hearing impairments, developmental retardation, neuromotor impairments (e.g., cerebral palsy), and affective/behavioral disorders (e.g., autism). Other resources provide more detailed descriptions of the adaptive assessment of these specific diagnostic groups including choice of measures (Bagnato, Neisworth, & Munson, 1989; Bailey & Wolery, 1989; Neisworth & Bagnato, 1987; Simeonsson, 1986; Wachs & Sheehan, 1988). This discussion reviews key guidelines in staging an assessment for each disability group.

Sensory Impairments

Visual Impairment

One of the most important staging considerations for children with visual impairment is allowing sufficient time for the child to orient and adjust to the unfamiliar environment. The use of a team approach using a vision specialist during the evaluation represents "best practice." These children must have time to explore toys gradually and to orient to the room arrangement through the combined use of hearing, smell, taste, and touch. The assessor must be sure of the child's *residual vision* as much as possible, since children are rarely totally blind; similarly, children often resist using their prescription lenses or parents forget to bring the child's glasses. Removing distractions, providing one toy or task at a time, and prompting touching of different toys and textures broadens the child's experience and gradually fosters awareness of surroundings.

It is vital that the child be provided with a distraction-free, well defined work area with accessible boundaries such as a table tray with higher sides. Next, choosing multisensory toys is in order; most toys in commercially available test kits are notoriously unmotivating even for the normal child! Carefully choose toys that seem to match the child's stage of play skills gauged by your observation and parental report. In general, toys must have the following attributes: movable, sound-producing, air-producing, oversized, textured, high-contrast colors and illumination, easily manipulated, and raised and single line features.

Psychologists must be skilled in using "instructional strategies" and knowledgeable about developmental expectancies for young blind children. Verbal directions must be more concrete and active than usual; a combination of verbal descriptions and manual prompts must be used in the presentation of assessment tasks. Preparatory descriptions of the toys/tasks being presented and what the child will be doing with them are helpful procedures. Children must be told also when to start and stop an activity to orient them in time. For example, "Sara, this is a fuzzy rabbit. He has big, long ears with bells on them that make noise. We can feel the ears with our hands and hear the bells with our ears. They are big and long! Hear the sound?" (Provide verbal and manual guidance.) "This toy over here is a big box. Let's feel how big and deep it is. You can almost go inside it." (Manually guide the child's hand into the box.) "Now, feel the rabbit on the floor beside you with your hands." (Assessor rings bells.) "Hear the bells? Get him! Now, put him in the big box." The psychologist has used auditory and tactile cues in working with the child to assess the ability to search for an object out of reach (object permanence) and to follow a direction regarding location. The reward is successful completion of the task and hugging and social praise. Exaggerated up and down voice intonations should be used to help the child distinguish between different feeling states, for example, happiness and excitement for task completion, surprise for a new event (Jack-in-the-Box pops up), and firmness for stopping inappropriate behavior (e.g., eye poking). Gradually present and remove tasks for the child to smooth transitions and to increase readiness for the next activity with little upset.

Know developmental expectancies for blind preschoolers. They show some general though prominent functional deficits that must be considered during assessment. Blind children may not use their well-developed gross motor skills until they have learned to move out in space toward a sound cue; thus, sounds must first have reinforcement value for them. They show delays in social communication and initiation such as smiling and reaching out to touch a familiar adult's face. Also, these children typically show gaps in knowledge of concepts. They may know the name for something but be unable to describe it accurately because of their lack of experience.

Finally, it is often necessary to deal with the child's self-stimulatory behaviors such as hand flapping, eye poking, and twirling or spinning. These "blindisms" can be managed through the use of combinations of various behavior techniques including sensory extinction, interruption, and alternate sensory activities (Favell, 1982).

Hearing Impairment

A screening for *residual hearing* is an essential first step in staging. The use of hearing aids and body pack amplifiers must be determined beforehand. Assessment of hearing-impaired children requires very specialized skills. Ideally, the psychologist should have previous experience with deaf and hearing-impaired preschoolers and must be trained in the use of a total communication approach including signing and gestures. However, this is rarely the case; thus, consultation with a communication disorders specialist and/or hearing specialist during the assessment is a key to accurate assessment; simply, a team approach is essential!

The room environment for the child should be as free as possible of visual distractions and ambient noise and vibrations. Consider the room arrangement beforehand, especially lighting and direct seating across from the child so that full facial attention is obtained. Again, multisensory toys and tasks must be carefully selected. Visual and motor/tactile characteristics are most important; thus, toys should be movable, vibrating, colorful, textured, and highly arousing (e.g., pop-up toys, computer displays).

Once again, instructional strategies are important. Physically prompt the child's eyes and face to the task; reward with smiles, touching, facial expressions, and clapping. Use demonstrations, pantomime, and manual guidance to teach trial tasks beforehand to prepare the child. Make gestures very demonstrative and exaggerate facial expressions to convey direction and meaning. At times, allow the child to feel your throat vibrations for help in distinguishing words and sounds.

The use of nonverbal assessment measures and deaf norms is absolutely critical. Developmentally, young children with hearing impairments generally show serious delays in speech and language production. However, behavior problems with shyness, wariness, and social withdrawal are not uncommon and must be considered in establishing rapport. With older preschoolers, puppet play and interactive computer games can help foster trust, interest, and cooperation. In language assessment with such toddlers, it is often helpful to demonstrate comprehension through the

---

GUIDEPOINTS

- Determine residual vision and hearing aided/unaided.
- Consult with sensory specialists.
- Provide a distraction-free, well-defined work area.
- Select multisensory toys and tasks.
- Be demonstrative and exaggerate gestures, facial expressions, and voice intonations.
- Know developmental expectancies for visually- and hearing-impaired children and use handicap norms when possible.
- Emphasize touching, sounds, and verbal descriptions with visually impaired children.
- Stress a total communication approach with hearing-impaired children.

paired use of concrete and pictured objects. For example, a toy rabbit can be used for the child to match it with a picture of a rabbit.

Developmental Retardation

For infants and preschoolers with severe cognitive deficits, blends of the strategies for other disabilities are necessary. *Psychologists must consider atypical patterns of development and behavior when assessing severely retarded preschool children.* These characteristics include variable attention and arousal, high and low muscle tone, changeable moods, fleeting social communication, little or no initiation of interactions, self-stimulatory patterns, seizures, and nonpurposeful and infantile play patterns (e.g., mouthing, banging, shaking, throwing).

Body position and choice of toys are two important staging dimensions with severely retarded preschoolers. It is important to conduct the assessment with another team member, preferably the teacher or an occupational or physical therapist. Such children can be positioned in feeder/car seats so that upright positioning and head control are promoted. Another technique is to seat the child in the therapist's lap to support the child upright. The use of visually stimulating, response-contingent, colorful, movable, sound-producing toys themselves will prompt and shape adaptive responses better than toys with single indistinct features. Nevertheless, manual prompts are necessary to allow the child to initiate behavior; then, the psychologist can redo a task and observe whether the adaptive behavior is repeated independently without prompts. Emphasize social interaction heavily in the assessment. Face-to-face vocal play with severely retarded children can be conducted with peek-a-boo games, gently blowing air on the child's face to stimulate smiling, matching vocalizations, and other emotional responses. Another simple game consists of placing the child on his/her back while the psychologist uses high-pitched, up and down vocalizations (like a slide whistle) and moves his/her face near and then away from the child. Using this game, you can assess sustained attention, social communication, arousal, and evidence of the child wanting the game to continue (secondary circular reactions). Often, a Piagetian framework for cognitive developmental assessment is very useful to suggest tasks and procedures for eliciting cause–effect, means–end, imitative, and object search behaviors from severely retarded preschoolers.

GUIDEPOINTS

- Interrupt atypical behavior patterns.
- Determine optimal positioning.
- Choose multisensory, response-contingent toys.
- Emphasize social interactions.

Neuromotor Impairments

Consistent with the cognitive deficits frequently accompanying neurological impairments, cerebral palsied children are not able to discover and explore their worlds through motor exploration. In addition, they often learn to be helpless since their motor deficits prevent them from gaining toys that they want; this establishes a cycle in which parents and others dominate interactions and do things for them. They then become dependent and passive while never having the experience of testing their own capabilities—the key to developing a sense of personal competence or self-efficacy.

The aim of the developmental assessment is to circumvent the neuromotor deficits as much as possible, in order to isolate evidence of intact conceptual, problem solving, and social communication skills—a tall, but not impossible order.

As an inviolable principle, *psychologists should never assess cerebral palsied children unless they pair with a physical or occupational therapist or teacher skilled in proper positioning techniques.* Proper positioning for each child all too frequently makes the difference between an accurate appraisal and a seemingly "true," albeit, dramatic underestimate of the child's concepts and competencies. The cerebral palsied child, for example, should be evaluated over two to three sessions so that rapport can be established and the child's typical methods of communication determined. Consultation with the therapist or teacher will provide direction on the most effective positioning arrangement according to the child's level of muscle tone, arm and hand use, and trunk and head support. Often, young physically handicapped children interact and perform best when seated in their adaptive wheelchair with a table tray. The chair offers the advantage of structure, confinement at a table, foot support for leverage, and trunk support by an H-chest strap and shoulder wedges that position the arms forward for better hand use at the midline of the body. At a table surface, it is usually helpful to use a sticky or nonslip surface through the use of a removable product called Dycem, which prevents toys from sliding. Another arrangement may involve seating at a corner chair with a high back and wedges and blocks for trunk support. For more severely disabled children, the use of a beanbag chair is recommended to mold body positions; also, working with the child in side-lying on the side that offers best hand use is important. Proper positioning alters muscle tone, reduces the negative effects of persistent primitive reflexes, and aligns the head and body for optimal facial orientation, reaching and grasping, and manipulating. Haeussermann (1958) is still the best detailed resource on assessing the young cerebral palsied child.

Assessing the child's most reliable response mode is another key step in staging. The psychologist must explore alternative modes such as eye localization to pictures and objects, changes in facial (emotional) expressions, eye blinks, global gestures for the athetoid cerebral palsied child, and yes–no head shakes. The use of microswitches on action toys for cause–effect play and alternate computer-based communication systems must be explored and used as part of the assessment.

In summary, the psychologist must use adaptive equipment, determine the best response mode, properly position the child, and allow sufficient time for the child to try a task before offering verbal or manual guidance.

GUIDEPOINTS

- Team with an occupational or physical therapist.
- Remember to properly position neurologically impaired children.
- Use adaptive equipment to minimize response limitations.
- Determine the child's most reliable mode of response.

Affective/Behavior Disorders

Staging an assessment for a child with autism or pervasive developmental disorder is one of the most challenging and frequently exhausting experiences for a psychologist. A team approach is necessary with such children; the use of a formal assessment protocol or set of procedures helps greatly to reduce ambiguity and to appraise comprehensively the child's capabilities and intensity of service needs. The protocol should be a multisource, multidimensional survey that synthesizes information from parent interview, observation of parent–child interaction, ratings of atypical and functional characteristics, and appraisal of verbal and, especially, nonverbal concept development and problem solving. The use of curriculum-based measures and severity checklists such as the Childhood Autism Rating Scale (CARS) (Shopler, Reichler, & Renner, 1988) are extremely useful, since they allow all team members to contribute to the assessment and help to determine the diagnosis, severity of the disorder, and range of functional competencies to direct intervention.

Two aspects of pervasive developmental disorder or autism seriously disrupt developmental progress: a presumably neurochemical basis that distorts sensory input and often results in self-stimulatory behavior; and serious deficits in social interaction and communication. These same qualities make staging a formal assessment extremely difficult. A combination of table and free play activities should be chosen that alternates *verbal, nonverbal, and reciprocal tasks.* For structured activities, it is often best to use a chair and table to contain the child and/or an assistant *to interrupt inappropriate behaviors.* Often, these children show an unusual attachment to certain toys such as a "Gumby" doll or horse or typically toys that spin and move. These can be used as activity reinforcers for completing various assessment tasks. Interspersing verbal and nonverbal tasks is crucial; for example, object/picture identification followed by assembling a disjointed puzzle of a cat. Often, match-to-sample activities such as those on the Leiter International Performance Scale capitalize on the abnormal attachment to objects and reduced social interaction. Nevertheless, a portion of the session(s) should focus on observation of the interaction between the child and his/her parents, stressing expression and acceptance of affection, rhythmic habit patterns, symbolic play with toys, coping with changes, and above all, eye contact and initiation of social interaction. These observational sessions should be designed to elicit the child's typical responses to environmental stimulation, including negative reactions such as screaming, self-involvement, tantrums when routines are disrupted, and catastrophic reactions to transitions. A flexible clinical approach is necessary to provide overall organization for the session and to permit the psychologist to adjust to the child's behavioral cues.

GUIDEPOINTS

- Use a formal protocol for autism diagnosis and assessment.
- Limit self-stimulatory behaviors.
- Alternate verbal, nonverbal, and reciprocal tasks.
- Observe parent–child interactions.

SUGGESTED READINGS

Bagnato, S. J., Neisworth, J. T., & Munson, S. M. (1989). *Linking developmental assessment and early intervention: Curriculum-based prescriptions* (2nd ed.). Rockville, MD: Aspen.

Bailey, D. B., & Wolery, M. (1989). *Assessing infants and preschoolers with handicaps.* Columbus, OH: Merrill.

Haeussermann, E. (1958). *Developmental potential of preschool children.* New York: Grune & Stratton.

Neisworth, J. T., & Bagnato, S. J. (1987). *The young exceptional child: Early development and education.* New York: Macmillan.

Simeonsson, R. (1986). *Psychological and developmental assessment of special children.* New York: Allyn & Bacon.

Ulrey, G., & Rogers, S. J. (1982). *Psychological assessment of handicapped infants and young children.* New York: Thieme-Stratton.

Wachs, T. D., & Sheehan, R. (1988). *Assessment of young developmentally disabled children.* New York: Plenum.

BEST PRACTICE SUMMARY CHECKLIST

Chapter 3

How Does the Preschool Psychologist Stage an Assessment?

[ ] 1. Help your preschool staff evaluate and order an array of toys, furniture, and assessment materials so that they can better accommodate all types of special needs.

[ ] 2. Devise a team protocol that lists special considerations for staging an assessment of preschoolers with specific disabilities that all can use.

[ ] 3. Brainstorm creative tactics that team members can use to guide preschool behavior: attention, compliance, play, turn-taking, adjustment to unfamiliar situations, special interactions.

[ ] 4. Include an observation of parent-child interaction as a routine part of the child's assessment.

[ ] 5. Always ask parents to bring the child's favorite toys from home to be used as rapport-builders and even as actual toys for assessment tasks.

[ ] 6. Assess within the preschool setting or make the assessment room as home-like as possible.

[ ] 7. Invest in a wide array of nontest toys and games covering the infant to kindergarten range that are multisensory, response-contingent, social, and adaptive.

4

What Is Convergent Assessment?

ISSUES IN PRACTICE

- How important are technical psychometric considerations in constructing preschool assessment batteries?
- What are the components of a convergent assessment battery?
- What are eight major types of instruments?
- What type of assessment is the most useful for early childhood in instructional programming?

The status of preschool children cannot be assessed in the same way as school-age children. In fact, recent surveys of clinics and early childhood special education programs indicate that one third to one half of children evaluated initially for program eligibility were declared "untestable" because of language, behavioral, and sensorimotor impairments (Bagnato, 1990). Intelligence tests such as the WPPSI-R, McCarthy Scales, K-ABC, Binet IV, Woodcock-Johnson Preschool Cluster, and other similar norm-referenced measures were employed for these eligibility evaluations. One could ask, *For whom are publishers designing these measures if they cannot be used with half the children who need to be assessed?* These measures do not include young handicapped children in the test's normative samples. Few extant measures even contain handicap-sensitive adaptations or developmentally appropriate skill sequences to sample relevant behaviors adequately. These facts bring into dispute the common admonitions concerning "technical adequacy," which posit that psychologists should use only certain types of instruments under certain conditions to validly "test" young exceptional children (Danielson, 1989). In fact, some assessment specialists have concluded that many traditional norm-referenced tests are *invalid* for use with handicapped children because of these limitations (Fuchs, Fuchs, Benowitz, & Barringer, 1987). Early childhood assessment must be grounded in a developmental rather than a psychometric perspective. Unquestionably, fundamental changes in conventional psychological assessment methods are imperative with many preschool children.

As was stated in Chapter 3, psychologists must learn to be good playmates, astute observers of preschool behavior, persistent "detectives," adaptive assessment specialists, and, above all, comfortable with ambiguity. They must be willing to leave behind the psychometric security of their Binet kits, Wechsler scales, and time-worn biases. Early childhood assessment requires a broader outlook, flexible procedures, a practical understanding of development, and a more spontaneous and flexible interpersonal style that is antithetical with "lock-step" standardization procedures. Assessment for early intervention requires new perspectives and new practices; a Convergent Assessment is a contemporary approach to early childhood appraisal—an approach to meet legal, ethical, and practical requirements for the early intervention profession.

This chapter provides the rationale, purposes, and procedures for Convergent Assessment. Related topics discussed include the following:

- survey results regarding early childhood measurement in psychology and special education
- a classification system for early childhood measures
- criteria for selecting Convergent Assessment batteries

STATUS OF SCHOOL PSYCHOLOGY IN PRESCHOOL SETTINGS

Recent surveys of psychologists in preschool settings make clear that psychologists understand what specialized professional training and information they need to work effectively with preschoolers and their families (NASP/APA Preschool Interest Group, 1987). However, old habits die hard! Knowing what is correct and doing what is correct may have little relationship. Many professionals continue to force-fit and misapply school-age practices to preschool circumstances; administrative constraints and outmoded service delivery arrangements may account somewhat for this situation. A survey of 105 psychologists in preschool settings (NASP/APA Preschool Interest Group, 1987) underscores the discrepancy between knowing and doing. Forty-two percent of the psychologists indicate that their traditional preschool assessment techniques are inadequate; they want updated information on alternative methods. Yet, traditional measures, such as the Stanford-Binet (64%) WPPSI (37%), K-ABC

(33%), Vineland (49%), and other measures are still used predominantly. Only about 15% of psychologists use developmental or curriculum-based assessment techniques while over 90% of early childhood special educators and therapy staff depend on such systems (Johnson & Beauchamp, 1989). Psychologists also report other needs: knowledge of alternative play, observation, and nonverbal assessment methods (91%); knowledge and skills useful in intervention, especially curriculum planning and early education (27%); ways of developing rapport with young children (21%); knowledge of normal (95%) and atypical development (30%); and understanding and working with family systems (44%).

Several conclusions emerge from the survey that have direct implications for assessment and intervention.

1. Current school psychology practices and administrative procedures in preschool settings are at odds with both Public Law 99-457 and the National Association of School Psychologists (NASP) position statements on early intervention and early childhood assessment.

2. School psychologists continue to emphasize norm-referenced measurement, despite the evidence that children with special needs cannot be adequately assessed through standardized procedures and that normative information is of little instructional relevance.

3. Assessment and intervention are generally viewed as separate activities. Early intervention is based on intraindividual assessment (i.e., curriculum-based) while school psychologists continue to be preoccupied with interindividual assessment (i.e., norm-based).

4. School psychologists still spend much time on assessment for categorical diagnosis and placement, although this is at odds with the federal noncategorical mandate and best practices in the early intervention field.

5. There exists little understanding about the developmental, ecological, and multidimensional nature of early childhood assessment or the need for serial rather than one-time assessments to profile child skills, deficits, and needs.

GUIDEPOINT

- By necessity, use alternative versus traditional assessment
  methods with most special preschoolers.

A CONVERGENT ASSESSMENT MODEL

It is naive and misleading to use a single criterion for early childhood appraisal. The complexity of developmental delays in young children, their lack of self-regulatory capabilities, the need for parent involvement, and the necessity of interdisciplinary input demand a multidimensional approach to assessment and intervention. Early childhood assessment relies upon the confluence of information across multiple measures, domains, sources, settings, and occasions to accomplish multiple purposes. We refer to this approach and outcome as convergent assessment. *Convergent assessment refers to the synthesis of information gathered from several sources, instruments, settings, and occasions to produce the most valid appraisal of developmental status and to accomplish the related assessment purposes of identification, prescription, and progress evaluation.* It also combines both quantitative and qualitative information about the child in his/her physical and social environment. If different sources of information provide similar results, the early intervention team can more confidently detect child and family needs (see Figure 4.1).

Convergent assessment offers at least two strong advantages:

- A richer and broader sampling of child functioning across people, settings, and occasions; this enhances the social validity of assessment.
- A composite picture of the child's service delivery needs based on consensual information from teams of professionals and parents; this fosters the social as well as treatment validity of assessment.

Multiple Domains

Cognitive abilities in young children are so functionally dependent on other competencies that they cannot be isolated for assessment. Assessment of cognition in the preschool years is neither an exclusive dimension for assessment nor is it the most important. Psychologists must sample and examine numerous developmental and behavioral dimensions and cognition is only one of many. Some of the more critical dimensions include social competence, attention, language understanding and use, basic concepts, emotional expression, motor control, coping with new sit-

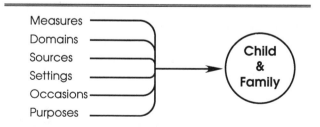

FIGURE 4.1. Convergent Assessment Model for early intervention.

uations, self-regulation, and play. The fact that most preschool programs emphasize these domains within their curricula makes assessment immediately more relevant for intervention.

Multiple Measures

Accurate assessment of special needs preschoolers relies upon the use of complementary sets of scales. These batteries are based on each child's functional limitations and the need to prescribe goals and strategies for child services. *These and other objectives are accomplished through the use of an individually selected multidimensional battery.* Research has demonstrated that a battery comprised of a combination of norm-based, curriculum-based, judgment-based, and ecological scales generates a broader and more valid and useful profile of functional capabilities that not only describes the child but guides selection of program objectives and intervention (Bagnato, 1984; LeLaurin, 1985).

Norm-based measures are diagnostic and determine the degree of developmental deficit by comparing a child with peers. Curriculum-based measures analyze attainment within and across sequences of developmental objectives; this curricular analysis helps to identify a child's intraindividual needs, suggests adaptations for response limitations, and aids in planning a treatment program and monitoring progress and impact. Judgment-based scales enable parents and professionals to contribute equitably to the decision-making process and to appraise ambiguous response classes. Ecological scales enable the team to assess the situations and contexts of the child and family providing a measure of the developmental quality of the environment.

Table 4.1 displays a generic model for a minimum convergent assessment battery. "Modal" batteries are suggested in Appendixes A and B for specific ages and handicaps. These are referred to as modal batteries because they provide an optimal combination of scales for use with most children of a particular age and handicap. These suggested modal batteries should not be considered the only possible combinations. Additional instruments and changes in some measures are dictated by particular child and family characteristics; most often, however, the suggested modal batteries will be an effective one or at least provide a "starter set" of tools. *The fundamental aspect to be considered is the developmental curriculum that is comprised of sequences of goals and activities targeted within the program.* All other measures are chosen in terms of their compatibility with the program's content and objectives.

As a prerequisite to battery selection, psychologists must first be adept observers of behavior—"detectives" in search of clues to solving the puzzle of the child's strengths, weaknesses, and developmental profile. Being a good detective requires the observation of behaviors that can be sorted

TABLE 4.1. A Convergent Assessment Battery Model

Scale Type	Purpose of Measure
Norm-based	Determine degree of developmental deficits through normative comparison.
Curriculum-based	Identify curricular objectives, offer handicap adaptations, and monitor child progress/program impact.
Judgment-based	Include parent and professional perceptions of child status and progress.
Eco-based	Characterize the social and physical qualities of the child's developmental context, especially the family.

into categories of age-appropriate, delayed, and atypical. Knowledge of development is the essential prerequisite, not what test to administer. In fact, there will be many cases in which psychologists can only use a "clinical sampling" approach (as discussed in Chapter 5), rather than a formal test. *There is no child who cannot be assessed; there are only professionals who cannot assess.*

Multiple Sources

Test performance in a controlled clinic situation with one person is not a representative sample of behavior! A convergent approach allows the psychologist to collect information from several sources using different techniques. Through a process of *triangulation*, professionals can identify areas of agreement among people about the extent of the child's needs and whether the child evidences the same skill for different people.

Multiple sources include family members, the several team members (teacher, speech therapist, psychologist), baby sitters, and others. These various sources would provide diverse types of data, including information from interviews, observations, ratings, and test scores.

Multiple Settings

Assessments must be conducted within and across different situations. This is the only way in which professionals and parents can accurately analyze the effect of physical and social settings on the child's performance in familiar and new circumstances. Also, cross-situational assessment detects whether a child's learning is context-specific or whether it is generalized to new people, materials, and circumstances. Multiple settings include home, preschool, clinic, playground, and different social arrangements (e.g., with parent present, one–one, peer-pairing, group circle time).

Multiple Occasions

Psychologists in preschool settings must work diligently to eliminate the school-age practice of single-session assessments. Young children with special needs must be appraised longitudinally in order to identify patterns of skills and deficits; this can be accomplished only through repeated observations and trials. Most importantly, PL 99-457 discourages early diagnostic classification; it bases service eligibility on estimates of delays in any of several developmental and behavioral areas. Accurate prediction of developmental status can be made only after serial assessments document the young child's response to intervention over an extended time (i.e., months, years). *Developmental status cannot be predicted in the absence of intervention.* Professionals regularly misdiagnose and underestimate the capabilities of children with sensory, neuromotor, language, and affective/behavioral disorders when these estimates are based on single occasion/source/setting information. A series of assessments (e.g., quarterly, semiannually, yearly) rather than a single session assessment is crucial for young children. Single-session diagnostic assessment with preschoolers is not only unjustifiable and unethical, it is illegal.

Multiple Purposes

Convergent assessment serves several interrelated purposes. The ultimate purpose is to plan instructional and therapeutic programs. Four major interrelated and sequential purposes are screening, prescriptive assessment, individualized curriculum planning, and child progress and program evaluation. This sequence is known as the Developmental Assessment/Curriculum Linkage Model (Bagnato, Neisworth, & Munson, 1989).

GUIDEPOINTS

- Employ a convergent assessment model to ensure the most representative appraisal of the child and environment.
- Focus on multiple developmental and behavioral domains.
- Gather information from multiple sources and multiple settings.
- Use a child-tailored battery of scales.
- Monitor gains serially during intervention.
- Link assessment and intervention via progress/program evaluation.

THE RIGHT TOOL FOR THE RIGHT JOB

Convergent assessment involves formal and informal measurement tools and methods to accomplish several aims for the young exceptional child and family. This approach fits both "best practices" and the legal mandate that no single criterion be used to diagnose a child or to determine eligibility for services. We should not select scales based upon some arbitrary and restrictive administrative requirement. Scales should be chosen based upon a specific purpose—the right tool for the right job. Ultimately, all scales in a battery must contribute to the treatment validity of the assessment—how well the assessment contributes to the guiding and monitoring of intervention.

Classification schemes often make a problem clearer and decisions easier. The myriad appraisal tools available to professionals in early childhood can be classified to assist in selecting appropriate measures based on a match between child/family needs and purposes. Such a classification should enable professionals to choose instruments for description, placement, prescription, and prediction. In a previous publication, a typology of dependent measures (Neisworth & Bagnato, 1988) was offered to help professionals choose assessment instruments. This classification scheme was offered to bridge a distinct gap in the early intervention field; it presents a way to organize available formal and informal assessment instruments into eight categories. Within the typology there is a description of the content and purpose(s) for measures that fit each category, examples of appropriate scales, and a sample of the clinical and research questions that the scales could address. Professionals can and should choose scales based not on popularity or administrative directives, but on child needs and purpose. The eight types of assessment tools are summarized in the sections below. Additionally, examples of exemplary scales are listed in tables that accompany the discussion of each type. A complete analysis and discussion of these and other measures can be found in *Linking Developmental Assessment and Early Intervention: Curriculum-Based Prescriptions* (Bagnato et al., 1989).

Curriculum-Based Measures

Curriculum-based developmental assessment is the preeminent form of measurement within early intervention programs (Bagnato et al., 1989; Johnson & Beauchamp, 1987) (see Chapter 6). The hallmark of curriculum-based assessment (CBA) is the direct congruence of testing, teaching/therapy, and progress evaluation. Task-analyzed sequences of developmental skills form the structural foundation and content for preschool CBA (see Table 4.2).

Curriculum-based measures have four major purposes: (1) to assess entry status in the curriculum, (2) to prescribe a child's individual plan of intervention goals and adaptations, (3) to provide a common instrument to coordinate interdisciplinary team members' assessments, and (4) to document the child's progress along the continuum of objectives and the program's efficacy.

TABLE 4.2. Selected Curriculum-Based Scales

Scale	Age range (mos)	Feature	Publisher
<u>Infant</u>			
E-LAP	0–36	One of first available Norm-related Uses motivating toys 500+ objectives	Kaplan
<u>Preschool</u>			
HELP and Help for Special Preschoolers (1981, 1986)	0–72	Most widely used (HELP) HELP at home materials	VORT
BDIED (1978)	0–72	Best criterion-referenced preschool system	Curriculum Assoc.
HICOMP Preschool Curriculum (1983)	0–60	Integrated programs 700+ objectives Behavioral strategies Track records for progress evaluations	Psychological Corp.
<u>Kindergarten</u>			
BM (1986)	36–60	Developmental and preacademic Handicap accommodations Activities handbook	DLM/ Teaching Resources

BDIED, BRIGANCE Diagnostic Inventory of Early Development; BM, Beginning Milestones; DLM, Developmental Learning Materials; E-LAP, Early Learning Accomplishment Profile; HELP, Hawaii Early Learning Profile; HICOMP, Higher Competencies Preschool Curriculum.

Two kinds of CBA instruments are available. *Curriculum-referenced* scales sample the types of skills included in most preschool curricula, although they are not specific to any particular curriculum. The most prominent example is the BRIGANCE Diagnostic Inventory of Early Development (Brigance, 1978) which is not itself a curriculum. *Curriculum-embedded* scales are those in which the assessment and instructional objectives and task sequences are nearly identical and specific to that curriculum. The Hawaii program, Help for Special Preschoolers (Furuno et al., 1985) is the most popular curriculum-embedded system.

Adaptive-to-Handicap Measures

Sensory, neuromotor, and behavioral deficits prevent many young children from showing what they have learned. These same functional impairments limit the acquisition of basic communication, attention, play, conceptual, and social skills. Children with neurodevelopmental disabilities are penalized when traditional measures are used. Measures that allow only one type of response to standardized stimuli assess the child's *disabilities* rather than *capabilities*. Their use is clearly discriminatory.

Adaptive-to-handicap measures are designed to circumvent the child's disabilities to produce a more accurate picture of abilities. Adaptive-to-handicap measures allow the use of alternate response modes (e.g., light wand, eye localization, computer) and varied stimulus presentations (e.g., color contrast, magnification, handles on form boards, textures) to assess knowledge and capabilities. Adaptive strategies are available most often within developmental curricula. Some newly developed norm- and curriculum-based hybrid measures, such as the Battelle Developmental Inventory (Newborg, Stock, Wnek, Guidubaldi, & Svinicki, 1984), contain adaptive modifications.

Adaptive-to-handicap scales help to achieve two primary missions: (1) to obtain a more valid or "fair" appraisal of the child's capabilities, and (2) to determine the types of instructional and therapeutic modifications necessary to help the child learn despite the impairment (Table 4.3).

Norm-Based Measures

Although norm-based measures have legitimate purposes, they are overused and misused in early intervention (Garwood, 1982; Shonkoff, 1983). Measures of cognitive and conceptual abilities are the most ubiquitous kinds of norm-based measures. It is often important to compare a child's abilities with those of age peers. Norm-based scales provide *interindividual* comparisons in order to determine the child's relative standing with expected performance. Thus, norm-based scales can screen, diagnose, and gauge the relative extent of problems (Table 4.4). In contrast, curriculum-based scales offer intraindividual comparisons. They enable professionals to chart the child's individual progress with previous performance, not the performance of others, as the referent. Nevertheless, norm-based scales continue to be misused to evaluate program effects and individual response to treatment. Normative instruments are insensitive to small increments of change and most often do not sample the types and scope of behaviors important in early intervention programs. Further, their rigid standardization does not allow adaptations to circumvent the child's impairments.

Norm-based measures do have, however, three distinct purposes: (1) to describe the child's functional skills in comparative terms, (2) to classify the degree of the child's deficits via a preexisting diagnostic category, and (3) to predict the child's development in the absence of intervention or other major life changes. This last purpose is a dubious one, at best, and does not seem warranted since the job of early intervention is to maximize developmental progress; dire predictions without reference to the effects of intervention are counter-productive.

TABLE 4.3. Selected Adaptive-to-Handicap Scales

Scale	Age range	Adaptation	Publisher
Infant			
Carolina Curriculum for Handicapped & At-risk Infants (1986)	0–24 mos	Visual, motor, auditory	Brookes
Mullen Scales of Early Learning (1990)	0–68 mos	General modifications	TOTAL Child, Inc.
Preschool			
Carolina Curriculum for Preschoolers with Special Needs (1990)	24–60 mos	Motor, sensory, social, language	Brookes
Developmental Programming for Infants & Young Children (1981)	0–72 mos	Visual, motor, auditory	U of Michigan Press
Oregon Project Curriculum for Visually Impaired & Blind Preschool Children (1979)	0–72 mos	Visual	Jackson, CO Service Dist.
Kindergarten			
Developmental Communication Curriculum (1982)	12–60 mos	Language, auditory	Psychological Corp.
Adaptive Performance Instrument (1980)	0–9 yrs	Motor sensory impairments	CAPE U of Idaho
Pictorial Test of Intelligence (1964)	3–9 yrs	Physical limitations	Riverside

Process Measures

Sometimes, children appear to be untestable by any means. Atypical behavior patterns and other severe limitations in functioning compromise the child's ability to attend, interact, and comply with task requirements. Yet, as emphasized, it must be a matter of principle that no child is untestable. Process assessment strategies include both formal and informal clinical methods for estimating the child's capabilities and probing information processing abilities (Vietze & Coates, 1986). Neisworth and Bagnato (1988) state that process assessment methods

> examine changes in child reactions (e.g., smiling, vocalizing, heart rate, surprise, latency, duration of attention) as a function of changes in stimulus events, to produce, by inference, an indication of the child's level of cognitive abilities, or qualitative advance in cognitive stage. (p. 32)

TABLE 4.4. Selected Norm-Based Scales

Scale	Age range (mos)	Kind	Publisher
Infant			
Bayley Scales of Infant Development (1969)	0–30	Development	Psychological Corp.
Kent Infant Development Scale (1985)	0–12	Development	Developmental Metrics
Preschool			
Battelle Developmental Inventory (1984)	0–84	Development	DLM/Teaching Resources
Preschool Language Scale (1979)	12–84	Language	Psychological Corp.
Kindergarten			
McCarthy Scales of Children's Abilities (1972)	24–102	Cognitive	Psychological Corp.
Kaufmann Assessment Battery for Children (1984)	30–244	Cognitive	American Guidance Service
Differential Ability Scales (1990)	30+	Cognitive	Psychological Corp.
Bracken Basic Concept Scale (1986)	30–96	Basic concepts and readiness	Psychological Corp.

The primary purpose of process assessment is to estimate the status of children who have absent or impaired response modalities and to discover obscured competencies in discrimination, comprehension, and recall that are not evident through standard means (Table 4.5).

Judgment-Based Measures

Perceptions and clinical judgment of children are an important component of early childhood assessment. Judgments are perhaps the most natural way to document the child's behavior in social circumstances; if various people in various settings hold similar judgments about the child's behavior, then those congruent, collective judgments provide social validity to assessment. Judgment-based assessment provides an economical and natural way to broaden the assessment beyond the limited clinical or program setting. Ratings from professionals, parents, and other caregivers are valuable for appraising the child's perceived strengths and weaknesses

TABLE 4.5   Selected Process Assessment Scales

Scale	Functional level	Type	Publisher
Infant			
Fagan Test of Infant Intelligence (1986)	Mild to severe	Computer-based	Infantest
Uzgiris-Hunt Infant Psychological Development Scales (1980)	0–24 mos	Piagetian	PRO-ED
Preschool to Kindergarten			
Dynamic Assessment (1984)	Mild to moderate	Feurstein	Psychological Corp.

GUIDEPOINTS

- Prescribe, coordinate, and monitor team intervention via curriculum-based scales.
- Accommodate sensory/response deficits with adaptive-to-handicap scales.
- Compare, classify, and predict functioning with norm-based scales.
- Probe possible hidden capacities through process measures.

---

and progress. An intervention may produce a change as detected on a test; if that change is not socially noticeable or important, it has no social validity. Only judgment-based assessment registers social perceptions.

Judgment-based assessment is appropriate for four purposes: (1) to sample ambiguous characteristics and response classes that are not discrete (e.g., normalcy of appearance and behavior; consolability; self-control); (2) to supplement and challenge the results of more formal but less natural measures; (3) to offer parents a nonthreatening way to contribute their impressions and intuitions about their child's capabilities; and (4) to socially validate assessment across time, people, and settings (Table 4.6).

Ecological Measures

By necessity, special education services have been child-centered. PL 99-457 ensures that this exclusive emphasis will change with the recognition

TABLE 4.6. Selected Judgment-Based Measures

Scale	Age range (mos)	Focus	Publisher
Infant			
Early Coping Inventory (1988)	4–36	Adaptive	Scholastic Testing Service
Carolina Record of Individual Behavior (1985)	0–48	Development Behavior	Rune Simeonsson
Preschool to Kindergarten			
Developmental Specs (1990)	24–72	Development	American Guidance Service
Child Behavior Checklist (1986)	24–72+	Behavior problem severity	Achenbach
Social Skills Rating System (1990)	36+	Social competence	American Guidance Service

that family support is vital to child progress; this broader ecological emphasis is operationalized in the Individualized Family Service Plan (IFSP) and requires teams to evaluate, not only the child but also the child's physical and social environment. Family "self-appraisal" is an important part of this trend.

Ecological assessment probes the child's developmental context, including preschool and home environments, peer interactions, caregiver responsiveness, child management techniques, safety features, parent/family program participation, and provision of handicap-sensitive toys. Ecological assessment promotes a transactional view of child development.

Ecological assessment measures can be properly used to accomplish two major missions: (1) to describe the nature and qualities of child/environmental interactions, and (2) to identify specific child and milieu dimensions that can be added or rearranged to improve interactions (Table 4.7).

Interactive Measures

Child interactive assessment concentrates on the character of caregiver-child dyadic transactions and is especially important in that development does not occur in isolation, but is the result of reciprocal interactions in which the behavior of each person in the dyad shapes the other.

Interactive assessment fulfills two purposes: (1) to dissect the typical elements of a caregiver–child interaction involving giving, receiving, and responding to cues; and (2) to highlight matches between the child's interactive competencies and the content and pacing of the caregiver's responses (Table 4.8).

Systematic Observation

Fundamental to any comprehensive and convergent assessment effort is the direct observation and recording of behavior. Systematic observation is a structured way to gather measurable data about ongoing discrete behaviors. It can occur in the naturalistic situation, under "staged" circumstances, or in prompted or role-playing situations. For example, sys-

TABLE 4.7. Selected Ecological Measures

Scale	Age range	Focus	Publisher
Infant–Preschool–Kindergarten			
Infant Daycare Environment Rating Scale	0–36 mos	Infant Daycare	Teachers College Press
Home Observation for Measurement of the Environment (1979)	0–72 mos	Home	Betty Caldwell
Early Childhood Environment Rating Scale (1980)	Pre-K	Preschool	Teachers College Press
Family Needs Survey (1985)	All	Family	Bailey

TABLE 4.8. Selected Interactive Scales

Scale	Age range	Focus	Publisher
Infant			
Brazelton Neonatal Behavioral Assessment Scale (1984)	Newborn	Infant	Lippincott
Parent Behavior Progression (1978)	0–36 mos	Interaction status and change	PRO-ED
Preschool–Kindergarten			
Teaching Skills Inventory (1984)	Preschool	Parent competencies	Robinson
Parenting Stress Index (1983)	1–60+ mos	Perceived stress	CPPC Press

tematic observation can detect the degree of interaction and extent of integration among handicapped preschoolers and nonhandicapped peers. Direct observation of behaviors in the preschool and home settings should be an violable prerequisite of any interdisciplinary assessment.

Systematic observation accomplishes multiple purposes in three major areas: (1) to detect emerging or present behavior patterns, (2) to closely analyze treatment-specific target behaviors, and (3) to quantify small increments of learning undetectable by other means (Table 4.9).

GUIDEPOINTS

- Validate functioning socially through judgment-based scales.
- Describe child/environmental dimensions via ecological scales.
- Analyze reciprocal interaction patterns with interactive measures.
- Record ongoing behavior by systematic observation.

TABLE 4.9. Selected Systematic Observation Techniques

Scale	Features	Publisher
Preschool–Kindergarten		
Planned Activities Check (1972)	10-min intervals	Doke & Risley
	All children engaging in an activity	U of Kansas
Social Interaction Scan (1988)	Time sampling of play behavior	Guralnick
	Uses Parten play categories	U of Washington
Direct Observation of Social Behavior	Focuses on one child	Early Childhood Research Institute
	Nine categories of social behavior	

SUGGESTED READINGS

Bagnato, S. J., Neisworth, J. T., & Munson, S. M. (1989). *Linking developmental assessment and early intervention: Curriculum based prescriptions* (2nd ed.). Rockville, MD: Aspen.

Neisworth, J. T., & Bagnato, S. J. (1988). Assessment in early childhood special education: A typology of dependent measures. In S. Odom & M. Karnes (Eds.), *Early intervention for infants and children with handicaps: An empirical base* (pp. 23–49). Baltimore, MD: Brookes.

Simeonsson, R. J. (1986). *Psychological and developmental assessment of special children*. Newton, MA: Allyn & Bacon.

BEST PRACTICE SUMMARY CHECKLIST

Chapter 4

What Is Convergent Assessment?

[ ] 1. Examine the available assessment tools for your program in order to choose a "modal battery" that is developmental, curriculum-based, adaptive, and ecological.

[ ] 2. Reach a consensus with your team to select and order an array of norm, curricular, judgment, and ecological instruments that can apply to all the primary disabilities and developmental needs including infants.

[ ] 3. Review, as an initial attempt, such scales/systems as the Battelle Developmental Inventory (DLM/Teaching Resources), Hawaii Early Learning Profile and Curriculum (VORT), and System to Plan Early Childhood Services (AGS).

[ ] 4. Establish team assessment procedures and schedules that enable you to assess children in a multidimensional manner: across time, people, settings, domains, and occasions.

[ ] 5. Help your staff to critically examine, revise, and broaden the criteria used for various assessment purposes including classification and program eligibility, progress monitoring, child-find and screening, and goal planning.

[ ] 6. Persuade your staff to rely more on appraisals of parent-child interaction and naturalistic observations of behavior in the home and preschool settings.

5

How Can the Psychologist
"Test Without Tests"?*

ISSUES IN PRACTICE

- Why is standardized testing an "unnatural" approach to assessment of special needs preschoolers?
- Can preschool children be validly assessed using their own toys and games?
- How can the psychologist use parents to test their own children?
- Why is the psychologist's knowledge of child development more important than the test chosen?

Preschool children naturally display patterns of development and behavior which frequently limit the use of formal and standardized evaluation procedures. Handicapping conditions including sensory impairments, motoric involvement, and speech/language disorders further compromise the utility of such measures. Based on direct experience, an alternative strategy for the assessment of young, handicapped children is necessary. Brief clinical sampling can be used as the basis for making structured

*From "Clinical Sampling in the Assessment of Young, Handicapped Children: Shopping for Skills," by R. LeVan, 1990, *Topics in Early Childhood Special Education*, *10*(3), 65–79. Copyright 1990 by PRO-ED, Austin, TX. Reprinted by permission.

judgments regarding development. In the context of skill hierarchies, this information is useful in designing programs for intervention. This chapter describes principles and techniques of brief clinical sampling. Examples of the applications of brief clinical sampling with young, handicapped children are given.

ADVENTURES IN ASSESSMENT

To say that Clarence was an active child would have certainly understated the case. This 3 1/2-year-old was clearly hyperactive, impulsive, and constantly on the go. Gross motor skills were good. Those who knew Clarence were fully aware of his agility. Observed expressive language was limited. Clarence communicated using an intricate blend of noises and gestures. No limitations of vision or hearing had been reported. Development of instructional programs for Clarence had been difficult. He also presented management problems both at home and in his preschool classroom. Behavioral and medical interventions had not been successful in producing any notable gain in self-regulation.

The assignment was to conduct further assessment with Clarence and obtain information that would be useful in promoting his overall development. As far as testing Clarence, others had tried before. They came away exhausted with no more than a qualified IQ somewhere in the range of 35–50. The assignment was accepted with determination. Instruments were selected and the assessment which was conducted at home began. A few short minutes later it was over. Even with the best attempts to structure the setting, the tiny toys of the test were of little value in drawing and holding attention. Once neatly organized in small boxes, they were left in disarray. Beads and blocks had become projectiles and were scattered about the floor. Because of the "less than optimal" level of cooperation, testing was discontinued.

This assessment had given Clarence a chance to work up an appetite. His mother placed him in his high chair, strapped him in, and securely snapped on the tray. Lunch was served. When the phone rang, mother left the kitchen to take the call. In a matter of seconds, Clarence unbuckled his strap and quickly released the latches to his tray. He pushed his chair to the edge of the counter, climbed up, opened a cabinet, and removed two large rings of keys. Fast thinking about what action should be taken to manage Clarence in his mother's absence was not fast enough. He unhooked top and bottom latches of the back door, selected the proper key to open the lock, and exited to the back yard. He darted into the garage where he unlocked the car, inserted the key in the ignition, and was preparing to take himself for a ride. At that point, mother interrupted his travel plans and escorted Clarence back to the kitchen to finish his lunch. Evidencing no surprise, she calmly announced, "He does it all the time."

In this brief scenario, Clarence displayed several important developmental skills. Intentionality was clearly present as Clarence executed the steps of his escape in a purposeful and well-directed manner. Observed skills included basic problem solving, perceptual discrimination, an understanding of objects by use, and an awareness of cause–effect relationships. This story of Clarence illustrates a theme known all too well to the veterans of assessment with young children. Skills that are not demonstrated in more formal testing may be elicited and observed later in other less structured and less formal settings.

PRESCHOOLERS AND TESTS

It is fortunate that not all preschool children are as active or as difficult to manage as Clarence. However, individuals working with young children do understand that they typically are quite active and their ability to maintain attention on tasks is limited. Young children like to be on the go rather than sitting still. They are highly inquisitive and enjoy exploration of their surroundings. The unique characteristics of the preschool child have been noted (Paget & Nagle, 1986).

From a Piagetian perspective, preschoolers show patterns of cognitive development that are qualitatively different from those of older children and adults (Piaget, 1952). Their preoperational thought is idiosyncratic and highly intuitive. Concept development is limited. Young children assimilate new experiences into existing patterns of thinking much more readily than they can accommodate or change these patterns to meet external demands. For this reason, they do much better in imaginative play than in conforming to structure or rules.

Reviewing the characteristics of preschool children in this context initially appears to be an unnecessary exercise. Who does not understand that very young children have patterns of development and adjustment that are qualitatively different than older children and adults? Perhaps because of its simplicity, this concept is typically overlooked in the design and construction of tests for preschool children.

Within the tradition of psychometric measurement, tests have been developed to appraise developmental skills. Standardized procedures are used to present selected tasks. The child's performance is judged according to set criteria and then translated into a score which provides an indication of standing in some normative group. Hopefully, this information will then be used to answer original assessment questions.

In testing, emphasis is placed on control of the child and on compliance to standard procedures. These materials are supplied. These materials may or may not be of interest to the child. To insure uniformity, the manner and sequence of eliciting responses is fixed. Verbal instructions may be quite formal and the complexity of such instructions may often exceed the concept development of the child at risk, let alone, the handicapped child.

The value of such standard procedures in preserving reliability and validity in normative measurement is certainly supported. However, procedures which emphasize control, uniformity, and direction are incompatible with the identification characteristics of young children. Preschool children are not too content working in one spot for very long and their curiosities are not well satisfied by most of the "fun" materials in test kits.

While completing a formal test with any young child is a challenge, the task becomes even more difficult when conditions that may adversely affect the child's ability to receive information and make responses are encountered. Limitations of vision or hearing, language problems, and impaired motor skills all may significantly limit performance. Problems with compliance associated with shyness, separation difficulties, or oppositional features which are frequently seen in young children may also compromise the demonstration of skills.

The adverse effects of these difficulties on performance are even greater when standardized procedures associated with testing place additional limits on the presentation of tasks and the evaluation of performance. Under such conditions, it is very difficult to make appropriate adaptations in materials, manner of presentation, or in criteria of evaluation to accommodate special needs.

SAMPLING DEVELOPMENTAL SKILLS

In the assessment of young, handicapped children, adherence to procedures which permit the quantification of performance may actually thwart efforts to obtain richer, more valuable information about what the child does and does not do in several domains of functioning. This information is essential in designing and implementing appropriate programming for the child. The value of identification of skills and the establishment of a "linkage" between assessment and intervention has been discussed (Bagnato, Neisworth, & Munson, 1989).

With a recognition of the limitations of more formal or test-based evaluation procedures, alternative strategies for obtaining valuable information regarding emergent and established skills are available. A creative strategy in the assessment of young, handicapped children involves the use of structured "clinical judgment" in appraising development and functioning in several domains (Bagnato & Neisworth, 1990a,b; Simeonsson, 1986). The use of clinical judgment in assessment represents an effort to overcome the limitations of more traditional psychometric approaches and provide information that is more directly useful in guiding appropriate instruction for the child.

In applying judgment-based assessment strategies, it is extremely important to discover what the child does do. Assessment will always be based on identification of emergent and established skills within several developmental areas. This information could be obtained from parent/ teacher report, observation, or direct interaction with the child. While reports are of value, observation and direct interaction with the child often provide more useful information. A critical limitation of observation is that the observer will only see behaviors that are elicited by natural demands of the situation. More information may be obtained through direct interaction with the child, as the observer then has the opportunity to elicit or "draw out" specific skills that may not be readily identified through observation alone.

The use of observation and direct interaction with a child to obtain a sampling of skill development is certainly not an innovative assessment technique. *The innovative component is the attempt to free such observation and interaction from the constraints of standardized procedure and to place the focus properly on the child's natural skills.* The objective is to make the assessment strategy conform to the characteristics of the young handicapped child rather than to force compliance to specific standardized procedures.

In sampling, the emphasis shifts from controlling the child to providing the child with multiple opportunities to express developmental skills. The objective of sampling developmental skills is to describe the child's capabilities. Efforts are directed at obtaining the very best sample of behavior which documents skill development. Sampling of skills provides a basis for formulating clinical judgments and designing appropriate programming.

GUIDEPOINT

- Recognize that a preschooler's "misbehavior" makes valid, standardized "testing" suspect in most instances.

SHOPPING FOR SKILLS: AN ASSESSMENT ANALOGUE

Have you done your grocery shopping this week? A trip to the supermarket is hardly an adequate analogy for conducting developmental assessment with young children. Those who study the complex neurological bases of cognitive development would certainly shudder at such simplistic comparison. However, there are points of similarity worth exploring. In the market, goods are shelved in a somewhat orderly fashion based upon group or use. Although the precise arrangement may vary from market to market, there is a general pattern of organization that is recognized by most shoppers. To promote efficiency, the shopper prepares a list to guide the pursuit. Knowing the layout of the market may be helpful in preparation of the list and in procuring the goods. Of course, the list does not map out an exact route. You can start at any point, pick up items as you go, and come back to get what you missed. Bargains can be selected from special displays in any aisle and at any time.

Much like the shopper in search of supplies, the evaluator is searching for samples of behavior. The child's repertoire of developmental skills may be seen as following some logical groupings. Although the precise arrangement will vary from child to child, there are generally recognized patterns of organization. Like the efficient shopper, the evaluator prepares a "shopping list" to guide the sampling of child behavior. Knowing the patterns of child development is helpful in preparing the list and in obtaining samples of skills. The list does not map out an exact route for eliciting and observing specific developmental skills. You can start at any point, pick up additional skills as you go, and always go back to find those skills that may have been missed. A bargain or unexpected demonstration of skills can be picked up at any time. The shopping list provides the evaluator with clear indication of essential skills that should be sampled to assess development. With the list, assessment time is used in the most efficient manner. Emphasis is on procuring the skills rather than on the order or techniques of procurement.

Several inventories or surveys of developmental skills that can serve as appropriate models for the design of shopping lists are available. The BRIGANCE Inventory of Early Development lists skills in 11 areas or domains (Brigance, 1978). The Early Intervention Developmental Profile (Rogers et al., 1981) and the Preschool Developmental Profile (Brown et al., 1981) provide listings of developmental skills in cognitive, language, gross motor, perceptual/fine motor, social/emotional, and self-care domains.

Commercially available developmental inventories often are based on detailed analyses of skills. Under ideal circumstances with competent and cooperative preschoolers, such refinement may promote precision. Under the more typical conditions of assessment, highly detailed skill analysis may not be possible. The detailed list can be a distraction and the user may become overly involved in procedures for defining and eliciting responses. As a result, the focus on the child's response and capacities becomes blurred and much valuable information may be lost.

An example of a fairly simple shopping list to guide sampling of developmental skills in the communications area is provided in Table 5.1. A shopping list for basic cognitive skills is presented in Table 5.2. These lists are based, in part, upon skills noted in common developmental inventories.

TABLE 5.1 Shopping List for Communication Skills

Developmental area	Skills to be sampled
Pre-speech	
Orienting	Orients to sound
	Orients to voice
Responding	Responds selectively to voice
	Responds to name
Gesturing	Gives greetings
	Indicates needs
Vocalizing	Makes cooing, babbling
	Imitates sounds
Receptive language	
Identifying	Identifies body parts
	Identifies common objects
	Identifies colors
Following directions	Follows one-step direction
	Follows two-step direction
	Follows complex directions
Developmental areas	Skills samples
Expressive language	
Naming	Names people
	Names body parts
	Names common objects
Stating needs	States need to eat, drink
Describing action	Describes own actions
	Describes action of others
Speaking socially	Responds to questions
	Initiates discussion

They are not comprehensive lists but rather offer suggestions for sampling representative behaviors in several skill areas. Similar listings covering these and other skills in the fine/gross motor, self-help, personal-social areas could be easily developed. The idea is to follow basic developmental sequences and age/stage expectatancies and create a list to meet your own shopping needs.

GUIDEPOINTS

- Use a "shopping list" of developmental skills to flexibly guide the systematic sampling of behavior.
- First, be well versed in typical and atypical child development stages and patterns.
- Sampling the skill is most important, not how it is sampled.

TABLE 5.2 "Shopping List" for Basic Cognitive Skills

Developmental area	Skills to be sampled
Association	
Matching	Matches objects one-to-one
	Matches by color, shape, size
Sorting	Sorts on one dimension
	Sorts on two dimensions
Organization	
Classifying	Assigns to class by use
	Assigns to class by category
Ordering	Orders by size
	Orders by quantity
Comprehension	
Displaying awareness	Attends to persons
	Attends to objects
Exploring relations	Affects circular reactions
	Affects cause–effect patterns
	Shows intentionality
	Follows complex directions
Understanding	Shows use of common objects
	Shows use of uncommon objects
	Shows action sequences
	Shows action for situation
	Recognizes absurdities
Memory	
Attending	Tracks visually
	Pursues objects
	Listens in sustained manner
Retention and recall	Matches visually by memory
	Matches auditorily by memory
	Identifies object by recall
	Identifies objects by recall
	Repeats digits or sentences
Concepts	
Identifying direction	Demonstrates up, down
	Identifies object's position
Quantifying	Identifies big, little
	Tells "how many"
	Counts
Identifying time	Shows temporal sequences

SAMPLING STRATEGIES

In sampling, the focus remains on the child. The setting and materials used serve only to facilitate the demonstration of developmental skills. The objective is to elicit and describe developmental skills in a functional manner. Techniques involved in sampling are directed toward eliciting the child's best performance.

Setting

Sampling of developmental skills can be accomplished in any setting. However, young children can more readily express skills in familiar surroundings where they can be given some latitude to freely engage in exploratory activities. The child's home or preschool classroom are often good settings. In cases where children must be seen in an office, clinic, or hospital setting, it is important to provide space and materials that will allow simulation of a more comfortable setting. The assessment can move from place to place and, in each new setting, the child and evaluator may identify opportunities for demonstrating skills.

The child's parents and teachers can often be very helpful in obtaining a good sampling of the child's capabilities. They can be enlisted to assist in all phases of the assessment. Attention can be given to how parents and teachers can be most helpful rather than to the plotting of schemes for "separating" the child from them. Only in those cases where the presence of others is clearly detrimental to the child should separation be considered.

Materials

Materials which come with many commercially produced tests or developmental inventories are often unfamiliar, too small, and not particularly attractive to the child. Young children respond notably better to three dimensional, larger, more colorful, materials. In most cases, appropriate materials are available in the child's home, school, or play setting. Young children will frequently demonstrate a specific developmental skill with such materials that they did not demonstrate with unfamiliar, less attractive materials.

Sampling does not require any specialized materials. With appropriate consideration to age, just about anything that can be used by a child to demonstrate a skill can and should be used in sampling. Objects in the room (e.g., chairs, tables, doors, phone, toys) can be materials for sampling both receptive and expressive vocabulary skills. Anything of which there is more than one (e.g., shoes, cups, bananas, gloves) is a suitable material for matching activities. Things that come in sets (e.g., toy blocks, plates, toy cars) or things that represent a category (e.g., fruits, tools, clothing) can be used in sorting tasks ranging from simple to complex. Objects that have specific uses (e.g., telephone, can opener, paint brush) are suitable for sampling basic comprehension skills. Collections of objects or toy representations of such objects that are often used together (e.g., can, can opener, pan, stove, plate) provide an opportunity to elicit complex sequences of behavior which reflect sophisticated understanding. Any objects that provide sensory feedback when acted upon (e.g., bells, light switches, remote control carts) present opportunities for demonstrating awareness of cause-effect relationships. Objects of varying sizes (e.g., large Teddy bear, small Teddy bear) can be used to demonstrate concept development. Other than concerns for safety, there are no limits to the possible uses of available materials in the sampling of skills.

Procedures

Using the shopping list of skills as a general guide, the assessment can proceed in a sequence that is most convenient. It is often helpful to work within general skill areas or domains (e.g., language, basic problem solving, basic concepts). Within the identified area, assessment moves from more basic to more complex skills. Attempts may be made to elicit responses in areas which correspond to the child's interests. Following the child's natural exploratory activity and eliciting skills associated with such activities may be useful in engaging children. Adaptations for children with handicapping conditions can be made as needed. Simultaneous expression of skills in several domains is frequently noted and increases the efficiency of the assessment strategy. Skills and capabilities are noted and recorded as they are demonstrated.

Helpful Hints

1. Begin with a relaxed approach focusing on establishing and maintaining rapport with the child. Sampling is a "child-centered" approach and retaining this orientation is of critical importance. Pace and scope of the assessment are adjusted to accommodate the needs of the child.

2. Enlist the help of parents, teachers, therapists, and others who are familiar with the child. They can often be very helpful by identifying routines, activities, or settings in which the child may commonly demonstrate the skill or skills you are attempting to elicit.

3. Incorporate familiar toys, games, and play activities. They offer multiple opportunities to elicit skills in a comfortable manner. Ask for help in identifying the games and activities that are familiar for this child.

4. Do not hesitate to try out new ways of eliciting responses in a creative manner. Adapt presentation and response modes to accommodate children with sensory, motor, or speech/language impairments.

5. As children may be encountering many different toys and materials, care must be taken to protect the safety of children.

6. Take time to enjoy your work. Assessing young children is fun. This is particularly true when the assessment strategies conform to the characteristics of the children.

CLARENCE: THE ADVENTURE CONTINUES

Back in the kitchen, under close surveillance, Clarence was finishing lunch. It would soon be time for another try. Efforts would be directed at obtaining a brief clinical sampling of emergent and established developmental skills using a shopping list to guide the assessment.

GUIDEPOINTS

- Be child-focused, not test-focused.
- Conduct the assessment in the "natural" home or preschool setting for best results.
- Include the parents as partners in the assessment interaction.
- Use the child's own toys or familiar home/preschool objects.
- Provide toys with multisensory features.
- Be natural, creative, and responsive in your interactions with the child.

Identification, Directions, and Concepts

Observation has established good orientation to sounds and voices. He was clearly responsive to his name. Clarence was invited to play the "show me" game. Moving from room to room, Clarence pointed out objects as they were named. Fairly common and easy items (e.g., ball, television, doggie) were introduced first. More difficult items were requested as the assessment progressed. Items were interspersed to maintain a successful response pattern and avoid frustration. Receptive skills were much stronger than suggested by previous performance on receptive vocabulary tests. Finding real objects in the context of a game was far more productive than pointing to black and white line-drawn pictures in a static and structured setting.

Building on this success, it was relatively easy to involve Clarence in other receptive language activities. In formal assessment, he had little interest in pointing to body parts on himself or in pictures. In play, he readily pointed out body parts as named on a large Teddy bear in the corner of the play room. When asked to "put his hat on Teddy's head" or "put this shoe on Teddy's foot," he quickly complied. Other one-step directions involving play with Teddy were readily followed.

It was a good time to produce a few directional concepts. Clarence placed Teddy in, under, and on top of a box as directed. He liked the idea of another "bear" joining the activities and identified "big bear" and "little bear." He also took the bears "up the steps" and "down the steps" with good compliance.

Attempts were made to elicit more advanced skills. Clarence did not correctly identify objects that were less common and he was not successful in identifying colors. He did not complete directions involving more than one element. With consideration to age, these skills may be included as objectives in programming for Clarence.

Exploration and Understanding

Clarence was an active explorer of his environment. He had already discovered many cause-effect relationships. Turning on lights, ringing the doorbell, operating water faucets, and changing the channel with the remote control were all comfortably in his repertoire.

It was time for a different version of the "show me" game. The objective was to find objects by described use. He evidenced good understanding of common uses. In response to "show me what we cook on," he identified his sister's play stove. This attracted his interest. With the toy pots and pans, he cooked a meal. Steps in the process were performed in the correct order with proper use of food and utensils. Even the finer details of proper seasoning were not neglected.

Toy dishes and cups were used to set the table. When Clarence was busy in the kitchen, one of the cups was turned upside down. When Clarence came to pour the coffee, he quickly noted the incorrectly placed cup and turned it right side up. He also smiled curiously when he noticed the shoe placed on the plate. Clarence was quick in identifying this odd entree and the other contrived absurdities.

Matching, Memory, and Classification

Two shoes, two apples, and two cups were placed on the floor. The two shoes were held up, the match was noted, and they were placed together. The cup was then held up and Clarence was invited to find the "match." He matched cup, book, and performed well with other paired objects.

Once ability to match was documented, it was quite easy to assess visual memory. One set of objects (shoe, orange, cup) was kept in clear view on the floor while the "mates" to these items were placed out of sight behind the sofa. When Clarence was not looking, one of the objects was covered with a box and Clarence was asked to go behind the sofa to find the mate to the hidden object. Short-term memory for one object was good.

On the toy farm, there were many animals and people. There were also cars, trucks, and tractors. Efforts were made to assess more sophisticated classification skills by moving people to one pile and animals to another pile. Clarence was asked to place toy animals and people in the appropriate piles. He was not successful with this task.

As in the other areas assessed. It is possible to document specific skills evidencing association, organization, and memory. With an understanding of developmental hierarchies, appropriate objectives can be established and strategies for promoting skill acquisition designed.

Naming and Expressing Needs

Throughout the assessment, Clarence did not produce any discernible words. Sounds were used for naming with "vroom" for car and "woof" for doggie. He did well in gestural expression. When given toy musical instruments (e.g., guitar, horn), he did well in demonstrating their appropriate use. Needs to drink, eat, use bathroom, and go for a ride were all clearly expressed in gesture. Attempts to elicit some easy sounds (e.g., ball, mom) were not successful.

CONCLUDING COMMENTS

The case of Clarence illustrates some applications of brief clinical sampling in the assessment of a young, handicapped child. Only a few of many possible strategies are described here. The actual assessment of Clarence was continued over time to document a range of skills in several areas. Following the child's natural interests, developmental skills were sampled in a comfortable manner using materials readily available in the natural setting. A shopping list was used to guide the sampling in an ordinal fashion moving from more simple to complex skills in the communication and cognitive areas. There were frequent opportunities to sample skills across domains (e.g., matching and memory) while the child was engaged in one activity.

Clarence was an active child with good motor skills, good receptive skills, and no identified sensory impairments. However, the principles of brief sampling as described here can be readily applied in the assessment of young children who are experiencing a range of significant neurological, motor skill, or sensory handicaps. Appropriate shopping lists can be developed. Materials and strategies to elicit samples of skills can be freely adapted to meet the needs of the child.

The objective of brief clinical sampling is not to complete a normative evaluation of the child's development. Rather, the emphasis is clearly on documenting identified capacities that are, however, stage and age-related. Although not specifically described in the context of this discussion, many important behavioral characteristics (e.g., attention, self-regulation, task persistence, cooperation) are observed. A structured system of clinical judgment such as the System to Plan Early Childhood Services

(Bagnato & Neisworth, 1990a,b) or play assessment system like the Transdisciplinary Play-based Assessment proposed by Linder (1990) could be readily used to organize identified skills and behaviors. Within the context of developmental skill hierarchies, eligibility for services could be supported, appropriate objectives could be established, and meaningful programming prescribed.

SUGGESTED READINGS

Cohen, M. A., & Gross, P. J. (1979). *The developmental resource: Behavioral sequences for assessment and program planning* (Vols I & II). New York: Grune & Stratton.

Wachs, T. D., & Sheehan, R. (1988). Developmental patterns in disabled infants and preschoolers. In T. D. Wachs & R. Sheehan (Eds.), *Assessment of young developmentally disabled children*. New York: Plenum Press.

Linder, T. (1990). *Transdisciplinary play-based assessment: A functional approach to working with young children*. Baltimore, MD: Paul H. Brookes.

Simeonsson, R. J. (1986). Qualitative-developmental assessment. In R. J. Simeonsson, *Psychological and developmental assessment of special children* (pp. 133-178). Newton, MS: Allyn & Bacon.

BEST PRACTICE SUMMARY CHECKLIST

Chapter 5

How Can the Psychologist "Test Without Tests"?

[ ] 1. Refresh your memory about normal and atypical child development patterns by reviewing Piaget's stages and reading pertinent resources:

> Cohen, M. A., & Gross, P. J. (1979). *The developmental resource: Behavioral sequences for assessment and program planning* (Vols I & II). New York: Grune & Stratton.

> Wachs, T. D., & Sheehan, R. (1988). Developmental patterns in disabled infants and preschoolers. In T. D. Wachs & R. Sheehan (Eds.), *Assessment of young developmentally disabled children.* New York: Plenum Press.

[ ] 2. Conduct a practical exercise with your staff to have someone select six toys appropriate for a 3-year developmental range (e.g., 18–54 months) and use them to test a child's developmental skills while others observe. Then, hold a brainstorming session to analyze what you saw and reach conclusions about the child's levels of functioning.

[ ] 3. Order, under 30-day examination, assessment resources that rely on naturalistic, play-based observation of behavior as an alternative form of child appraisal and goal/activity planning:

> Linder, T. (1990). *Transdisciplinary play-based assessment: A functional approach to working with young children.* Baltimore, MD: Paul H. Brookes.

> Fewell, R., & Vadasy, P. (1981). *Learning through play: A resource manual for teachers and parents.* Allen, TX: DLM/Teaching Resources.

6

What Is Curriculum-Based Developmental Assessment?

ISSUES IN PRACTICE

- Is "teaching to the test" justifiable?
- Why is CBA the ideal method for team assessment?
- Why may psychometric test items be poor CBA tasks?
- What is "treatment-utility" in assessment?
- Why are serial assessments critical with CBA?

Professionals know the value of norm-based, standardized assessment. Instruments with adequate technical qualities enable us to determine the status of a child with respect to a referent group. Such assessment is thus useful for diagnostic purposes (i.e., determining the clinical category closest to the child's performance and attributes). Thus, normative, diagnostic assessment is important in its own right; however, it does not generate detailed or specific information for immediate program planning. Diagnostic assessment (i.e., finding the category of handicap) with preschoolers is not particularly useful vis-a-vis the mission of early intervention. But assessment serves several functions: diagnosis, prediction of developmental status, and program planning. Therefore, comprehensive assessment permits placement, prediction, and prescription (Neisworth & Bagnato, 1988).

Educators and therapists are much more concerned about what children can or cannot do—rather than what they are or are not (i.e., retarded, "disturbed," "learning disabled"). Thus, for years educators have complained about the low "treatment utility" of psychometric, trait-based assessment. Intelligence quotients, personality profiles, and other measures of global ("g" factors) or alleged characteristics offer little guidance to the teacher or parent who must decide what to teach and what materials and strategies would be most effective. Further, diagnosis of infants and young children is especially difficult and fraught with pitfalls. Very young children may be most uncooperative during formal testing. Infants, toddlers, and preschoolers are difficult to assess, change rapidly, and often require adaptations in assessment which may violate the standardization procedures required for norm-based assessment.

In addition to the usual problems associated with accurate and reliable assessment of youngsters, various handicapping conditions produce stimulus and response limitations that further complicate normative testing, making it questionable at best. Given the treacherous nature and low treatment utility of even well-calculated diagnostic appraisal, it is no wonder that teachers and therapists have demanded assessment that is more relevant, practical, and linked directly to intervention. Indeed, Public Law 99-457 requires assessment that is *noncategorical* and yields a profile of the child's *specific* developmental strengths and weaknesses across multiple developmental areas. Curriculum-based assessment (CBA) is widely accepted by both special and early educators as the best means for supplying the specificity and relevance needed for preschool program planning (Bagnato, Neisworth, & Capone, 1986; Johnson & Beauchamp, 1989). Note, again, that it is the *purpose* of the assessment that must be considered when selecting best practices and measures. It is essential for psychologists to be skilled in developmental CBA to increase their credibility and value to other early intervention professionals (Neisworth & Bagnato, 1986).

DEFINITION OF CBA

CBA is a form of criterion-referenced measurement wherein curricular objectives act as the criteria for the identification of instructional targets and for the assessment of status and progress. Criterion-referenced assessment has been employed for some time in therapy and applied behavior analysis. The major purpose of such assessment is to evaluate attainment of preset standards. Behaviorally-based instruction and therapy often involve a changing criterion design wherein the requirement for reinforcement is progressively raised. Similarly, programmed instruction and precision teaching involve measurement of behavior to check for mastery of objectives. CBA is clearly an application of criterion-referencing or goal attainment scaling for educational purposes (Simeonsson, Huntington, & Short, 1982). Even more specifically, *developmental* CBA uses developmental landmarks or expectancies as potential instructional goals and objectives (see Chapter 4 for curriculum tables).

PURPOSES OF CURRICULUM-BASED DEVELOPMENTAL ASSESSMENT

Expert use of CBA is central to quality early childhood intervention. Developmental CBA can be the major approach for accomplishing four important tasks: identifying program entry points, program planning, progress monitoring, and program evaluation. Each of these functions of CBA is discussed and illustrated later in this chapter.

CBA provides the needed closeup of child developmental status. It not only identifies where the child is within an array of objectives but permits monitoring of progress. It detects what the child can and cannot do, giving clear entry points within the program's curriculum. The monitoring function of CBA is particularly useful: it tracks child progress (formative assessment), demonstrates accumulated progress (summative assessment), and offers continual information on the effectiveness of instruction (corrective feedback). Clearly, CBA is a most direct means for identifying the entry points within an instructional program and for pacing and altering instruction.

Besides providing entry points and tracking progress, it is important to note a third distinct advantage of developmental CBA: it can invite and evaluate interdisciplinary team collaboration. Developmental curricula and corresponding assessment usually include several areas of development (i.e., motor, language, cognitive, and social). Teaching, therapy, and tracking of curricular progress in each developmental domain can be done by specialists. The child's progress within and across developmental domains can be charted, reflecting the contributions of specialists and detecting special areas of difficulty. CBA can "pull together" a team involving a physical therapist, psychologist, speech/language therapist, special education teacher, parent, and even pediatricians (Bagnato & Hofkosh, 1990). Each member can contribute to and assess relevant developmental objectives. No other form of assessment encourages and structures interdisciplinary collaboration as specifically as CBA.

Finally, there is yet another advantage of *developmental* CBA: it provides an indirect form of norm-based assessment. Normal developmental curricula are based on developmental landmarks (i.e., skills manifested by most children at various ages) that have been validated over years of clinical experience. The use of two-word sentences is generally characteristic of 2-year-olds. This capability is a norm (developmental landmark) and a curricular objective. When curricular objectives are based on child development norms, child achievement can be judged relative to other same age children. The 3-year-old who learns to walk shows mastery of the curricular objective but also a serious delay relative to the 12–15-month norm for walking. Good developmental CBA, then, also yields a normative picture of the child's development.

The curriculum-based scale within the developmental curriculum lays the foundation for profiling specific child strengths and weaknesses and for mapping and evaluating the course of intervention. Clearly, then, the choice of an appropriate developmental curriculum is crucial and fundamental.

GUIDEPOINTS

- Recognize CBA's wide historical use in early intervention.
- Use developmental CBA to plan program prescriptions.
- Monitor goal mastery and progress with CBA.

BENEFITS OF A DEVELOPMENTAL CURRICULUM

Most curricula include objectives across several major developmental domains. Because of its specificity, curriculum-based developmental assessment provides direct guidance for writing instructional objectives— a kind of outline or blueprint for treatment. Using a map metaphor, we can conceive of CBA as a way of finding specific directions for starting on a "developmental journey." The curriculum is the map which includes crucial landmarks, many potential destinations, and clear routes toward the destinations. The curriculum "map" should be detailed enough to permit progress checks (how far we have gone), accommodations for various handicaps (alternative routes), and comprehensive and balanced objectives (covers a large territory). Without a curriculum, Individualized Educational Program (IEP) objectives must be generated piecemeal, perhaps without a broader view of where the child is going or should go. Without a curriculum, it is difficult, confusing, and hazardous to specify entry objectives, individualize program planning, monitor progress, and evaluate program impact. If getting the right map for a trip seems important, the necessity of selecting the right curriculum cannot be overestimated. A child service program without a curriculum will benefit from using one that is program appropriate (i.e., that fits the children's needs, staff philosophy, and capabilities). If a program does not employ a curriculum, the psychologist can use a curriculum that includes developmental goals and objectives that span the areas of concern for most children and is feasible for staff use.

DEVELOPMENTAL CURRICULA

The developmental milestones recognized in child development are organized into curricula that comprise developmental objectives for teaching children who experience developmental delays or dysfunctions. A developmental curriculum, then, is composed of developmental objectives (i.e., critical capabilities that are targets for instruction and therapy). A given milestone (e.g., uses two-word sentences) obviously has dozens of precursive or prerequisite skills. Since much of development is incremental and involves a "building" process of increasing differentiation and integration of competencies, hierarchies of developmental objectives can be described. Through task analysis, observation, and logic, curricula incorporate sequenced developmental hierarchies that become "ladders" or sequences for instruction. Figure 6.1 illustrates a developmental task analysis or hierarchy of skills for the area of Attention/Task Completion from the *HELP for Special Preschoolers* (Furuno et al., 1985) curriculum. Note the increasing complexity and independence in skills required with increasing age and the graduated scoring by functional level (2 = mastery, 1 = emerging, 0 = absent). Such scoring aids in curriculum entry determinations, progress evaluations, and goal planning.

Determining where a child is within a curriculum yields a profile of current capabilities (i.e., curriculum-based appraisal of developmental status). Identifying subsequent developmental objectives for instruction and therapy becomes *prescriptive* developmental assessment. It should be noted that developmental objectives are not—and should not be—psychometric test items. Only *functional* developmental objectives should be emphasized, since they contribute to the child's increasing mastery of the social and physical world (e.g., initiates social interactions with adults; operates mechanical toys; attends to a talk for 3 minutes with distractions). When assessment instruments designed for diagnosis are normed and subjected to psychometric refinements, the items that survive the process are included in a test because they differentiate statistically between age or diagnostic groups; these items may or may not be worthy of teaching. Standing on one foot and stacking three blocks, for example, are familiar items on norm-based developmental assessment devices. It is dubious that such skills in isolation should actually be instructional objectives.

Domains and Subdomains

Curricular content is usually grouped into useful developmental categories or *domains*. Typically, developmental curricula include the domains of cognitive, language, social–emotional, and motor development. Other domains are often variations or combinations of these basic four categories. Self-help, sensorimotor, psychomotor, social competence, communication,

D.A.	Developmental Task Analysis: ATTENTION/TASK COMPLETION	Functional Level
30 - 36 mo.	Starts task only with reminders and prompts	2
36 - 48 mo.	Completes 10% of task with little sustained attention	2
42 - 48 mo.	Attends to task for 5 minutes with no distractions	2
42 - 48 mo.	Remains on-task for 5 minutes with distractions	1
48 - 60 mo.	Starts task with no reminders or prompts	1
46 - 50 mo.	Completes 25-50% of task with some prompts	1
48 - 60 mo.	Attends to task for 10 minutes with no supervision	0
48 - 60 mo.	Remains on task for 10 minutes with distractions	0
60 - 66 mo.	Completes 50-75% of task with some prompts	0

FIGURE 6.1. Curriculum-based assessment through developmental task analysis. From *Help for Special Preschoolers* by Santa Cruz County Office of Education, 1987, Palo Alto, CA: VORT Corporation. Copyright 1987 by Santa Cruz County Office of Education. Reprinted by permission.

problem solving, and affective development are some of the terms that will be encountered when examining the numerous available curricula.

Domains are usually broken into two or more *subdomains* (i.e., dimensions of developmentally related but different capabilities). Language development, for example, can be analyzed into such subdomains as expressive, receptive, pragmatic, gestural, and imitation. These subcategories are useful for organizing and planning instruction, even though the assignment of a skill to one category or another may sometimes be arbitrary.

Subdomains are composed of developmentally related objectives arranged in hierarchies—from easier to harder or from primitive to advanced development. These objectives can readily be tailored to the child and written into lesson plans and IEPs. A few new curricula are organized within *strands;* these are interrelated skills that cut across domains and can be taught or practiced concurrently. Using a telephone, for example, includes language, social, cognitive, and motor objectives: strands or cross-referencing are practical ways to avoid teaching fragments and to optimize balanced progress. One practical approach to implementing interrelated developmental objectives is to weave them into the existing program's schedule of activities (Figure 6.2). Some teachers design a matrix with the several scheduled activities as rows and a child's (or group's) several domain objectives as columns. Lessons centered around an activity such as snack time can include specific language, social, motor, and cognitive objectives. These same objectives can continue to be taught, generalized, and maintained in other routines and activities. Indeed, most daycare or preschool scheduled activities provide opportunities for the building of interrelated and colateral developmental competencies.

Lessons

In the narrow sense, a curriculum refers only to the organization and content of developmental objectives; increasingly, however, published curricula include several other components. Lessons or suggested activities are also usually included. Indeed, some curricula feature recipe-type lesson cards that many teachers and aides are more than happy to use. Lessons are sometimes described, along with suggested materials, in a booklet or three-ringed binder. Some curricula provide discussions of selected teaching strategies and learning principles. Behavioral and Piagetian principles and related methods are the most frequently cited.

Many early childhood educators are eager to use "canned" lessons, activities, materials, and room arrangements. The day is busy enough without the burden of inventing lessons for small groups and individuals. On the other hand, many teachers resent too much "scripting" of lessons, preferring suggested activities that can be tailored to their situations. Staff preferences in this regard should be determined before curricula are purchased.

Curriculum Placement Estimates

A number of curricula include a form or procedure for rapid placement of the child in the curriculum. An estimate of capabilities is done through testing, observing, or interviewing to discover roughly where the child may be functioning in each domain (and sometimes subdomain). Entry behaviors are then identified as starting points for instruction.

Parent Materials

Parent materials and home-based activities are highly desirable components of some new curricula. With the increasing emphasis on family

ACTIVITY BY OBJECTIVES MATRIX

Child's Name ___**Roxanne**___

Date ___**9/90**___

Current Program Titles (abbreviated): _____

Language 1—vocalizing 3 word sentences; Language 2—g, h, k, initial sounds
Social 1—vocalizing peer names; Social 2—initiating interaction using play
organizers; Cognitive 1—identifying letters; Personal care 1—street crossing; Personal
care 2—coat (dressing); Gross motor 1—tricycle riding; Fine motor 1—name writing

ACTIVITY	CURRICULAR DOMAIN					
	Language	Social	Cognitive	Personal care	Gross motor	Fine motor
Greeting	1^ax^b	1xxxxx		1x^c		1x
Play		2xxxxx^c			1xxxxx	
Circle	1x 2x	1xxxxx^c				
Centers	1x 2x		1xxxxx^c			1xxxxx^c
Story	1x 2x					
Break/rest rooms	1x 2x					
Art/Music	1x 2x					1x
Game (gross motor)				2x		
Lunch	1xxxxx^c 2xxxxx^c					
Break/rest rooms						
Play		2xxxxx			1xxxxx^c	
Departure	1x 2x	1xxxxx		1x 2x^c		

^{a} Numerals correspond with IEP objectives; ^{b} refers to number of trials; ^{c} denotes
when skill is to be measured.

FIGURE 6.2. A sample matrix of developmental objectives reoccurring across different activities. From unpublished manuscript, 1979, by S. Lyon and L. Schneider. Reprinted by permission.

involvement and indeed, new infant legislation that requires a family focus, parent–child activities are a welcome component. Further, older, more widely used curricula are now being published with supplemental materials to be used at home to accommodate families.

It should be noted that "parent involvement" can mean several things. Sometimes materials and activities supplied to parents assist them in teaching toward the same objectives as in the preschool program (parents-as-teachers approach). Increasingly (especially in view of PL 99-457), parent materials and activities are becoming focused on helping *parents-as-parents,* emphasizing parent–child reciprocity, constructive interaction, and "joint action routines." This approach broadens the scope of curricular objectives and attempts to enhance the quality of family–child development.

Progress Charts and Forms

Finally, most good curricula have some means for tracking child progress and displaying developmental status. Some use a simple check-off sheet or form for noting date of mastery; others provide some useful profile chart or actual progress "tracks." These CBAs can and should be shared with parents. Usually, graphic displays of child *change* are appreciated most by parents. Quarterly and annual curriculum progress summaries are valuable when summative assessment or program evaluation is attempted.

In summary, then, published curricula contain hierarchies of developmental objectives organized into domains and subareas or strands, and often include quick entry appraisals, continual and periodic progress monitoring, parent materials, and suggested lesson plans.

SELECTING DEVELOPMENTAL CURRICULA

Since the selection of a curriculum and its assessment components is a most important program decision, it must be done with deliberation. The topics included in this selection should help in the selection process (Figure 6.3). The three major dimensions to consider are child, setting, and curriculum characteristics.

GUIDEPOINTS

- "Map" a child's program with a developmental curriculum.
- Focus on functional goals within multiple developmental domains.
- Consider the parallel use of parent materials.
- Evaluate the developmental sequences and skill hierarchies.

Child Characteristics

Obviously, the nature of the children enrolled in a program is the preeminent consideration. Developmental age and handicap are the two major aspects of importance with regard to child characteristics.

Developmental Age

Programs for youngsters are usually organized around age levels. The most frequent groupings are infant (0–2), toddler (2–3), preschool (3–5), and kindergarten or readiness (5–6) programs. Infant and transition/readiness programs are increasingly seen as important services beyond the usual preschool age group. Armed with fairly convincing evidence and professional support, infant advocates have successfully lobbied for federal policy and public law. The result is seen in the language of PL 99-457 (see Chapter 1).

Transition/readiness programs are proliferating to smooth the transition between preschool/child development type programs and education/school-based programs. Transition programs are especially important where the differences between early childhood and elementary programs is greater and when children need structured programs to shape school readiness.

Note that the developmental age (not chronological) is the major information usually needed. The comprehensive services of many toddler/preschool programs can usually accommodate children of chronological and developmental age 2–5.

A complication may arise with certain developmental disabilities when one area of a child's development (e.g., motor) is at an infant level when other areas are well within the preschool developmental age. In such cases, it might be necessary to use two curricula. Again, some curricula do include infant through readiness content. These age-comprehensive curricula are most useful when children evidence uneven development.

Handicap/Severity

The more specific and severe a handicap, the more likely a specialized (dedicated) curriculum will be the optimal choice. Children with relatively severe vision, hearing, neuromotor, or behavioral/emotional difficulties often require specialized techniques and materials. Further, clinical technique and teaching methods must be adapted to meet sensory/response limitations. Curricula dedicated to a specific handicap will usually be the best choice when teaching groups with same handicap (e.g., deaf) or severe disorder (e.g., autistic).

Many newer curricula do provide general suggestions and sometimes specifics for accommodating various (usually mild to moderate) handi-

CONCERNS IN SELECTING A DEVELOPMENTAL CURRICULUM

Curriculum _____ Publisher _____

Address _____

Phone _____

1. What is the population?
   Developmental Age————   Handicap Specific/Adaptable ————
   Program type: —— Home   —— Center   —— Clinic
                    —— Individual   —— Small Group

2. What areas are covered?
   —— Gross Motor   —— Fine Motor —— Own Care
   —— Language   —— Cognitive/Problem Solving
   —— Social/Emotional   —— Other

3. Are these areas covered in a balanced manner?————

4. Are the areas presented in a sequential manner?————

5. Does the organization provide or permit cross-referencing or strands?————

6. Does the material lend itself to normalization and integration?————

7. Type of family involvement:
   —— Parent Centered —— Notes/Information Sheets   —— Sibling Activities

8. What training is needed?
   —— Study of the Manual —— Workshop   —— Consultation

9. How are lesson plans formatted?
   —— Clear   —— Require extra preparation time
   —— Easy to use   —— Adaptable to handicapping conditions

10. Is curriculum-based assessment facilitated?
    —— Formative (day-to-day)   —— Summative (long-range)
    —— Clear   —— Easy to use

11. Is data support available?
    Field Tested ————————   Teacher Recommended ————————
    Number of children ————   Type of programs ————————

12. How durable are the materials
    Sturdy constructed materials ———— Amount needed ————
    Consumables ————   Extra materials ————
    Special features ————————————————————

13. What is the cost?
    Basic curriculum ————————   Extra manuals ————
    Consumables ————————   Other supplies ————

FIGURE 6.3. Checklist for evaluating and selecting developmental curricula.

caps. Hopefully, the "adaptive-to-handicap" feature will become part of most new curricula.

Setting Characteristics

Most early childhood curricula have been developed for use in preschool centers; other settings that provide programs to many special needs youngsters are best served by a setting-appropriate curriculum. Setting-specific curricula are available for use in the home, hospital, and daycare situations. Home-based curricula are certainly not new, but are now even more important when infant education and family involvement are considered.

Sometimes home-based curricula are used in conjunction with part-time center-based programs. Additionally, a few curricula focus on parenting skills, which are especially important for new parents of handicapped/at-risk infants.

Hospital and clinic settings deserve special curriculum content. The staff and techniques involved with the intensive care unit or high-risk nursery require objectives and activities tailored to the situation. These restrictive settings are temporary, but child development activities are crucial to offset early developmental problems and delays if not the negative effects of medical treatment itself.

Curriculum Characteristics

We have already discussed the benefits and components of a good curriculum. Here, we refer to qualities to look for after child and setting characteristics are satisfied. These eight qualities are summarized below and are included on the curriculum evaluation form at the end of this chapter.

Age and Domain Inclusiveness

Full age and domain coverage may be important to a program. Obviously, a mixed category, mainstreamed program would require a curriculum capable of accommodating a wide age range. Important also is coverage of all major areas of development. Children's weak areas must not be addressed at the expense of progress and even regression in other developmental domains. Parallel, balanced progress is feasible with a curriculum that covers all major dimensions of child development. Inclusiveness also refers to comprehensiveness of objectives within each domain. Some curricula include many more objectives per domain than others. Generally, a greater number and more detailed objectives are desirable when working with more severe and specific handicaps.

Family/Parent Involvement

Sometimes we make progress with children *in spite* of the parents. Wherever possible, however, active involvement of parents in the child's early education yields greater benefits. Parent–professional collaboration may greatly enhance child learning, generalization across setting, and maintenance of progress. Further, there may be benefits to siblings, relatives, neighbors, or others who come in contact with better parenting and teaching. Some curricula offer specific suggestions and even plans for home-based activities, teacher–parent discussions, and parent skill training. Often, teachers will be able to involve a parent in the center as well as at home. In any event, the family is increasingly seen as the focus for concern, rather than the child isolated from the home context. Curricula that include family participation have distinct advantages: they are in the spirit of the new laws and policies that emphasize family collaboration and they greatly assist in maintenance and generalization of center-based learning.

Developmental Integration and Normalization

As more integrated, mainstreamed early childhood programs are offered, curricula that promote integration become especially needed. Objectives should move the handicapped child progressively to more normal, age-appropriate capabilities. Likewise, the management and instructional methods suggested must, when feasible, become more "normal" and compensatory (i.e., less contrived and prosthetic). Social integration can be encouraged through activities that include cross-age tasks, where children at differing developmental levels can participate. Through integration activities, cross-age tutoring, and other suggested projects and unit plans, some curricula especially offer opportunities of normalization and integration; these integration qualities are usually emphasized in the promotional material for the curriculum.

Progress Monitoring

Curriculum-based developmental assessment presumes a developmental curriculum that includes developmental hierarchies within the several domains. Much has already been said about how progress tracking and program evaluation can easily be accomplished when a good curriculum is in use. As discussed, most newer curricula offer some mastery check-off sheet or some way to keep track of what objectives that have and have not been achieved.

Criteria for mastery are often recommended, although the teacher may want to use other standards. The often seen "90% of the time" may not make as much sense as "three consecutive times correctly," or "four days in a row." Teachers will usually want to construct criteria suitable for use not only within a daily lesson, but that reflect a recognition of maintenance and generalization.

Effort/Benefit Ratio

To be effective, a curriculum must be properly implemented. Some curricula seem excellent until put into practice. The needed time and effort may not be tolerated, even though the later payoff may be great. Sometimes well-designed thorough curricula take longer to put in place; a consultant or model program can be quite instructive and save much trial and error.

An admonition about the cost of curricula may be helpful: excellent curricula are commercially available for $50 to $75; there is no need to pay much more. Those curricula in the $100+ range often include materials (e.g., puppets, blocks) that are easily found elsewhere. Few curricula are worth more if they are age inclusive (0–8), handicap-adaptive, and include a tracking system to facilitate formative and summative evaluation.

Information Base

One of the best ways to select a curriculum is to examine research literature, brochures, or curriculum manuals for information regarding the efficacy and utility of the curriculum during field-based research.

Unlike assessment tools, statistics such as reliabilities and validities are less relevant. Rather, outcome-related information regarding child progress in terms of numbers of curriculum objectives achieved with and without prompts, time needed to train staff, or staff satisfaction reports are most useful. When available, technical reports are a valuable resource for selecting a curriculum; when no information is available, the consumer should beware.

GUIDEPOINTS

Select an appropriate developmental curriculum by:

- Developmental age
- Severity of handicap
- Program characteristics
- Age and domain coverage
- Parent involvement
- Normalization emphasis
- Field-research base
- Progress evaluation components

TWO TYPES OF DEVELOPMENTAL CBAs

Curriculum-referenced and curriculum-imbedded assessment are both forms of CBA, each with its own strengths and weaknesses according to the purpose for assessment. In practice, it is likely that school psychologists will more often employ curriculum-referenced devices (see Chapter 4 and Appendix A for a summary of commonly used developmental curricula and their imbedded assessment instruments). For a complete review of the features and use of 25 developmental CBA systems, refer to Bagnato, Neisworth, and Munson (1989).

Curriculum-Referenced Assessment

A number of "generic" curricular scales are now available that might be described as composites of specific curricula. Instruments such as the BRIGANCE Diagnostic Inventory of Early Development (BDIED) (Brigance, 1978) and the Battelle Developmental Inventory (BDI) (Newborg et al., 1984) provide a means for assessing specific skills that are common to most developmental task curricula. Developmental scales that are readily cross-referenced to similarly-based curricula may be termed curriculum-referenced.

Professionals who are skilled in the use of curriculum-referenced scales are able to profile the child's specific strengths and weaknesses and make recommendations that are cast in terms of a program's specific curriculum. Thus, results on the BDI, for example, may be used to recommend entry objectives and IEP objectives based on Hawaii Early Learning Profile (HELP), HICOMP, or other similar curricula. Curriculum-referenced scales provide a bridge or common base applicable across program-specific curricula.

Curriculum-Imbedded Assessment

If the curriculum itself is used as the source for both testing and teaching, the instructional and assessment items are, of course, identical. Curriculum-imbedded assessment, also termed content-referenced assessment, refers to use of the specific program curriculum for assessment purposes. Many curriculum-imbedded scales have adequate reliability and validity with neurodevelopmentally disabled preschoolers (Bagnato & Murphy, 1989). As the content of the CBA scale departs from the actual curricular items, the assessment results may require some extrapolation or interpretation. Using this approach, assessment can take much time. If the teacher is conducting the assessment, the curriculum-imbedded method may be feasible. (Once this is done, however, progress monitoring is relatively easy.) Another major disadvantage of this approach is that preschool programs use a variety of curricula. A child's status in his/her former curriculum at best only roughly corresponds to the new program's curriculum. (Obviously, if curricula are the same, movement across programs would not require renewed assessment.)

EXAMPLES OF CURRICULUM-REFERENCED AND CURRICULUM-IMBEDDED ASSESSMENT DEVICES

Curriculum-Referenced Scale

Perhaps the most widely used curriculum-referenced preschool assessment instrument is the BDIED (Brigance, 1978) designed by a school psychologist. The BDIED analyzes the acquisition of 98 developmental skills within 11 major domains across the birth to 7-year age range. The major domains are Preambulatory Motor Skills and Behaviors, Gross Motor Skills and Behaviors, Fine Motor Skills and Behaviors, Self-Help Skills, Pre-Speech, Speech and Language Skills, General Knowledge and Comprehension, Readiness, Basic Reading Skills, Manuscript Writing, and Math. Behaviors within these clusters are sequenced hierarchically and are also referenced to general age range placements with research citations. The BDIED can be scored by various means including interview, natural observation, diagnostic teaching, and direct assessment. In addition, tasks from the BDIED can be flexibly modified to accommodate the sensory and response limitations presented by various handicaps. The BDIED is most effectively used with preschoolers having mild to moderate developmental disabilities. Finally, behaviors within the BDIED match favorably with those emphasized in various commercially available developmental curricula used in early intervention programs; however, the BDIED is also referenced to a companion curriculum, BRIGANCE Prescriptive Readiness: Strategies and Practice (Brigance, 1985).

Curriculum-Imbedded Scale

The Hawaii package of assessment and curricular materials, Hawaii Early Learning Profile (HELP) and HELP for Special Preschoolers (HELP-SP), is the most widely used and comprehensive curriculum currently in use by infant and preschool programs serving young handicapped children and their families. The HELP Checklist (Furuno et al., 1985) analyzes 685 developmental skills in the birth to 36-month age range within six developmental domains: Cognitive, Language, Gross Motor, Fine Motor, Social–Emotional, and Self-Help. The HELP-SP: Assessment Checklist surveys 625 developmental skills across the 36- to 72-month range within the areas of Self-Help, Motor, Communication, Social, and Learning/Cognitive. In all, 28 separate goal areas or subdomains are appraised within these five domains. Fully acquired, emerging, and absent skills are scored and adaptations for handicaps are allowed within both scales.

GUIDEPOINTS

- Select curriculum-referenced scales for linkage with many curriculum types.
- Choose curriculum-imbedded scales for linkage with a specific curriculum.

ASSESSMENT FOR INSTRUCTION

Curriculum-based developmental assessment is the primary technique used to plan instructional and therapeutic programs for young exceptional children. Among all other forms of assessment, CBA is unique: assessment items are also curricular objectives based on developmental norms. This offers a way to pinpoint specific strengths and weaknesses, track curricular progress, synchronize team efforts, and provide estimates of normative status.

Early intervention programs include finely graded CBA developmental skill sequences to identify appropriate goals for even the most severely handicapped preschool child. Perhaps the most critical assessment feature of CBA is serial or repeated evaluations over time to document progress in learning and the effectiveness of instruction. Clearly, CBA is exemplary of "best practice" in psychology and education. In the future, more ecological methods of CBA are anticipated. This means that curricula and assessment strategies will be devised to identify the characteristics of the child's environment, including parents, family circumstances, stress, and classroom arrangements and adult–peer interactions. The objective is to identify and treat not only the child's individual skill needs but also dimensions of the physical and social environment. Creative advancements in curriculum-based developmental assessment technology are clearly in the works. Curriculum-based developmental assessment is a natural partner of developmental instruction and is used before, during, and after programming; a close-up of these three assessment phases follows.

Before Instruction

The "before" measure is certainly important; it tells the teacher where to begin with instruction. Children who have developmental differences cannot be presumed to possess all the skills of same-age "typical children." By using a hierarchy of developmental landmarks and competencies, the professional can identify what skills a given child displays, which ones are missing or delayed, which ones would be reasonable IEP goals, and which skills should be taught next. The assessment information can be collected by diverse means: observation, interview, and elicited performance. The "before assessment" provides valuable *program entry* information that matches initial instructional objectives with a child's current capabilities; this makes sense from both behavioral and cognitive–developmental perspectives.

Most good programs use comprehensive developmental curricula—organized lists of sequential and hierarchically arranged skills in the several areas of development. Great precision for entry into the curriculum is possible, of course, when the child is assessed on the actual objectives within the program's specific curriculum. CBA includes a graduated scoring system that can detect small increments of learning (0, 1, 2 or +, −, ±). As pointed out earlier, this procedure may be more thorough, but quite time consuming. Often, extended observation and testing are needed to check the child's mastery of actual, detailed, program-specific curriculum objectives. Sometimes an abbreviated procedure is used for program entry assessment. A program may use an assessment device that *samples* the developmental objectives contained in its specific curriculum. Using such assessment devices provides at least rough estimates of where a child is in a specific developmental curriculum. This method is much faster but, as indicated, does not provide the exact position of the child in all areas of a specific curriculum. Use of a good curriculum-referenced device is often the best procedure—assuming someone will have the time and skill to administer the procedure.

During Instruction

Assessment of the child's progress during program participation might also be estimated through an instrument that samples the curriculum. Many teachers, however, prefer to use the program's curricular objectives as a kind of checklist. In this fashion, the teacher can continually track the child's (intraindividual) progress within the program curriculum. This information is useful, of course, in guiding instruction and for planning the next objectives. This feedback function is a crucial strength of CBA and is central to direct instructional technique.

Parents are especially interested in their child's progress, and CBA is most valuable in this regard. Some commercially available preschool curricula actually include a chart or form that permits a graphic display of child progress. The LAP, HELP, and HICOMP curricula, for example, emphasize progress tracking that can be shared with parents.

After Instruction

Finally, summative assessment after program involvement (end of year, transition to new program) may also be accomplished by using the curriculum itself or an assessment device that samples the content of typical preschool curricula (i.e., a curriculum-referenced instrument). Professionals often encourage the use of a standardized curriculum-referenced assessment device as well as the curriculum itself for summative assessment (see Chapters 4 and 10). When properly chosen, the standardized device will sample the same or similar objectives as in a given program. Further, since the assessment device is not based on any single curriculum, it roughly relates to many curricula and, thus, acts as a comparative concurrent measure to check accuracy. When a child moves from one program to another, it is cumbersome to compare child status in curriculum A with that in curriculum B. The curriculum-referenced device can act as the information bridge between developmental programs.

GUIDEPOINTS

- Emphasize a "test-teach-test" approach with CBA.
- Appraise preintervention, baseline competencies.
- Monitor skill acquisition (daily/monthly) during intervention.
- Evaluate overall progress in multiple areas comparing beginning versus end-of-year levels.

SEQUENCE OF STEPS FOR
CURRICULUM-BASED DEVELOPMENTAL ASSESSMENT

Repeated appraisals during instruction can document change and determine whether modifications may be needed in instructional strategies. This assessment–prescription–evaluation model has been referred to as a "test-teach-test" approach or developmental assessment/curriculum linkage (Bagnato et al., 1989). Evidence of the child's progress is not based on comparative evaluations with other similar children, but rather with the child's previous performance levels as a reference point and higher level goals as criteria to be mastered. In practical terms, an initial comprehensive appraisal of skills within several developmental domains and subdomains provides a baseline assessment of current skills and deficits. Early intervention specialists can then determine individualized goals along the developmental or instructional sequence that become the focus of teaching and therapy. Finally, with these goals as benchmarks, the child is reevaluated at some predetermined time to detect evidence of progress.

With progress, more challenging clusters of related skills are then established to amplify the child's individualized plan. The following five-step sequence forms the basis for developmental CBA:

1. Appraise the status of developmental skills within the major functional domains.
2. Determine functional ranges in each developmental domain.
3. Identify "transitional points" of skill acquisition in each domain.
4. Select related objectives that match the child's current level of skill acquisition in each domain within the developmental sequence and teach to mastery.
5. Reevaluate to monitor developmental change and generalization of learning across persons, situations, and materials.

Chapter 12 presents a case study which emphasizes and details the use of developmental CBA for monitoring child status, goals, and progress during intervention.

Step 1: Appraise Developmental Status

Certain norm-based scales such as the BDI (Newborg et al., 1984) can function as curriculum-referenced measures since they are "curriculum-compatible." They are hybrid norm-based scales that contain similar but more global developmental sequences compared with the curriculum-based scales. However, unlike school-age curricula and intelligence tests, the parallel content of norm-based developmental skill measures and preschool curriculum-based measures generates some valid "assessment/curriculum linkages" (Bagnato et al., 1989).

The skills and developmental domains surveyed in both types of instruments are similar. Thus, a diagnostic specialist such as the developmental school psychologist or the early childhood special educator can use norm-based scales to appraise landmark developmental skills then calculate developmental ages and developmental quotients which describe a particular child's level in each developmental domain and subdomain, including cognitive, language, perceptual/fine motor, social–emotional, gross motor, and self-care.

Curriculum-imbedded scales, however, may be used more directly to appraise developmental levels. Both curriculum-referenced and curriculum-imbedded scales can be used to establish developmental levels and thus enter a child into an appropriate level within the curriculum, such as skill sequences appropriate for the 24- to 36-month level.

Step 2: Determine Functional Ranges

Once the child has been entered into appropriate curriculum levels for each developmental domain, an analysis of each item or task within the sequence at that developmental level must be made to determine the extent to which the infant or preschooler has acquired that skill and its behavioral components. The procedure involves an appraisal of which skills are fully acquired (+), absent (−), or emerging (±) within all major developmental areas. Thus, a range of functioning can be ascertained within each developmental domain.

Step 3: Identify "Transitional Skills"

The next step in the sequence involves isolating those specific skills that are only partially acquired or emerging (±). Examples include an infant's beginning coordination of eyes and hands in reaching for a brightly colored mobile or a preschooler's beginning discrimination of 12 different forms in a shape-matching task. In both instances, the child may have acquired components of the final skill but be unable or inconsistently able to complete the task as expected. Intervention is now directed toward full skill acquisition on these tasks in the developmental sequence. Transitional skills are ideal instructional objectives since they are usually at the optimal "challenge level" for the youngster—not too hard, not too easy. These transitional competencies are curriculum-entry points or *linkages* for individualized curriculum planning and progress evaluation purposes.

Step 4: Link Curriculum Goals to
Transitional Skills and Teach to Mastery

With identification of the child's transitional skills, individualized goal-planning is accomplished by designing lessons which involve these transitional skills in various *purposeful* and natural activities such as when drawing and writing, matching shapes in group circle time activities, labeling pictures during story-telling and prereading groups, and during lunch and toileting routines. Instruction is most effective when clusters of related skills are taught together across people and settings and also across curriculum areas so that uneven development is prevented. This also prevents teaching to isolated tasks which produces the learning of nonpurposeful splinter skills. Most commercially available developmental curricula include field tested strategies for grouping transitional skills for individual and group instruction and for matching appropriate instructional techniques (such as shaping and prompting) for teaching certain tasks. Mastery criteria are established by the program and each teacher; however, criteria typically involve 80%–90% completion of a task without prompting over a number of trials or when the skill occurs under several conditions. Most intervention specialists believe that mastery and generalization of trained skills occur when that skill is repeatedly displayed with different people, in different settings, with different materials, and under circumstances distinct from the training conditions.

Step 5: Reassess Developmental Skills and Profile Gains

Frequent formative evaluations are needed to provide evidence of developmental changes in the transition skills that have been the focus of instruction. Such evaluations typically occur on a monthly, weekly, or even a session basis depending upon program resources. The curriculum-imbedded scale is used once again to assess gains within several curricular areas. Again, the emphasis is not upon rote, isolated completion of splinter skills, but rather on the functional or purposeful use of such skills in play, social, and/or self-care routines. Frequent reevaluations enable the program staff to determine areas of change and also to detect domains in which no progress is apparent. These clinical evaluations allow the team to reconsider the ineffectiveness of their teaching and therapy methods. Once this reevaluation is completed, the process is repeated by determining the next range of fully acquired, emerging, and absent skills so that a child's individualized goal-plan can be revised. This reciprocity between CBA and developmental instruction is the sine qua non of contemporary early intervention.

GUIDEPOINTS

- Appraise developmental levels.
- Determine ranges of acquired, emerging, and absent skills.
- Link transitional skills and curricular goals.
- Teach skills to mastery.
- Reevaluate skills and profile gains.

SUGGESTED READINGS

Bagnato, S. J., & Hofkosh, D. (1989). Curriculum-based developmental assessment for infants with special needs: Synchronizing the pediatric early intervention team. In B. Gibbs, & D. Teti (Eds.), *Interdisciplinary assessment of infants: A guide for early intervention professionals.* Baltimore, MD: Paul Brookes.

Bagnato, S. J., & Murphy, J. P. (1989). Validity of curriculum-based scales with young neurodevelopmentally disabled children: Implications for team assessment. *Early Education and Development, 1*(1), 50–63.

Bagnato, S. J., & Neisworth, J. T., & Munson, S. M. (1989). *Linking developmental assessment and early intervention: Curriculum-based prescriptions* (2nd ed.) Rockville, MD: Aspen.

Neisworth, J. T., & Bagnato, S. J. (1988). Assessment in early childhood special education: A typology of dependent measures. In S. Odom & M. B. Karnes

(Eds.), *Early intervention for infants and children with handicaps: An empirical base.* Baltimore, MD: Paul Brookes.

Neisworth, J. T., & Bagnato, S. J. (1990). CBA in early childhood education. In J. Salvia & C. A. Hughes (Eds.), *Curriculum-based assessment: Testing what is taught.* New York: Macmillan.

BEST PRACTICE SUMMARY CHECKLIST

Chapter 6

What Is Curriculum-Based Developmental Assessment?

[ ]   1. Meet with your preschool staff at least yearly to reexamine the mix of children in your program to assess their special instructional/therapeutic needs regarding curriculum materials.

[ ]   2. Collaborate with your staff and your administrator to select a commercially available core developmental curriculum and other auxiliary curricula that match the program's philosophy and goals with the special needs of your children.

[ ]   3. Select and use norm-based scales whose items match the tasks and content of the program's curricula.

[ ]   4. Help team members to focus their work on instructional objectives that are truly functional for a child.

[ ]   5. Gain agreement among team members about an efficient way for using the developmental curriculum as the "team's instrument" to share assessment responsibilities and monitor progress.

[ ]   6. Design a team-approved timeline for regularly monitoring child progress that fits your program's resources and demands (e.g., daily, weekly, monthly, quarterly, semiannually).

7

What Is Unique about Working with Infants?

ISSUES IN PRACTICE

- Is it practical and useful for parents to take an active part in infant assessment?
- Why must psychologists simultaneously consider parents' and infants' needs?
- Can an infant be assessed in about the same time and under the same circumstances as older children?
- What techniques, other than formal testing, are needed to assess an infant?
- What are the unique qualities of infants that create special requirements for staging the assessment?
- Why blend infant assessment and intervention?
- Why should infant assessment be a continual process?

Several aspects of working with infants alter how assessments must be staged. Such factors as state control, fatigue, hunger, medical complications, and physiological limitations have an impact on how long a session can be or even whether it can be held at a scheduled time. *Psychologists must show sensitivity and patience and put the infant's needs above the need to complete an assessment on schedule.* This chapter discusses some of the unique qualities of infant assessment and intervention. Four topics are covered: parents as part of the assessment team, multidimensional aspects of infant assessment, staging the assessment, and blending assessment and intervention.

PARENTS ARE PART OF THE ASSESSMENT TEAM

When older children are assessed, parents may observe or not even be present. When an infant is assessed, parents take an active part in the assessment. One or both parents usually accompany and hold the child part of the time. The psychologist has the interesting challenge of paying attention to and talking with parents while observing and assessing the infant. *Infant assessment is infant intervention*—as it provides a continuous observation and dialogue with the parents and response opportunities for the infant at risk (Bagnato, Munson, & MacTurk, 1987; Brazelton, 1982).

Parent-Focused Process

Give parents time to express themselves at the beginning of the assessment. It is often their first chance to discuss in detail their concerns and needs regarding their child. They may not be aware of the reason for referral and their concerns may be very different from the referring professional's concerns. Listen to what they think is the purpose of the assessment. What issues are most important to them? Start your discussion with parents' concerns and help them take an active role in deciding what areas should be emphasized in the assessment and in planning for services.

Interviewing parents at the beginning of the assessment can provide an overview of the pregnancy, birth, health history, and information concerning previous evaluations by other professionals. Pertinent information about immediate and extended family members can also be obtained. The psychologist is able to learn a great deal in a short time about the reporting ability and observational knowledge of parents during this initial conversation. It gives an indication of how to deal with parents during the assessment. Much developmental and behavioral information about the infant is obtained from parents, and your comments and questions should encourage them and make them feel adequate.

A hypothetical example will illustrate this "parent-focused" process. "John," 12 months old, has been referred by his pediatrician because of suspected developmental delay. His uncle was in special education classes. His parents, while aware of the doctor's concerns, are more worried about John's sleep problem which is disrupting family life. The uncle who had had delayed development leads a relatively happy life, so John's parents are not too scared by the developmental delay. However, John's screaming at night is so disruptive that they cannot stand it any longer.

What issue should you address? Start the discussion with the sleep problem. What can be learned in this session that will ameliorate the immediate problems of sleep and family disturbance? How may they relate to the suspected developmental delay? Certainly, be alert to developmental indications of delay but do not let it be the focus of the session unless the parents seem ready to discuss it. Save the pediatrician's concerns for another day. *Show parents that their concerns have a direct influence on what you do.* This is particularly important, since the assessment may lead to intervention. Parents' active participation, goal-setting abilities, and decision-making will be essential for effective intervention (Dunst, Trivette, & Deal, 1988).

GUIDEPOINTS

- Conduct a "parent-focused" assessment.
- Establish a partnership with parents to learn as much as possible about infant and family during assessment sessions.
- Promote goal-setting and decision-making by parents.

Parent Participation

Have parents actively participate in the assessment procedures by holding the infant and giving physical support. Separation anxiety may need to be relieved, feeding may be necessary, or diapers may need to be changed. Parents often are able to give the psychologist suggestions on how to manage difficulties during the assessment.

Ask parents to help interpret the infant's actions, vocalizations, and expressions. Assess baby's ability to send readable cues, parents' abilities to read baby's cues and respond in a sensitive manner, and baby's ability to respond to parents. This reciprocal understanding is the best of parent–infant interaction, upon which much development depends (Bromwich, 1981). It is also helpful to have the parents present certain activities to the child. This may result in baby's optimum performance as well as allowing the psychologist another opportunity to observe parent–infant interactions.

Establishing Confidence and Communication

The assessment of their baby is often parents' first exposure to psychologists and special services. Try to arrange the initial session at a time when

---

GUIDEPOINTS

- Promote active parent participation.
- Assess parent–child interactions observed in assessment sessions.

---

both parents can be present to give and receive information. Mothers and fathers often have different views of their baby and the presenting problems. They both need to know that you are interested in their points of view, fears, and priorities.

Convey to them that they are authorities on their child and have much to offer to the assessment. Let them know that while you have expertise in development and children, you do not know their child as they do. Therefore, you will be asking them for information about their infant.

Remember, parents usually do not know what an assessment is all about. Because the client is an infant, it is probably one of the first assessment sessions the parents have experienced. Explain such issues as confidentiality, what happens in an assessment, why certain activities are done and questions asked, and how this information will be used. Get parents' reactions to these procedures, and if they do not understand or if they seem uncomfortable with what is being done, try to learn why. Use language the parents can understand to explain what is happening and why it is important. The mission is to collaborate and communicate.

GUIDEPOINTS

- Gain trust of both parents by being open and honest with them.
- Establish good communication so they understand you and the assessment, and you understand them.
- Convey to parents that they are authorities on their child.

MULTIDIMENSIONAL ASPECTS OF INFANT ASSESSMENT

Multiple Sources of Information

The emerging system of infant assessment seems to be the use of transdisciplinary assessment teams made up of parents, psychologists, therapists, early intervention specialists, and medical personnel. Gather information from these sources if the team approach is not available to you.

Medical

Review a complete medical report including vision and hearing assessments, when available, *before* seeing the infant. Occasionally, there are important considerations for handling the infant because of seizures, a heart condition, or other medical concerns.

Medical reports include information such as (1) Prenatal Risk Factors scale—an assessment of maternal obstetric history and abnormal events during pregnancy, labor, and delivery; (2) Apgar scores, which measure heart rate, color, reflex irritability, respiratory effort, and muscle tone at 1 and 5 minutes after birth; (3) neurological examinations of neonatal reflexes, neuromotor development, alertness, and specific cranial nerves; (4) the Neonatal Behavior Assessment scale, which looks at such factors as the infant's state of control and ability to modulate reactions, attend to stimuli, and control motor activity; (5) measurements of vision and hearing; and (6) other reports of possible neurological, physiological, genetic, behavioral, and health factors.

Parents

As mentioned, parents are a rich source of information. They can supply the family history and extensive reports of the baby's behavior. Easy-to-use rating scales and other instruments are available to help estimate and quantify parent reports. (See Table 7.1 for examples of available scales.)

Therapists

Make use of physical, occupational, and speech therapists as needed. Work closely with a physical and/or occupational therapist if seeing a child with cerebral palsy, Down syndrome, or other condition with a motor impairment. Therapists' help is invaluable in positioning the child, as well as sorting out what behaviors and movements are being influenced by muscular and neurological impairments. They often have immediate suggestions for handling and positioning techniques that are helpful for parents. Have a speech therapist assist in assessing infants with involvements such as cleft palate, facial paralysis, and breath control problems. Collaborate with a speech therapist or occupational therapist when assessing an infant with feeding or neuromotor problems. Consult with hearing or vision specialists if the infant has known deficits in these areas. If therapists or specialists are not able to be present, consult with them ahead of

TABLE 7.1. Selected Infant-Related Scales

Instrument/Publisher	Age range (mos)	Type/Features
Judgment-Based/Family/Ecological Focus		
Family Needs Survey U of North Carolina, Chapel Hill, NC	Infant/ preschool	Judgment-based, self-report by parent
Home Observation for Measurement of the Environment U of Arkansas, Little Rock, AR	0–36	Judgment-based, ecological, parent interview
Parent Behavior Progression PRO-ED, Austin, TX	0–36	Interactive, parent–infant dyad, individualized
Norm-Based Child Focus		
Bayley Scales of Infant Development Psychological Corp., San Antonio, TX	2–30	Developmental, mental, motor, behavior record
Gesell Developmental Schedules Developmental Evaluation Materials Houston, TX	0–36	Neurodevelopmental, somewhat adaptive-to-handicap
Infant Psychological Developmental Scales—Dunst Revision PRO-ED, Austin, TX	0–30	Process oriented, somewhat adaptive-to-handicap
Judgment-Based Child Focus		
Brazelton Neonatal Behavioral Assessment Scale J.B. Lippincott, Philadelphia, PA	0–1	Interactive, developmental, and neurophysiological
Carolina Record of Individual Behavior U of North Carolina, Chapel Hill, NC	0–48	Adaptive-to-handicap, useful for severe handicaps, checklist for observation
Developmental Profile II Western Psychological Services Los Angeles, CA	0–108	Parent interview, norm-based, developmental
Curriculum-Based: Programming Focus		
Carolina Curriculum for Handicapped Infants and Infants at Risk (CRIB) Paul H. Brookes Co., Baltimore, MD	0–24	Adaptive-to-handicap, developmental, checklist for observational use
Developmental Programming for Infants and Young Children, Vols. 1–3 Early Intervention Developmental Profile University of Michigan Press (EIDP) Ann Arbor, MI	0–36	Adaptive-to-handicap, developmental, checklist for observational use
Hawaii Early Learning Profile (HELP) VORT Corp., Palo Alto, CA	0–36	Adaptive-to-handicap, developmental, checklist for observational use
Transactional Intervention Program University of Connecticut Health Center Farmington, CT	0–60	Ecological, interactive, observational

time regarding possible area of concern, and call them in as needed for future consultation.

Include early interventionists in assessment if at all possible. They may have completed a family assessment which can give you valuable information. They will usually coordinate intervention services after the assessment. Parents may look to them for further clarification of the assessment because they will be the ones working directly with the family on an ongoing basis. Therefore, it is most helpful for interventionists to be present during assessments.

GUIDEPOINTS

- Review medical reports before assessment.
- Make full use of parents' knowledge in assessing their infant.
- Collaborate with therapists and other specialists whose expertise is invaluable.
- Work closely with ongoing early intervention service providers.

Multiple Settings

The infant should be seen in the family home (Hanson & Lynch, 1989) as well as in the clinical setting. When meeting in the home, parents are in control of the setting, if not the assessment. This ensures that they have some power and influence over what happens. Professionals must collaborate with parents, not dictate to them.

Having part of the assessment in the home provides an opportunity to see parents and infant in their natural context. Possible environmental causes or contributors to problems can be observed, such as risk of lead poisoning, lack of stimulation, extremely high levels of stimulation, poor physical care or conditions. This is information not easily available from an assessment in a clinic nor from parents' verbal reports.

The interactions between parents and infant observed in the home are certainly more "typical" than those seen in the clinic. The assessment time could be scheduled to overlap with baby's feeding time, an opportune time to observe behaviors in many developmental areas. This observation is much more valuable when completed in the infant's home.

There are, however, several advantages to holding part of the assessment in a clinical setting. The psychologist can stage the assessment to meet the needs of more formal assessment. Observations can be made of the infant's separation anxiety and reactions to strange surroundings. The parents' ability to act as an advocate for their child in a professional setting can be observed. A clinical setting usually does not have space limitations and distractions which may be present in family homes. Of course, neither home nor clinic assessment can give a full picture of the infant; performance must be appraised across settings.

GUIDEPOINTS

- Conduct part of the assessment in the family home.
- Conduct part of the assessment in the clinical setting.
- Observe parent–infant interactions in both settings.

Multiple Occasions

Infant assessment almost always requires more than one session. Conduct at least one in the home and one in the clinic. Conduct them when the infant is awake and alert. The infant's state is likely to vary during a session. The baby may be rested and attentive at the beginning but quickly become tired, upset, or inattentive. *Psychologists must be constantly aware of the state of the infant* and be willing to stop direct assessment even though the assessment is not complete. Sometimes, if the baby has a short break to rest or eat, more testing can be completed. However, this does not always suffice and another session may be needed.

Some infants have frequent illnesses. Even though the infant may have only a slight upper respiratory infection or be nearly recovered from an ear infection, performance in the assessment can be influenced. Parents may say, "She can usually do that, she just doesn't feel very good today." When parents say their child is being underestimated, they may well be accurate and a second visit to the home may be needed.

Parents are an active part of an infant assessment. Therefore, their "state" must also be taken into account. Other stresses in the family, such as poor health, financial problems, or extreme anxiety about the assessment, can influence the assessment outcome. The infant is likely to behave in a less than optimal way if parents are under stress. Parents' ability to report accurately and completely about the infant's history and behavior may be influenced if they are very stressed. When parents are seen on more than one occasion, a basis of comparison is formed and influences such as those mentioned can be more readily recognized and reduced.

Planning multiple assessment sessions reduces the pressure to "finish the assessment today." Such issues as the infant's state, poor health, or parental stress are reasons to stop and complete the assessment at other times. Planning a second meeting ahead of time lessens the likelihood that parents will feel their child "failed."

```
┌─────────────────────────────────────────────────────────────┐
│                       GUIDEPOINTS                            │
│                                                              │
│   • Plan multiple assessment sessions from beginning.        │
│   • Attend to infant's and parents' states during session.   │
│   • Stop session when optimal performance is not possible.   │
│   • Continue on another day, if necessary.                   │
│                                                              │
└─────────────────────────────────────────────────────────────┘
```

Multiple Methods

Assess an infant with interview, observation, and elicited performance methods to get a complete picture of the baby and family that will lead to intervention, not just diagnosis. Use both structured and unstructured interview styles. An informal style may help parents relax. Strive to make them as comfortable and as relaxed as possible. While the assessment may be rather routine to the psychologist, it is often very stressful for parents. *Remember, parent cooperation and involvement are being actively sought.* By starting with an informal interview, you can set the stage for cooperation.

Birth history, age of infant when reaching certain developmental milestones, and specific knowledge regarding home environment can be acquired through a more structured interview with parents. Use a less structured, active-listening style when obtaining information on the family, parents' concerns; level of acceptance or denial of the child's developmental capabilities, perceptions of the infant; involvement of or problems with extended family. (See Table 7.1 for suggested interview instruments.)

Also, use interviews with other professionals to obtain details not included on written reports. After having release-of-information forms signed, call doctors, therapists, or other specialists who have seen the child to get updated reports or more complete information.

Many published tests and scales are available for the more formal assessment process (Bagnato, Neisworth, & Munson, 1989; Hanson & Lynch, 1989). Some possible scales are presented in Table 7.1. Formal observation of performance on a standardized instrument or rating on a developmental scale is important but insufficient for assessing an infant.

Make extensive use of informal methods of interviewing and observation. Judgment-based assessment instruments can be used to record and quantify clinical observations and judgment (Table 7.1). Observe functional disabilities and link these to intervention needs.

Informal Observations

Informal observations of infants should be a large part of the assessment process (sometimes as much as 50% of the time). *Flexibility is essential in*

GUIDEPOINTS

- Informal initial interview with parents helps set stage for cooperation.
- Use both structured and unstructured interview styles.
- Use a battery of tests.

---

assessing infants. Any number of things may crop up to interrupt a formal testing situation, so use informal observation as much as possible. This places fewer limitations on the infant and hopefully lessens the stress. *Observe the infant's spontaneous play behavior,* what the baby does rather than what you can convince the baby to do. You will be observing what is more nearly the infant's normal repertoire of behaviors (Linder, 1990).

Observe incidental occurrences of developmental tasks during infant and parent play sessions. Record these on a checklist such as the Early Intervention Developmental Profile (Rogers et al., 1981) (Table 7.1). Look for the following types of behaviors in informal observations:

1. Posture items: lifts head, sits with support, rolls supine to prone, gets to sitting, pulls self to standing.
2. Mobility: crawling movements, pivots, crawling, creeping, and walking.
3. Fine motor manipulation: reflexive grasp, hand to mouth, grasps with palm, reaches, bangs two objects, grasps with finger tips.
4. Social development: looks at adult, smiles, reciprocal smile, and cries when mother leaves, moves away from and returns to parent.
5. Communication: coos, reciprocal vowel sounds, repetitive syllables, responding to parent's language, "words," follows direction, and two words combined.
6. Concept understanding: plays peek-a-boo, looks for hidden object, stacks objects, uses "tool" to obtain object, recognizes use of common object.
7. Temperament: activity level, distractibility, adaptability, and attention span.

Emerging behaviors may also be evident during this "play time."

These incidental or opportune observations can save the psychologist time and frustration. Many behaviors are much more easily elicited in informal play with a parent than sitting at a table with a stranger. The fact that behavioral items have been observed in an informal setting does not lessen their legitimacy. Make full use of these opportunities to record the infant's developmental behaviors.

Use parent–child interactions to gain understanding of the parents. Parent–child play can indicate the parents' understanding of the infant's development, capabilities, and limitations. Does the parent seem to be aware of an infant's postural insecurity? Does he/she recognize the infant's sensitivity to touch? Does he/she move slowly to avoid startle reactions? Address these things in the first assessment session, giving parents helpful suggestions to take home with them. This will support the idea that assessment is worth while and parents will get something out of it. Informal observation of parent–child interactions are an essential part of any infant assessment.

GUIDEPOINTS

- Make informal observations an important part of every infant assessment.
- Allow spontaneous play to observe infant's normal repertoire of behaviors.
- Record incidental occurrences of checklist items.
- Opportune observations save you time and frustration.
- Observe parent understanding of child in "play time."
- Give parents helpful suggestions to take home from first session.

STAGING THE ASSESSMENT

Assessment Setting

Stage the clinical sessions of an infant assessment in a "homelike" environment. Have homelike furniture, carpeting, adequate incandescent lighting, and pictures on the walls. Provide extra chairs for family members (grandmothers have been known to come, as well as siblings). Have a separate room available for these family members if possible. A high chair, child table and chair, space to play on the floor, and/or a large table on which to place the infant is needed, depending on age and disabilities of the infant.

Provide a well-supplied diaper changing area. You may need to ask if a diaper change is needed. Some parents are reluctant to interrupt a professional session to change their baby. Have a bathroom nearby for siblings. It is wise to provide a means of warming a bottle and a private place for nursing. For older infants (and siblings) some animal crackers and juice can "save the day" as well as provide you with an opportunity to observe eating skills.

Have the setting as free of distractions as possible. Sounds and clutter that may be ignored by one use to that room may be very distracting to a new-comer. Arranging the environment means paying attention to detail.

GUIDEPOINTS

- Conduct assessment in a "homelike" atmosphere.
- Have facilities and supplies for toileting and feeding needs.
- Provide a distraction-free environment.

Assessment Adaptations

Infant assessments require some staging adaptations by the psychologist. Most notable, perhaps, is the importance of parents in the assessment. First establish rapport with parents, then with the infant. This will facilitate the baby's acceptance of you. Time spent in waiting for the infant to warm up to you will usually be saved by avoiding clinging or crying if you advance too rapidly. Eventually you or a therapist will need to hold the child to complete some gross motor and reflex items on the scales so it is important to establish trust.

Wait for the child to make the first advance and then use facial expression and/or vocalizations as your first contact. Sometimes it is necessary to avoid even eye contact with the infant until he/she starts looking at you. The first step might just be looking and smiling at the infant momentarily and then averting your gaze away from the baby. The next step could be holding out a toy for the child. If the baby refuses it, give it to a parent, who can give to the child. Take time to establish a rapport with the infant, and respond with small steps to the infant's tentative approaches .

Voice quality is important. The infant may not understand words, but will usually react to vocal inflections. Speak in a gentle, low volume voice. Some very young infants seem to respond better to higher pitched voices. Use lots of intonation to show happiness, excitement, surprise, and humor. Avoid "baby talk." An exception to this might be if the infant has a particular "word" for an object and you want to test for receptive language. Then you might want to use the infant's "word" or the parents' version of this word if you get no response with the correct form of the word. Remember, voice quality is the most salient part of language to infants.

Pace the assessment to suit the infant. Correct pacing of entire sessions, sections of sessions, and individual interactions is critical. The infant, particularly if very young, may tire easily and change states rapidly. Sudden awareness of discomfort can cause a dramatic change in the baby's behavior. Try to learn the infant's signals which precede changes in state. Make each section of the assessment short to avoid fatigue. Yet conduct each interaction in an unhurried way, allowing time for the infant to manipulate things. The child may become frustrated if an item is presented, one activity takes place, and the item is whisked away. (This is one reason informal play activity needs to be a large part of an infant assessment.) Always get the infant's attention on a replacement item before taking away a toy. If an item is refused, try again later, or let the parent try to interest the infant in it.

Position the infant for optimal performance. Consider the child's needs and create the most advantageous positioning arrangement. Use furniture of proper size, adaptive equipment, parent's lap—whatever is needed to facilitate the infant's best performance. The infant must feel posturally secure and have freedom of movement as needed for performance. If the infant has tonal abnormalities, positioning can help facilitate optimum tonal quality. For instance, if an infant tends to sit rigidly with an arched back, placing a blanket roll beneath the hips and knees to form a 90° angle may help reduce the arching. The assistance of a physical or occupational therapist is needed to position infants with severe tonal or neuromotor impairments. *If you are not sure of the positioning needs of a particular infant, consult with a therapist.* Each infant's needs are different and the importance of positioning cannot be overemphasized.

Consider the infant's condition during handling. Consult with a nurse or therapist if the condition is known before the assessment. A premature baby may need slow, gentle movements to avoid being startled. An infant with low tone may need extra head and trunk support. A baby with spasticity or high tone may need to be held with one knee flexed to help nor-

---

GUIDEPOINTS

- Establish a rapport with parents first.
- Let infant make first advances to you.
- Use voice quality to communicate with infant.
- Create short segments in assessment.
- Proceed at a relaxed, calm pace.
- Position infant for optimal performance.
- Have therapist assist in adaptive positioning.
- Adapt handling techniques to individual needs.

malize tone. Ask parents what handling techniques they use and what suggestions they have for you in handling the infant during assessment.

BLENDING ASSESSMENT AND INTERVENTION

Parent Involvement Leads to Intervention

Parents have been active participants in the assessment. Encourage them to continue their active involvement during intervention. Help them learn from the assessment and see it as an integral part of services available to them and their infant. Explain what and why you are doing things during the assessment so the parents can begin learning to understand their special infant immediately. Listen to parents. *Behaviors that have an impact on family interactions must be assessed.* Parents' areas of concern may indicate intervention that is needed to help with the infant's development, or they may indicate a need for the family to adapt to the infant's limitations.

Assess the infant with intervention in mind. Start intervention during the assessment by teaching parents to recognize their baby's strengths. The reasons for behaviors are not always obvious. A certain behavior that parents view as a problem may in fact be a functional adaptation the infant has made in an attempt to communicate, move, or manipulate objects. An example is a blind infant who insists on touching the faces of people holding her. This may be an adaptation to "see" who is holding her. Some infants who are multiply handicapped may appear to have very few strengths. But help parents find some positive behavior to encourage them.

Help parents see the infant's areas of need that could be a focus of intervention. Parents may unknowingly encourage behaviors that appear "cute" which actually are detrimental to development. Give suggestions on how they could encourage appropriate responses or minimize inappropriate responses.

Parents should leave the assessment with some concrete suggestions of intervention activities they can do. It is important these these immediate services have value to the parents and infant. Are there medical or caregiving concerns that require immediate attention? Do they need a written list of service providers to contact? Would they benefit by talking to another parent who has been through this before? Write things down for them, they may not remember all you said.

Let parents know what happens next when the current assessment is completed. *Explain to them that assessment is not a one-time occurrence but a continuing process of monitoring developmental progress that is closely intertwined with intervention.*

GUIDEPOINTS

- Listen to parents.
- Assess behaviors that have impact on family.
- Help parents see infant's strengths and areas of need.
- Give concrete suggestions for parent action.
- Explain assessment as continuing process.

Purpose of Infant Assessment

Consider the purpose of infant assessment from the parents' viewpoint. Two prominent questions are, "What is wrong with our baby?" and "What can be done to help us?" Therefore, you need to address both these questions if asked. The assessment needs to provide some diagnostic indication of what is "wrong" but even more, it needs to be part of the services offered to "help" the baby and family. Use caution when giving an infant's "diagnosis" to parents. Diagnoses usually are not clear cut unless there is a definite genetic or medical disorder. Emphasize instead what you have learned during the assessment that will help in planning intervention services. Concentrate on the qualitative and quantitative indications of the infant's strengths and weaknesses. How can strengths be used to help this infant develop to his or her full potential? Indicate what behavioral modalities this baby can use for interactions with the family and environment. This will help the family and early interventionists in planning activities to enhance development. Point out specific behaviors the infant can accomplish and others that are difficult or impossible. Explain what adaptations the baby makes in order to accomplish certain results. These details are needed to develop an Individual Family Service Plan (IFSP).

GUIDEPOINTS

- Assessment purpose is more than just diagnosis.
- Assessment is a planning tool for intervention.
- Include quality and characteristics of behaviors.

Reporting

Parents of infants, unless they have had an older child who needed psychological testing, have not had an opportunity to learn the professional jargon. It is imperative that they understand reports of the assessment. Therefore, *do not use jargon.*

Give a prompt, lucid report to parents. At the close of each session, let them know in general terms what has been learned about their infant. *Parents are part of the assessment team* and have ultimate control over decisions. Keep them informed. Obviously, a detailed report will take some time to formulate. When a written report is prepared, parents receive a copy. However, give an oral report after each session. Do not leave parents without giving them new information. Graphs and pictorial aids can be helpful with some parents.

Follow up the first session with a phone call a few days later. Give parents an opportunity to ask questions and take time to clarify any misunderstandings. Invite them to call you any time they have more questions, especially following subsequent sessions.

GUIDEPOINTS

- Do not use jargon.
- Report orally at close of each session.
- Make follow-up phone call for clarification.
- Send parents written report.

Individual Family Service Plan

Assessment is one part of the process of early intervention. It should be planned to blend directly with planning and providing services to the infant and family. In addition to the infant assessment being discussed here, there is a family assessment which identifies family strengths and needs. This is often completed by early interventionists.

Hold a team meeting to write the IFSP after assessment reports are completed. IFSP team members include parents and all, or representatives of, service provider agencies. Writing an IFSP is a team effort. If all the professionals are not included in the IFSP meeting, their input should be available in the form of written or oral reports. Formulate general long-term goals and specific short-term goals for the family and infant based on information from assessments.

Certain parts of the IFSP are required by Public Law 99-457. The infant's strengths in each developmental area must be reported along with strengths and needs of the family. These should be the foundation of goals. Specific short-term goals are written in areas of need for infant and family. *Family input is required and extremely important when writing goals.*

Intervention should address those goals which parents have prioritized, both for the infant and for the family. Some parents will be capable advocates for themselves and their baby. Other parents will need more help in deciding what their immediate needs are and what goals are reasonable for the family and situation. Goals need to be feasible in the setting where intervention will take place (Thurman & Widerstrom, 1990). Figure 7.1 gives a sample page of an IFSP for a family served by a combination home-based and center-based intervention agency. [See Hanson and Lynch (1989) and Thurman and Widerstrom (1990) for more instructions for IFSP development.]

Explain in detail to parents what will go on at the IFSP meeting. If needed, role play with them to help them gain confidence in presenting their goals or priorities. Appoint one of the professionals to guide or assist parents during the meeting if it is deemed necessary.

Remember, parents are the final decision makers, either on their own or with varying amounts of guidance. *The IFSP should not be written before the team meeting with parents.*

GUIDEPOINTS

- Assessments are foundations for IFSPs.
- Prepare parents for the IFSP meeting.
- Have input from all team members and all who contributed to assessments.
- Parents may need help in the "professional" atmosphere of the IFSP meeting.

Continuing Assessment

Typically, intervention goals are written for a period not longer than 6 months. Reassess the infant and family before writing new goals. Infant assessment needs to be conducted frequently because development may change rapidly. Families change too, so reassessment of the infant must be integrated into the family's reassessment of their own total family situation. Remember, blend continuing assessments into interventions that are in place or may be needed in the future. Include the family and the infant in assessments and intervention plans (see Chapter 8).

GUIDEPOINTS

- Assessment is a continuous process.
- Reassess infant and family before writing new goals.
- Blend continuing assessments and interventions.

FAMILY GOALS

Child's name: _John P_   Date: _4/16/90_

Family strengths: _Mr. and Mrs. P. have a strong desire to work together to help John. They have realized during the assessment process that they want John to get more out of life than his uncle has been able to do. Mr. and Mrs. P can both arrange some time to meet with intervention staff._

Family's prioritized needs: _The P's want assistance with: (1) John's sleeping problems; (2) understanding more about what they can do to help John's development; and (3) explaining the situation to John's grandparents who don't think John has any problems._

Family's long-range goals: _For immediate and extended family to understand John's developmental needs._

Family's short-term goals:

Objective	Resources	Strategies	Review Date
Help John overcome sleep problem by carrying out behavior modification.	*Infant Program Teacher (Mrs. S)*	*Behavior modification*	*6/90*
Get respite care at bedtime so parents can go out.	*MH/MR (Mrs. B)*	*Mrs. P will call and make arrangements*	*5/90*
Talk to IP staff to gain understanding of John's developmental level.	*IP staff, Mrs. C, Ms. L, Ms. H, Ms. S*	*Parents take turns bringing John to Center and have appointments*	*10/90*
Get grandparents to help transport John to Center.	*IP teacher (Ms. S)*	*Home visits to grandparents to explain John's needs are ready*	*About 6/90*

FIGURE 7.1. Sample Individual Family Service Plan (IFSP).

SUGGESTED READINGS

Bagnato, S. J., Neisworth, J. T., & Munson, S. M. (1989). *Linking developmental assessment and early intervention: Curriculum-based prescriptions* (2nd ed.). Rockville, MD: Aspen.

Bromwich, R. (1981). *Working with parents and infants: An interactional approach.* Baltimore, MD: University Park Press.

Dunst, C. J., Trivette, C. M., & Deal, A. G. (1988). *Enabling and empowering families: Principles and guidelines for practice.* Cambridge, MA: Brookline Books.

Hanson, M. J., & Lynch, E. W. (1989). *Early intervention: Implementing child and family services for infants and toddlers who are at-risk or disabled.* Austin, TX: PRO-ED.

Linder, T. W. (1990). *Transdisciplinary play-based assessment: A functional approach to working with young children.* Baltimore, MD: Paul Brookes.

Thurman, S. K., & Widerstrom, A. H. (1990). *Infants and young children with special needs: A developmental and ecological approach* (2nd ed.). Baltimore, MD: Paul Brookes.

BEST PRACTICE SUMMARY CHECKLIST

Chapter 7

What Is Unique about Working with Infants?

[   ] 1. Meet with your core team members to explore and discuss the use of a transdisciplinary, play-based style of assessment for infants that includes the parent as a central participant.

[   ] 2. Select "friendly," easily understood developmental rating scales or interview formats that allow parents to report their observations in the most reliable, nonthreatening fashion.

[   ] 3. Designate someone to be the parent advocate on the team during the assessment who can immediately elicit the parent's interpretations of what they are seeing and can also direct attention to and interpret important behaviors.

[   ] 4. Assess initially in the home setting with all infants to gain a more natural, ecological view of typical interactions.

[   ] 5. Collaborate with your team to design an activity-based timeline for the assessment that includes frequent breaks, time for feeding, spontaneous versus structured interactions, and interviewing.

[   ] 6. Engage in creative problem-solving with your staff to design easily understood ways to communicate developmental assessment results to parents including computer displays, colored graphs, goal sequences, and photos of expected and actual behavior by infants.

[   ] 7. Be sure that your program's IFSP format directly links child and family needs, goals, and interventions and is not merely an administrative tool.

8

What Are the Basics for Family Collaboration?

ISSUES IN PRACTICE

- Do families have a legal right to participate in the assessment of their children?
- Is it important to obtain parent information in child assessment and program development?
- Can parents effectively collaborate in the assessment of their children?
- What tools can be used to obtain useful information about parents and families?

The family is a complex, mutually dependent social system in which single situations influence others (Minuchin, 1985). In addition to the routine challenges of family life, having a child diagnosed as handicapped, developmentally delayed, or at-risk for further complications can cause dramatic changes within the functioning of a family (Byrne & Cunningham, 1985) and ultimately alter the quality of life for the child. Parents and family members are presented with choices and major decisions which will affect the development and life situation of the child. Management of life events and the decisions that must be made require the family to act when the family may not have the experience, knowledge, or competence to do so.

Professionals can provide opportunities for families to participate in decisions regarding their child. *As parents become active and effective participants in assessment and treatment decisions, this experience may have a positive impact on the welfare of the parents, family members, and the development and progress of the child.* Additionally, through effective interaction and collaboration with team members, parents can receive guidance, encouragement, and support, as well as realize that they have choices. This chapter will focus on ways the psychologist or other early intervention specialist can effectively involve parents and families in the assessment process.

REASONS FOR PARENT AND FAMILY INVOLVEMENT

Parental involvement is critical to the success of intervention programs (Bronfenbrenner, 1975) and parental participation in the assessment process is an initial part of their involvement. Reasons for parent participation in the assessment process include the following:

- Public Law 94-142 and PL 99-457 mandate that parents have the right to be involved with the identification and diagnosis of their child's disorder as well as with the child's placement and programming.
- Although special education professionals are trained in assessment and program development for special needs children, parents know their child better than anyone else.
- Parents and professionals should agree on the status and expectations of the child for success (Allen, 1980).
- Involvement in the assessment process may lead parents to become more skilled in dealing with family issues and decisions, especially those regarding the handicapped child (Dunst, Trivette, & Deal, 1988).
- Parental expectations, either positive or negative, may lead to a self-fulfilling prophecy; therefore, parent participation in the assessment process may adjust these expectations to a healthy and positive supportive level.

FACILITATING PARENT INVOLVEMENT

The needs of a preschooler who is at-risk or has a handicap must be addressed during assessment and development of the child's goals and program. Assessment should be a team effort and the psychologist and other early childhood professionals can involve parents in several important ways, which are discussed in detail in this chapter. Parents can—

- provide a health and medical history
- discuss their concern regarding their child's problems and potential
- participate in ecological assessment, including assessment of their family's functioning and assessment of their environment
- provide information from direct observation of their child and become agents in behavioral change
- participate in the identification of goals and program design
- participate in evaluating the acceptability of their child's program, including specific techniques and experiences planned for the child.

History and Health Record

An at-risk or handicapped preschooler often has a more eventful medical history than that of a nonhandicapped peer, and the child's medical history and developmental milestones provide valuable information to team members as they begin assessment. Parents often have permanent records of their child's illnesses or significant events which occurred in the earlier years. Pregnancy, delivery, and neonatal complications as well as doctor and/or hospital visits, medical diagnoses, or other relevant history may shed light on present conditions. Chronic medical conditions or frequent hospitalizations can often interfere with adaptive behavior and learning and may also contribute to a diagnosis of retardation (Rutter, 1972). Past and present prescribed medication as well as past therapy services (i.e., physical, occupational, language) provide information regarding the levels and amount of services the child has received. Asking parents to recount their child's history is frequently an opportunity to hear their concerns and to detect their fears, disillusionment, and hopes for the child.

Although functional goal and program planning should not be based on the cause of the handicap or condition, information regarding the child's developmental status and medical history is beneficial to have as a reference.

GUIDEPOINTS

- Ask parents to provide significant events in the child's health history.
- Provide parents with a well-designed health history questionnaire to complete.
- For thorough and accurate information, encourage parents to complete the questionnaire together, making sure that it is thorough and accurate.

Parent Interview

Meeting with the parents (or caregivers) for an interview can accomplish two important goals. First, it allows the professional to become acquainted with the parents and family members, the initial step in rapport building. Second, the parents may offer valuable and pertinent child and family information. The medical and developmental history mentioned above is often discussed during the parent interview. Information regarding the characteristics and behavioral repertoire of the child (e.g., behavior patterns, resiliency, and temperament) may also be discussed.

Interviews also provide the opportunity for the psychologist to gain insight into issues such as child-rearing style, attitudes, and values. Over-protective or uninformed parents, or those living in disorganized or unstimulating environments, can affect the developmental status of the child. Conversely, supportive and positive parental attitudes may lead the way for parental support and advocacy for the child.

In order to obtain a clear picture of parental perceptions regarding the child, professionals should consider involving both the father and mother (or other caregivers) in the interview. Unfortunately, however, interviews usually occur during the day when one or both parents are working. Also, many single-parent homes are usually headed by the mother. Researchers have found that both mothers and fathers of developmentally disabled children believe it is important for fathers to be involved in the problems of their children (Gallagher, Beckman, & Cross, 1983). However, the father may divorce himself emotionally from the child, forcing the mother to provide most if not all of the child care (Tavormina, Ball, Dunn, Luscomb, & Taylor, 1977). Also, because fathers typically provide less direct care for their children, they may have fewer opportunities to feel that they are doing something of immediate value (Cummings, 1976). These are important variables to consider when working with parents of a child with special needs.

Family interview techniques are a valuable tool for a psychologist, as the techniques employed during the interview affect the nature and content of the interview in the following ways:

- The manner in which questions are asked influences the responses given. Open-ended versus closed (yes/no or one-word responses) questions afford the parents an opportunity to elaborate on important details.
- As an interviewer, you must consider your philosophical viewpoint when prompting parents for information. A professional coming from a psychodynamic background may not "hear" the same information as a professional from a behavioral background. Caution must be used in the interpretation of the information.

- Retrospective information must be weighed cautiously. If parents have more than one child, they may be confused and give less than accurate information (Umansky, 1983).
- Parents should be reassured that the information they disclose will be kept in complete confidence and shared only with other team members.

Parent questionnaires regarding such areas as child behavior and parenting style should be *supplemental* to the interview in order to avoid redundancy of information and excess time consumption for the parents and professionals involved. Issues related to the use of specific questionnaires are discussed below.

GUIDEPOINTS

- Be sensitive to parents' concerns regarding their child
- Reassure parents that information will be held in confidence.
- Create questions before the interview to save time and effort as well as to prepare for the interview.

Participation in Ecological Assessment

In order to identify the child's needs and services, the psychologist must assess the "ecology" of the child's life. External components of the child's world (i.e., physical, psychological, and social contexts) are important variables to consider. Assessment of these components can be addressed in the following fashion: (a) assessment of general family functioning, parent–child relationships, family needs, concerns or issues directly related to the child; and (b) the physical environment (home- and intervention-based) the child is expected to function in and adapt to successfully.

Family Functioning

Assessment of the family–child situation is crucial and an effective procedure for collecting this information is direct observation of behavior. This refers to "structured procedures for collecting objective and quantifiable data on ongoing behavior" (Neisworth & Bagnato, 1988). Observation of the antecedents and consequences of the child's behavior as he or she interacts with family members or other caregivers provides information regarding the development of the child's behavioral repertoire. More importantly, this information should be considered when making decisions regarding behavior management and programming.

In addition to direct observation, the psychologist may use commercially made instruments designed to measure ecological variables. A primary consideration in selecting an ecological assessment scale is to obtain a "goodness-of-fit" between the type of information needed and the characteristics of the instrument (Bailey & Simeonsson, 1988). Factors that need to be considered in the selection process include the purpose or nature of the assessment and the characteristics and behaviors to be assessed. Examples of parent/child assessment instruments include (a) Parent/Caregiver Involvement Scale (Farran, Kasari, Comfort, & Jay, 1986); (b) Maternal Behavior Rating Scale (Mahoney, Finger, & Powell, 1985); and (c) Interaction Rating Scales (Clark & Siefer, 1985). Table 8.1 outlines these assessment devices.

In addition to family–child interaction assessment, the measurement of stress may provide important information. The Questionnaire on Resources and Stress (QRS) (Holroyd, 1974) is the oldest and most frequently used measure of stress. The QRS and the Parenting Stress Index (Abidin, 1986) were designed to give a general idea of the amount of stress the parents may be experiencing (see Table 8.1). Critical review of these measures prior to use is necessary. The information received from these measures can be used in the initial screening of the family or during program evaluation to determine effectiveness of intervention. The interpretation of information obtained with a stress measure should be analyzed with caution. Professionals should consider that intervention programs which require active parent participation may cause the parental stress level to increase (Winton & Turnbull, 1981).

The needs of the family in relation to their child are, of course, a major concern. Therefore, the psychologist may consider using a *needs assessment* in order to get an idea of the family concerns or issues. Two of the most widely used measures are the Family Information Preference Inventory (Turnbull & Turnbull, 1986) and the Family Needs Survey (Bailey & Simeonsson, 1989) (see Table 8.1). The items measure aspects of family functioning such as degree of concern over planning for the future, finding and using support, as well as financial considerations and explaining to others about the child. Early childhood specialists may find this information valuable for intervention and support planning.

Cultural influences are an important consideration in ecological assessment. The effects on the functioning of the individual members and the family as a unit can be powerful. However, many people deviate from their cultural roots and customs. Care should be taken to avoid expecting stereotypes in all cultures. Each family is different and professionals should be sensitive and flexible in adapting to and working with individual groups.

In addition to being sensitive to cultural differences in families, psychologists should exercise caution when becoming involved with family issues. Focus should be placed on those issues that are most directly related to the welfare of the child (e.g., developmental needs and concerns of the parents). Professionals should avoid involvement with issues that are less directly related to the child (e.g., long-standing family disputes or marital problems). Referral of the family to other professionals for assistance in dealing with these or similar issues can benefit the family and form a collaborative union with a wider network of helpful professionals.

Environmental Assessment

Considerable attention has focused on the importance of the physical environment and its effects on the child's situation and progress (Bronfenbrenner, 1979). Home and intervention settings are equally important to include in the assessment picture. Participation of the parents in the assessment of the child's environment may result in beneficial effects— that is, the parents may become aware of the need for a structured, yet stimulating home environment.

There are several commercially made instruments designed to assess the child's environment. Examples of reliable and valid tools include the Home Observation for Measurement of the Environment (HOME) (Caldwell & Bradley, 1978) and the Early Childhood Environment Rating Scale (ECERS) (Harms & Clifford, 1980). Parents may participate in the completion of these scales. Table 8.1 outlines these specific assessment instruments.

Parents as Observers

Parents can also be included in the assessment process by being taught to observe general and specific behaviors of their child and serve as agents in the child's behavior change. Does the child initiate interaction with family members? How often does the child go to the bathroom independently? As parents observe the frequency and intensity of behaviors, they become aware of the important behaviors professionals are trying to strengthen, decrease, or maintain.

Parents can also be encouraged to observe the therapists, preschool teachers, and assistants working with the child. As parents observe instructional and behavioral techniques, as well as examples of generalization of these skills to other situations or settings, they may learn to imitate these procedures at home. Parents who are familiar with teaching procedures and behavior management techniques are more likely to be more involved with the intervention. However, professionals must realize that long-standing behaviors that may have been accepted at home must be decreased before parents can effectively teach new or more appropriate behaviors (Alberto & Troutman, 1986). Helpful resources for teaching parents to use behavior-change procedures with their children may be found in Table 8.2.

TABLE 8.1. Selected Family-Related Measures

Scale	Focus	Author/Publisher
Parent–child interaction		
Parent/Caregiver Involvement Scale	Assesses parent interaction with child during play	Farran, Kasari, Comfort & Jay (1985) Dale Farran, Univ of NC, Greensboro, NC 27412
Maternal Behavior Rating Scale	Assesses maternal interaction with child during play	Mahoney, Finger, & Powell (1985) Gerald Mahoney, U of CT, School of Medicine, Farmington, CT 06032
Interaction Rating Scales	Assess parental interaction and sensitivity to child behaviors during play	Clark & Siefer (1985)
Stress		
Questionnaire on Resources and Stress	Sentence completion format used to assess caregivers resources and stress related to caring for a handicapped individual	Holroyd (1974) Clinical Psychology Publishing, Brandon, VT
Parenting Stress Index	Measures the amount of stress in the parents	Abidin (1986) Pediatric Psychology Press, Charlottesville, VA
Family Needs		
Family Information Preference Inventory	Assess parent needs related to their child	Turnbull & Turnbull (1986) Merrill Publishing, Columbus, OH
Family Needs Survey	Assess parent needs related to their child	Bailey & Simeonsson (1990) Univ of NC, Chapel Hill, NC
Ecological		
Home Observation for Measurement of the Environment (HOME)	Judgment-based assessment of the interactive needs of the parent/child	Caldwell & Bradley (1978) Univ of Arkansas, Fayetteville, AR
Early Childhood Environment Rating Scale (ECERS)	Judgment-based analysis of the child's preschool classroom	Harms & Clifford (1980) Teachers College Press, Columbia University, New York

TABLE 8.2. Resources for Behavior Change

Resource	Focus	Author/Publisher
SOS! Help for Parents	Practical advice and techniques for handling everyday behavior problems; book and audiotape available	Clark (1985), Parents Press, PO Box 2180, Bowling Green, KY 42102
How to Teach Series	Offers techniques for increasing desirable behaviors in children	Azrin, Besalel, Hall, & Hall (1981), PRO-ED, Austin, TX 78758
Living with Children	Practical techniques for parents to use in changing the behavior of their children	Patterson, (1976) Research Press, Box 3177, Dept S, Champaign, IL 61826
Parents are Teachers	Offers easy-to-understand child management strategies for parents	Becker (1971) Research Press Box 3177, Dept S, Champaign, IL 61826
Solving Child Behavior Problems at Home and at School	Provides step-by-step methods for improving children's behavior	Blechman (1985) Research Press, Box 3177, Dept S, Champaign IL 61826

Parents can also be encouraged to collaborate with professionals through use of the Behavioral Style Questionnaire (Carey, McDevitt, & Fullard, 1975). This judgment-based tool assesses qualitative dimensions of the child's individual mood and behavioral characteristics. The information can be quite beneficial to use during program development.

Program Development

Parent participation with the team's professionals in determining their child's goals serves three purposes: (1) the parents learn through the decision process the strengths of the child and can be encouraged to build on those strengths, (2) they may become aware of the weaknesses of the child and can be encouraged to work on emerging skills at home, and (3) involvement provides opportunity for parents to develop competencies and empowerment.

As described in Chapter 2, one particular program planning instrument which incorporates the parent in program planning and team decision-making is the System to Plan Early Childhood Services (SPECS) (Bagnato & Neisworth, 1990). This judgment-based assessment tool is the only commercially available assessment device which incorporates ratings of the child's behavior from the parents and team members for designing a treatment program.

Parents who become involved with planning and decision-making may feel more positive toward the child. Additionally, parents may take an active part in the skill development and growth of the child by working with the child on maintenance and generalization of learned skills in the home or other settings.

Acceptability of Program

As parents become active participants in planning, they will be more prepared to participate in the child's program evaluation and make sound decisions regarding acceptability of the program. Evaluation of acceptability is a critical component of any program. After the child has begun to receive services, the team and the parents must continue to communicate and collaborate to evaluate parent satisfaction and perceived value of services, and continue to discuss issues of concern (Bailey & Simeonsson, 1988a–c). Goals and progress should be reviewed in the evaluation process as changes in the child's program may be warranted.

The effectiveness of a child's program should be looked at closely to determine if progress is the result of training, maturation, or other variables (Fotheringham, 1983), and these considerations should be discussed by parents and team members. Parents should be encouraged to express their views concerning the child's program by discussing behaviors in which they have observed improvement. Also, new concerns may arise and should be addressed.

As program acceptability is determined, parents become active learners and participants in a process they are likely to be active in throughout the child's life. It is difficult to empirically measure the effects of participation of individual families, however, one would expect great benefits.

CONCLUSIONS

Each parent or set of parents has different background experiences, knowledge, and perceptions regarding their role as parents in their child's development and intervention program. There is no single approach that works best. Many parents may be very willing to cooperate and become advocates for their children. Others may choose to be passive participants, involving themselves with only the minimal requirements. Team members should attempt to be realistic yet encouraging. Creative problem-solving to increase parent and family participation may help to facilitate any situation, should it arise.

Successful assessment and delivery teams incorporate the parents and family members and support their efforts to contribute to the welfare and progress in the child's overall development. Not only is the family–team collaboration productive and ethical, it is the law!

GUIDEPOINTS

- Create opportunities for parent participation and success.
- Support the positive efforts and involvement of parents
- Praise parent endeavors.
- Be realistic in your expectations of parent participation.

SUGGESTED READINGS

Bailey, D. B., & Simeonsson, R. J. (1988). *Family assessment in early intervention.* Columbus: Merrill.

Clark, L. (1985). *SOS! Help for parents.* Bowling Green, KY: Parents Press.

Dunst, C. J., Trivette, C. M., & Deal, A G. (1988). *Enabling and empowering families: Principles and guidelines for practice.* Cambridge, MA: Brookline Books.

Patterson, G. R. (1976). *Living with children: New methods for parents and teachers.* Champaign, IL: Research Press.

BEST PRACTICE SUMMARY CHECKLIST

Chapter 8

What Are the Basics for Family Collaboration?

[ ] 1. Arrange circumstances to involve parents actively in assessing their child's status and in participating in team meetings.

[ ] 2. Encourage parents to help identify and appraise their child's objectives and progress.

[ ] 3. Interview both parents, preferably together; use forms and questionnaires sparingly at the interview.

[ ] 4. Avoid involvement in domestic issues that are tangential to the child's welfare; refer parents to other professionals and agencies for counseling, per se.

[ ] 5. Collect information on the family's perceptions of their child's needs and their own needs.

[ ] 6. Assess the child's family context by observing parent–child interaction and the physical–social qualities of the home.

[ ] 7. Assist the parent in becoming a good observer of child and professional behavior.

[ ] 8. Select some assessment instrument or structured format that both parents and other team members can use to provide a common denominator for team decision-making.

9

Can Professionals Forecast and Plan for Kindergarten Success?

ISSUES IN PRACTICE

- How can professionals ease a child's transition from preschool to kindergarten?
- Can transition prerequisites be incorporated into the preschool curriculum?
- Should the family participate in the transition process?
- Is there a time sequence for implementing transition goals?
- What is the proper role of screening and assessment for kindergarten transition?

Much controversy surrounds the issues of kindergarten readiness, generally, and kindergarten screening, specifically. Sparks fly in the clash between those who espouse a maturationalist viewpoint ("give them more time") and those who advocate early intervention ("earlier is better"). Unfortunately, children are harmed most in this clash when they are excluded from beneficial learning and socialization experiences. Kindergarten "readiness" screenings and "entrance testing" have been misused to exclude young children from school. For the young child who is at developmental risk, delays in getting help can be devastating. Arbitrary cutoff scores and restrictive eligibility criteria are the barriers that prevent children from getting important early experiences. Children are made to fit the mold of the schools rather than the schools making accommodations for diverse abilities and needs. Parents are dissatisfied, confused, anxious, and angered by this practice. School psychologists are uniquely positioned to champion alternate beliefs and practices which are child- and family-centered, rather than school-centered.

The real challenge is constructing procedures that better enable us to forecast kindergarten success and plan for preschool to kindergarten transition. We must develop and promote systems based on the philosophy of making available broader early childhood education options for young children who have both slower timetables and developmental disabilities. All young children with special needs have a right to individualized transition plans to ensure success in one of their first, most important, and enduring early childhood life events—public school entrance.

FACILITATING THE TRANSITION TO KINDERGARTEN

Two major concerns arise when the at-risk or special-needs preschooler reaches kindergarten age: How can a smooth transition to kindergarten be accomplished, and what are the best indicators for forecasting the child's success? These concerns can best be addressed through careful planning and a thorough understanding of the transition process.

Transitioning is a critical developmental step. It prepares the child for the stay in the new school environment and sets the stage for other transitions with which the child must cope throughout the early elementary grades. Thus, survival skills should be embedded within a child's preschool and kindergarten curriculum to ready the child for successive changes and new demands and expectations.

Too often a child is plunged into a new setting without adequate preparation; it is left to the resources and ingenuity of the new caregivers to help the child to cope with these changes. It is the professional's responsibility to maximize the educational benefit and minimize the trauma and confusion associated with transition. *Careful planning is the prerequisite for "errorless transition" and kindergarten success.*

Transition to kindergarten should be an *individualized* process. Children will be entering kindergarten with a variety of experiences and skill levels. Some will have spent several years in a preschool situation while others will be coming directly from home with little experience in socializing with peers. Professionals need a thorough understanding of the child's current environment to adequately meet the transition needs of each child. In addition, professionals must assess the receiving environment (i.e., the kindergarten classroom) and the related needs of each child and family. An understanding of these areas will form the basis for all planning and decision-making in the transition process.

Another important consideration is that transition is not an occurrence that affects only the child. Transition involves the entire family. *In each step of the transition process the parents must be actively involved and accurately informed.* Because the needs of special-needs preschoolers exceed those of their peers, professionals and parents need to collaborate in order to increase the chances for success in kindergarten. A major component in successful transition is to provide the family with options, support, and information that are appropriate to their needs, as well as to the needs of their child (Hains, Fowler, & Chandler, 1988).

GUIDEPOINTS

- Embed transition skills in preschool and kindergarten curricula.
- Plan carefully for "errorless" transition.
- Appraise thoroughly preschool, kindergarten, and home environments.

Planning for "Errorless" Transition

For infants and toddlers, transition planning should be started at least 6 months to a year prior to the change (McDonald, Kysela, Siebert, McDonald, & Chambers, 1989). Transition to a public school program or private kindergarten also requires considerations and planning for program options, scheduling of observations, and meetings over a 12-month period. Professional communication and organization are essential. Factors that should be considered by the person(s) responsible for transition organization are presented in Table 9.1. Establishing a timeline is the best strategy for organizing parents and professionals in accomplishing transition tasks (see Table 9.2).

Twelve Months Prior to the Transition Event

As the preschooler reaches the chronological age of 4 or 5 (depending on current developmental status), transition planning should begin. Development of the transition calendar for the year should be created and staff responsibilities determined. Ongoing assessment using a curriculum of prekindergarten and kindergarten expectancies is the "engine" that drives the transition planning process.

Curricular and child goals need to be defined to work on the readiness skills that prepare the child for kindergarten placement. Arrange to

TABLE 9.1. Considerations for Transition Organization

1. Organization and careful planning may facilitate a trusting relationship between parents and professionals. Considering that a school psychologist is often the primary caseworker and educational advocate for the handicapped child during his/her educational career, it makes sense to develop a positive and open parent–professional relationship as early as possible.

2. Organization facilitates productive involvement of professionals in the assessment and program development of the child.

3. Meeting scheduled timelines alleviates last minute decision-making. Working ahead of schedule allows time to reprogram if unscheduled complications arise.

4. Organized collaboration among all professionals associated with the transition process facilitates productive involvement in the assessment and program development of the child.

5. As a professional, one would like to appear organized and "on top of" the transition event. Disorganization only breeds frustration and uncertainty in parents and other professionals. Transition can be an anxiety-producing event for the parents. Organization on the part of the school psychologist may lessen the stress parents may be feeling.

---

meet with the receiving kindergarten staff to discuss the program (i.e., the schedule the child will be expected to meet and the curricula the child will be expected to follow). Ecological observation of the kindergarten setting is an effective way to get an idea of the quantity of planned structure and unstructured time and the level of independence the child is expected to show. Be sure to carry out observations at the beginning of the school year to assess the child's needs and the program's requirements so early intervention can take place.

Although the transition readiness assessment is ongoing throughout the year, a screening of the child's functional skills, as well as emerging and absent skills, is completed at this time. If the child is already enrolled in a preschool program, observations should be conducted in that setting and teachers and staff interviewed to monitor the child's skills and needs. The screening process will be discussed in more detail later in this chapter. In order to include the family in the assessment process, tentative transition goals can be collaboratively developed and discussed with parents, and they can be advised of the procedure that will be used for the follow-up assessment which will be used to determine specific goals and objectives for the child.

Ten Months

Upon completion of the screening, the professionals involved meet to review the transition schedule, screening results, and tentative goals. This

TABLE 9.2. A Timeline for "Errorless" Transition

Time	Task Initiated	Task Completed
12 Months		
1. Transition calendar of events created	————	————
2. Allocate team members responsible for events	————	————
3. Arrange to meet with receiving kindergarten teacher(s)	————	————
4. Ecological observation of receiving kindergarten setting	————	————
5. Begin screening to determine readiness strengths and weaknesses	————	————
10 Months		
1. Team members attend pre-planning meeting to review timeline, screening results and tentaive child goals	————	————
2. Schedule program planning with team members and parents	————	————
3. Provide parents with a list of activities they can use at home with child	————	————
9 Months		
1. Implement progress monitoring system with preschool teacher	————	————
2. Initiate preschool curriculum objectives for approximating kindergarten setting	————	————
3–4 Months		
1. Administer thorough follow-up assessment	————	————
2. Meet with multidisciplinary members to determine appropriate services and program goals	————	————
3. Meet with parent to discuss/receive input for child's program	————	————
4. Conduct visitations of kindergarten with parents and child	————	————
Post transition		
1. Schedule staff meetings to monitor child's kindergarten progress	————	————
2. Initiate progress reporting to parents	————	————

meeting facilitates organization and consistency among the team members. Next, the child's parents and the professionals meet to collaboratively discuss the screening results, determine goals, and detail the entire assessment and transition process. The parents should be encouraged to discuss concerns or ask questions they may have regarding the transition process, the child's developmental status, or current program.

At this time, it is also beneficial to provide the parents with a list of prekindergarten activities they can use at home with their child to foster independence. Also, while it may seem premature, professionals should provide the family with information and support regarding special support services available if the at-risk child continues to have learning or behavioral difficulties.

Nine Months

Monitoring the child's "readiness" progress should begin. Weekly or monthly progress reports, if used properly and consistently, can effectively fulfill two important needs: (1) facilitate communication between the school psychologist and the preschool teacher, and (2) provide a sequential developmental record of the child's progress in acquiring expected learning and behavioral competencies. This process insures that parents and professionals have a "common language" to monitor existing strengths and weaknesses in order to prevent possible problems from occurring. Keep the progress report simple, yet thorough to prevent excessive time usage. Figure 9.1 provides an example of a simple and effective model of a progress report. At this time, it is also appropriate to begin introducing and monitoring environmental and program changes in the preschool curriculum to gradually approximate those to be experienced in the kindergarten setting.

PROGRESS REPORT

Name of child: *Jeffery Royer*

Date: *December 3, 1990*

Program goal: *Language development–social development*

Status: *Jeffery continues to be delayed; however, this week we really saw a big difference in him!! While two other boys were playing in the kitchen, he wandered into their area and picked up a pan and said "me too?" The boys were pleased and let Jeff join right in.*

Program goal: *Fine motor development*

Status: *Jeffery continues to hold the large pencil with a fisted grip. The occupational therapist plans to have him use a "grip-rite" on his pencil beginning next week.*

FIGURE 9.1.   Sample brief progress report card for parents.

Three to Four Months

A thorough follow-up assessment to determine the strengths and weaknesses of the child should be carried out at this time. The assessment of a preschooler for transition and mainstream programming should emphasize two major competencies: *preacademic skills* (i.e., recognition of letters, numbers, and colors) and *social–emotional skills* (i.e., on-task behavior, attention, following directions, cooperation with peers and adults, and adjustment to new situations). Most preschool curricula (e.g., Hawaii Early Learning Profile, Beginning Milestones) include the academic and social readiness skills necessary for success in kindergarten. When the multidisciplinary assessment is completed, results are discussed with parents and team members, and the program and the child's goals are determined. *The transitional status of children is based on the discrepancy between their present level of skill development and the demands of the kindergarten curriculum they will be expected to follow.* Readiness for transition should not be determined exclusively by performance on nationally standardized norm-referenced tests, but by acquisition of skills in the local school curriculum as well.

During this time, it would be beneficial to familiarize the parents and child with the kindergarten setting. A visit to the kindergarten room and the kindergarten teacher should be arranged. If possible, several visits should be scheduled so the child can become accustomed to the new setting.

Post Transition

Monitoring of child progress should continue between the school psychologist and the kindergarten teacher after the transition has been made. Collaboration of both parties divides the responsibility and insures communication. Prepared weekly or monthly progress reports take very little time to complete and mail. This is an effective and efficient interim way to communicate the child's progress to the parents and address problems that may arise.

To insure smooth transition, the child, parents, present and receiving care-givers, and appropriate resource personnel should be involved in each step of transition. A checklist and time sequence for errorless transition is shown in Table 9.2.

GUIDEPOINTS

- Begin transition planning one year prior to the event.
- Develop a timeline for organizing transition.
- Determine regular times for reporting progress to parents.

Identifying Crucial Kindergarten Transition Needs

Through formal and informal assessments, professionals begin to determine the strengths and weaknesses of the child, as well as the needs of the parents and professionals. An analysis of the preschool and kindergarten curricula can identify areas of commonality and continuity. *A comparison of kindergarten objectives and the child's abilities can provide a quick assessment of skills that will need special instructional attention.* Obviously, all children will not be "ready" for kindergarten. Special needs will require special transition plans and, sometimes, referral for special education services. A special needs child will not be ready for mastery of kindergarten objectives in all areas. It is important, however, to ensure that every child masters skills that will foster mainstream integration to the greatest possible extent. Instruction in key areas has been found to be helpful in facilitating the move to kindergarten (Pollaway, 1987; Simner, 1983). Five key competencies best predict the child's ability to successfully make the transition from preschool to kindergarten:

- academic readiness skills
- social skills
- responsiveness to the type of instructional style provided
- responsiveness to the environment in which the child will be placed
- attention-span, distractibility

These competencies can be embedded in the preschool curriculum and gradually fostered in the early intervention program.

Academic Readiness Skills

Although academic skills are not always stressed in preschool programs, certain key skills are crucial for kindergarten success (Leigh & Riley, 1982; Simner, 1983):

- number and letter recognition
- ability to grasp pencils
- counting
- verbal fluency
- writing letters and numbers in recognizable form

These areas should be an integral part of the preschool curriculum and actively introduced to preschool children. Students with physical disabilities will have difficulty with the grasping and writing tasks or with verbal fluency and will need special adaptations. Most students, except the most severely delayed, should be able to approximate mastery of these areas with sequential and well-planned instruction.

Antecedent skills for both academic and social competencies are attention and memory span. Development of memory skills and on-task behavior should be a crucial part of any preschool curriculum.

Social Skills

Another important area of competence is the development of social interaction skills. *Children must be able to cooperate in groups of various sizes.* In kindergarten classrooms, large group instruction is often a drastic change for the child accustomed to individualized or small group instruction practiced in the preschool. Research comparing one-to-one versus small group instruction (Fink & Sandall, 1980) has indicated that group instruction in the preschool can enhance ability to function in typical school situations. The gradual increase in group size and time on-task in the preschool program facilitates successful transition.

Responsiveness to Instructional Style and Environmental Structure

Important differences exist between the preschool and the kindergarten programs in both the manner of instruction and the physical layout. As part of transition, it is beneficial to know the degree of change that will be experienced by the preschooler in both of these settings. Psychologists and teachers must collaborate to plan opportunities for preschoolers to practice and generalize both preacademic and social–emotional transition skills. However, preschools should not become mirror images of the kindergarten. The quality of preschools and kindergartens vary greatly. One of the opportunities present for the psychologist or other professional in charge of transition is to physically link the two programs. Arrangements should be made for the preschool staff to visit the kindergarten and vice versa. Supervised meetings between the two staffs should be held to discuss methods of facilitating transition. *The onus should not be exclusively on the preschool to modify its program to approximate the kindergarten program.* Positive developmental aspects of the preschool program and environment should also be adapted in the academically-oriented kindergarten classroom to ease transition.

GUIDEPOINTS

- Identify crucial transition skills and incorporate these into the preschool curriculum.
- Link preschool and kindergarten curricula and environments.

APPRAISAL FOR KINDERGARTEN TRANSITION

During the last decade, school involvement in early childhood education has proliferated. The impetus of Public Law 99-457 will certainly add momentum to this movement, primarily in the area of special needs students. To complement these programs, education agencies have been accelerating the use of developmental evaluations to aid in identifying and placing children classified as "at-risk." As of 1986, one half of the states had mandated developmental screening for children between 3 and 6 years of age (Meisels, 1987). For most educators and school psychologists this is new ground. *Traditional methods and technologies of assessment are of questionable value for this age range and are especially inadequate for dealing with children with a wide range of handicapping conditions.*

Several important aspects of the transition evaluation process are early warning signs of at-risk development, screening, follow-up developmental assessment, posttransition monitoring, and family and professional communication and collaboration. A schematic representation of the total prekindergarten assessment procedure is shown in Figure 9.2.

True Warning Signs

Developmental delays must be identified and treated early. Waiting for preschool screening programs to identify problems can waste precious time that could have been spent in intervention. Many developmental and behavioral inventories (Child Behavior Checklist, Learning Behaviors Scale) list warning signs of learning and behavior problems. It is important that parents, teachers, and other professionals dealing with children have a comprehensive knowledge of warning signs that might forecast problems. Table 9.3 presents a checklist of possible indicators of developmental and behavioral problems.

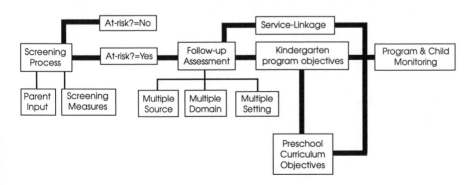

FIGURE 9.2. Kindergarten transition assessment model.

TABLE 9.3. Possible Indicators of Developmental Problems: A Checklist

Indicator	Occurrence		
	Often	Sometimes	Rarely
Vision			
Squints or holds objects close to eyes	_____	_____	_____
Rolls eyes around, is cross-eyed or does not use both eyes to track objects	_____	_____	_____
Doesn't return waves or in other ways doesn't imitate others	_____	_____	_____
Does not look at colorful, eye-catching objects	_____	_____	_____
Often rubs eyes	_____	_____	_____
Complains of itching or burning eyes or of double vision	_____	_____	_____
Holds objects close to eyes	_____	_____	_____
Has recurring styes	_____	_____	_____
Has difficulty doing many skills which require eye–hand coordination such as scribbling on paper with a crayon	_____	_____	_____
Auditory			
Does not react to sudden loud sounds	_____	_____	_____
Has many earaches and/or has fluid seeping from ear	_____	_____	_____
Often complains of dizziness and/or headaches			
Has little voice control or difficulty imitating sounds	_____	_____	_____
Repeats the same sound over and over or only repeats words after hearing them spoken by another person	_____	_____	_____
Significant delay in speech development	_____	_____	_____
Relies on gestures when speech would be more appropriate	_____	_____	_____
Neuromotor			
Constantly rocks back and forth or perseverances other gross-motor movements	_____	_____	_____
Displays difficulty controlling arm or leg movement	_____	_____	_____
Falls frequently and walks poorly	_____	_____	_____
Drools	_____	_____	_____
Poor muscle tone (lack of firmness or excessive flaccidity)	_____	_____	_____
Behavior			
Fears new experiences and people	_____	_____	_____
Withdraws consistently from situations where he or she is touched or held	_____	_____	_____
Does not play with other children and prefers to be isolated from peers	_____	_____	_____
Often hits or bites self or others	_____	_____	_____
Exhibits temper tantrums or significant mood shifts	_____	_____	_____

TABLE 9.3. *(cont'd)*

	Occurrence		
Indicator	Often	Sometimes	Rarely
<u>Other</u>			
Has difficulty understanding and remembering simple directions	_____	_____	_____
Does not speak in complete sentences	_____	_____	_____
Cannot attend to tasks for a duration approximating that required for preschool or kindergarten lessons	_____	_____	_____
Cannot identify numbers and letters prior to kindergarten	_____	_____	_____
Does not show interest or participate in group activities	_____	_____	_____

Unless a gross and obvious deviation from normal development is apparent, the use of warning signs as indicators of a condition is unwarranted. Early warning signs should only be used as general indicators that further assessment may be warranted.

Many of these warning-sign inventories include behaviors (or lack of behaviors) that are intended to be indicators of children at-risk for later school failure. When conducting a developmental assessment, or when observing a child either in the home environment or in the preschool, it is important to have a clear and unbiased view as to which skill truly predict later school failure.

Simner (1983) reviewed research findings on traditionally accepted warning signs of school failure. Of all the abilities we typically waste time assessing, only five signs showed moderate to high correlations with later school difficulties! Other factors commonly thought to be valid indicators of later success were found to have very low predictive validity. A summary of these findings are listed in Table 9.4.

The observation of warning signs in early childhood is a prescreening procedure. Parents and preschool teachers are most likely to notice at-risk types of behaviors. Children exhibiting these warning signs may be referred for screening prior to the traditional prekindergarten screening process. One of the primary objectives of prekindergarten screening is to find children who may need special prereferral intervention for mild or moderate developmental learning/behavior problems. Educating parents about warning signs and utilizing "outreach" and "child-find" programs can identify children with at-risk behaviors at an early age while providing them with effective prekindergarten services. Many children, however, are not identified early enough and show up for kindergarten registration or screening several months before the start of school. For these students, the timeline for transition will need to be condensed.

```
GUIDEPOINTS

• Use warning signs checklists for early prereferral for screening.
• Emphasize only true indicators for kindergarten success in the
  assessment.
```

TABLE 9.4. Valid and Invalid Indicators of School Success

A. Factors with moderate to high correlation to later school success
   1. Attention span, distractibility, or memory span
   2. In-class verbal fluency
   3. Interest and participation
   4. Letter and number identification skills
   5. Printing errors

B. Factors with low correlation to later school success:
   1. Gross or fine motor coordination
   2. Peer acceptance or adult cooperation
   3. Basic language skills (not including verbal fluency)
   4. Drawing and copying errors

From "The warning signs of school failure: an updated profile of the at-risk kindergarten child," by M. L. Simner, 1983, *Topics in Early Childhood Special Education, 3*, 17–27. Copyright 1983 PRO-ED, Austin, TX. Reprinted by permission.

Prekindergarten Screening

Purpose and Use

Traditionally, the major purposes of prekindergarten screenings have been to assess the readiness of children to enter the school environment and to identify children that might be considered at-risk for further referral and assessment. Readiness assessments must be differentiated from screening assessments. Technically, readiness tests are measures of achievement and their purpose should be to provide instructional information for educational planning. The term readiness carries confusing connotations and can be easily misinterpreted. *Readiness and achievement-format tests should not be used in the screening stage of assessment.*

Screening instruments are general measures that provide a global sample of landmark developmental and learning skills. They should be used only to identify children who exhibit skills that *seem* to indicate a questionable performance for age. Upon identification, these children should be referred for a more thorough assessment. This should be the only purpose for which screening tests are used.

Screening is the first step in the appraisal for kindergarten transition. Screening has two outcomes:

- early identification and intervention for the child with mild to moderate handicaps, and
- identification of children with special needs who have not previously been identified.

If there appears to be one or more areas of difficulty, a comprehensive assessment is indicated. *The only decision made at this point in the process is that the child is in need of further evaluation to confirm or refute the screening results.* Because the established risk for children with severe handicaps has probably already been identified, these children can be referred directly to the second, more comprehensive stage of the appraisal process.

While developmental screening has the potential to be a valuable tool, there are also dangers inherent in the screening process that must be avoided. Premature labeling and the effects of lowered expectations still exist and are evidenced in our school programs. Note that screening instruments are not designed to be either diagnostic or prescriptive. *In no way should screening tests be used for the exclusion, classification, or placement of children.*

Orientations to Screening

The use of screening devices for recommended inclusion or exclusion in kindergarten programs has become a prevalent practice. The ethics and legality of these practices are very questionable. Often the theoretical orientation of the screening instrument determines how it is used. Two theoretical orientations predominate. The *process orientation* stresses aspects of development that are theoretically related to underlying learning abilities. Some of these factors include constructs such as intelligence, visual and auditory discrimination, and perceptual–motor skills. The assumption is that if the child is developmentally mature in these areas, he or she is ready to receive instruction. Tests using the process orientation have several drawbacks. There is little evidence to support that the processes allegedly measured by these tests are predictive of success in kindergarten. There is also limited evidence that these processes are amenable to intervention strategies, thus limiting their application to instructional planning. A major misuse of these types of tests has arisen. Parents of children deemed "not ready" for kindergarten have been encouraged to hold back children from kindergarten until they have attained an "appropriate" level of readiness. The recent trend in kindergarten programs to adopt more academically-oriented curricula has contributed to the perception by parents and teachers that the child should attain a certain undefined level of readiness before kindergarten entry. This raises ethical and legal questions as to the actual role the school should play in early childhood education. In these situations we are asking for the children to meet the needs of the school rather than having the schools meet the needs of the children. The reality of the situation in schools is that process-oriented instruments are often used to exclude children from needed learning opportunities. Cutoff scores are frequently established (based on a "developmental age" as reported by a test) and parents are encouraged to hold back their child until the following year. This implies that no instructional adaptations will be made for individuals and that there is some mythical starting point necessary for kindergarten admittance. The pressure placed on parents having to make the placement decision is enormous and the responsibility for a successful kindergarten year transfers from the school (where it should be) to the parents. Alternatives to this type of procedure must be implemented. *Note that retention and exclusion are rejected as unethical by the National Association of School Psychologists in published position statements.*

The *skills orientation* examines directly what the child can and cannot do related to academics and instruction (e.g., What letters can the child identify, how far can he or she count, how many directions can the child follow at one time, can he or she recognize colors?). The screening aspect of the skills orientation is limited to identifying children in need of more thorough assessment. The follow-up assessment in the skills approach relies on developmental task analysis of skills and linking these to behavioral methods of instruction and treatment. Items from tests using a skills orientation are designed to be directly transferrable to objectives for a child's academic program. Professionals using the skills orientation are interested in linking specific skills demonstrated by the child to the new curriculum. There are no a priori decisions made about whether the child is ready for kindergarten. Rather, the results are used to determine instructional objectives and to link the child to services that will better facilitate his or her progress in the kindergarten program.

Selecting the Screening Instrument

Many screening instruments are currently available. Two surveys, in New York (Joiner, 1977) and Michigan (Michigan Department of Education, 1984), illustrate the range of instruments used for screening purposes. In the New York study, 177 school districts were polled to identify the instruments currently being used in their prekindergarten screening procedures. It was found that 151 separate tests or assessment instruments were reported in use! In the Michigan study, 111 different tests were in use in the state public schools! The use of locally developed instruments may account for a large number of the measures found in these surveys, but the heterogeneity of screening practices is apparent. The present situation is certainly even more complicated and problematic. With this wide array of screening instruments available the obvious question arises: What criteria should be used for selecting a screening test?

A good screening instrument should meet the same requirements as any other standardized test. It must have adequate reliability, validity, standardization procedures, and the data necessary to support claims made by the publishers. Other considerations include cost, ease of administration, and expertise needed for interpretation. Probably the most important consideration for selecting a screening measure is that it is a screening measure. Avoid tests that make extravagant claims that go beyond the basic purposes of the screening process. In reality, only a handful of screening tests have adequate reliabilities, validities, and discriminant function indexes (i.e., sensitivity, specificity) to be confidently or ethically used for screening purposes (Meisels, 1985).

Developmental screening instruments should be chosen carefully. Few available scales meet the strict psychometric criteria that are, arguably, most germane and most necessary when attempting to identify the child with problems (Table 9.5). Meisels offers important guidelines for the selection of developmental screening instruments. Choose only scales that meet the following criteria.

1. Contain brief tasks and procedures.
2. Sample only those behaviors that truly distinguish children at-risk for learning problems or handicaps.
3. Focus on developmental rather than academic readiness tasks.
4. Survey a wide range of developmental domains rather than one area (i.e., intelligence), exclusively.
5. Report reliability and validity data, especially predictive and sensitivity-specificity indexes.

Other researchers report that few individual screening measures have the technical adequacy necessary for early identification (Mercer, Algozzine, & Trifiletti, 1979). They echo the previous recommendations but offer other important considerations, particularly the use of multinstrument batteries which have higher accuracy rates. Other points include selecting scales that are curriculum-compatible, incorporating measures of physical health and socioeconomic status, emphasizing teacher judgments, and ensuring follow-up developmental assessments.

A good example of a technically superior, multidimensional developmental screening instrument is the Early Screening Inventory (ESI) (Meisels & Wiske, 1988). This instrument can be administered in 15–20 minutes, measures a wide range of skills, and includes a parent questionnaire. Scores obtained on the ESI result in one of three recommendations: "OK," indicating normal development; "rescreen," recommending readministration of the ESI within 8–10 weeks due to borderline perfor-

TABLE 9.5. Valid and Sensitive Developmental Screening Instruments

Scale	Age range (yrs)	Publisher
Development/Learning		
Early Screening Inventory (ESI)	4–6	Teachers College Press
Minneapolis Preschool Screening Instrument (MPSI)	3.7–5.4	American Guidance Service
Early Screening Profiles (ESP)	2.0–6.11	American Guidance Service
Behavior/Social Competence		
Child Behavior Checklist (CBCL)	2.0–6+	Psychological Corp.
Social Skills Rating System (SSRS)	3–6+	American Guidance Service
Learning Behaviors Scale (LBS)	Kindergarten	Psychological Corp.
Study of Children's Learning	Pre-K+	Psychological Corp.

mance; and "refer," indicating the need for immediate referral for a more thorough assessment.

Family Considerations

The first interaction between the schools, parents, and children often occurs during the prekindergarten screening procedure. It is not possible to overestimate the significance of this event in a family's life. Parents often view the entrance into a public school, preschool, or kindergarten as the first major milestone in a series of "rites of passage" for their child. For parents of a nonhandicapped or mildly delayed child, this may be their first encounter with the testing and assessment of their child. For the parents of the handicapped child, the developmental screening may present a first time comparison with regular school expectations. In

---

GUIDEPOINTS

- Identify children in need of more thorough assessment.
- Use screening measures to include rather than exclude children from learning opportunities.
- Select screening instruments that sample important skills for instruction and therapy.
- Involve parents in the appraisal of their child.

either circumstance, parents are understandably anxious and wary. It is critical that the prekindergarten evaluation be a positive experience for the child. It is of equal importance that parents come away from the assessment with valid and appropriate information about their child. The processes involved in communication with parents and in staging assessments with young children are addressed in other chapters of this book and will not be discussed in any detail here. What is unique in this situation is the introduction of a family to an institution which will house their child for the next decade or more. The onus is on the schools to offer a positive and informative welcome.

COMPREHENSIVE FOLLOW-UP ASSESSMENTS

Purposes

A comprehensive assessment should follow every questionable screening result. This follow-up assessment has two major goals:

- confirm and designate the degree of delay or deficit so that appropriate referrals and/or support services can be recommended for the child, or to refute the screening results; and
- provide the kindergarten teacher with precise educational information so that a link can be established between the assessment and the child's educational program.

A follow-up assessment includes a thorough overall team-based developmental assessment using a Convergent Assessment Battery (see Chapter 4). It requires the services of resource personnel from a variety of disciplines. Physical and occupational therapists, speech and language specialists, early educators, counselors (for parents and children), nurses or pediatricians, and psychologists should be available for this stage of the process. Traditionally, specialists have operated in isolation. Collaboration and communication across disciplines or with parents has not been a strong point of the evaluation process. A program designed to alleviate this problem is the System to Plan Early Childhood Services (SPECS) (Bagnato & Neisworth, 1990a,b) (see Chapter 2). The major goal of SPECS is to standardize parent–professional decision-making and to foster kindergarten transitions and service delivery.

A major goal of thorough developmental assessment is to receive input from multiple sources and across multiple domains. The use of multiple sources for information gathering accomplishes several purposes. A truer estimate of the child's status is provided when information originates from several sources. For example, low-incidence handicaps and situation-specific behaviors will require multisource appraisals across environments to produce representative assessments. Multisource evaluation increases the likelihood of parent and professional agreement, integrates decision-making, and enhances the external validity of both assessment and treatment.

Multiple domains that describe a child's total profile must be included in the developmental assessment. The assessment should include traditional areas such as language, cognitive, gross motor, perceptual–fine motor, socioemotional, and self-care. Ecological and interactive areas should also be appraised, which would entail assessment and/or observation in several settings. (The nature of the transition process makes these two areas of particular importance.) With more severely handicapped children, measures of self-regulation, endurance, emotional expression, and normalcy should also be included. It is important to include a wide range of skills in the follow-up developmental assessment. It is also important that skills measured in the assessment can be taught in the kindergarten curriculum. To accomplish these goals, it is necessary to use both norm and criterion-referenced scales.

Norm-Referenced Measures

Norm-referenced tests are important in determining the degree of the child's developmental deficit. Yet, a shortcoming of norm-referenced tests is that they have low treatment utility (i.e., they provide little information about a child's actual abilities or weaknesses that would benefit program planning, since they often do not sample skills emphasized in kindergarten curricula). Choose only those norm-referenced instruments that sample skills required in the early childhood setting. The questionable technical adequacy of many early childhood measures calls for a cautious approach to interpretation.

Criterion- and Curriculum-Based Instruments

In order to bridge the gap in communication and to link the assessment to curriculum, criterion and curriculum-based assessments (CBA) are necessary components of developmental assessment. The use of CBA can provide the receiving teacher with starting points for instruction, a clear indication of sequential steps in future instruction, and a useful tool in evaluating child progress and the program's impact.

For a child with a handicap who has been receiving services in a preschool setting, an Individualized Education Plan (IEP) is in place that will indicate already the child's skill attainment prior to the transition. This is valuable because it will establish starting points for instruction in kindergarten and will provide another source of information which will add to the strength of the validity of the assessment. Having a clear idea of the child's capabilities will facilitate program planning by the teacher and will allow for precise communication with the parents. *Developmental assessments during the transition process must stress the child's strengths and needs rather than the child's condition or disability.*

GUIDEPOINTS

- Use multidimensional assessment procedures.
- Collaborate with parents and other team members.
- Assess to determine appropriate developmental support services.
- Link child needs to curriculum objectives.
- Monitor child progress and program efficacy.

CHILD AND PROGRAM MONITORING

Once a child has been identified as needing special support services, a comprehensive plan for monitoring the child's progress and the program's effectiveness must be implemented. Close communication among professionals and parents is necessary. Regular staffing meetings would serve to aid communication among professionals. Progress reports, similar to those shown in Figure 9.1, and regularly scheduled parent conferences will keep parents informed and involved in their child's program (see Chapter 11 for more details).

SUMMARY

The transition to a kindergarten program is a crucial step for children, especially so for a special needs child. Every effort should be made to ensure errorless transition through careful planning and collaboration among professionals and parents. The transition can be facilitated by embedding key prerequisite skill instruction in the preschool curriculum, such as academics and social skills that can be linked directly to kindergarten curricula. As the actual transition time approaches, the child's environment can be altered to better approximate the setting and type of instruction in the kindergarten.

The assessment process must be approached with diligence and safeguards to ensure that the child receives appropriate services and interventions to meet his/her needs without the threats of labeling or self-fulfilling prophecy. It is important to select the screening and assessment instruments based on a careful analysis of the reliability, validity, and standardization procedures. The screening stage of the assessment should be designed exclusively to identify children who might be considered at-risk for developmental problems and to refer them on for thorough follow-up evaluation. The follow-up assessment should be designed to determine the degree of the problem, to link the child to appropriate services, and to provide a linkage between the assessment and curricular objectives. Continuous monitoring of the child's progress and program effectiveness should be an integral part of the overall transition plan.

The concept of *linkage* underlies the entire effort—child to kindergarten, test to curriculum, parents to teacher. For the most efficient, errorless transition, all the links in the chain need to be strong.

SUGGESTED READINGS

Beckoff, A. G. & Bender, W. N. (1989). Programming for mainstream kindergarten success in preschool: Teacher's perceptions of necessary prerequisite skills. *Journal of Early Intervention, 13*(3), 269–280.

Kochanek, T. T., Kabacoff, R. I., & Lipsett, L. P. (1990). Early identification of developmentally disabled and at-risk preschool children. *Exceptional Children, 56*(6), 528-538.

McDonald, L., Kysela, G. M., Siebert, P., McDonald, S., & Chambers, J. (1989). Transition to preschool: Parent perspectives. *Teaching Exceptional Children,* Fall issue.

Meisels, S. J. (1985). *Developmental screening in early childhood* (rev. ed.) Washington, DC: National Association for the Education of Young Children.

Neisworth, J. T. (Ed.) (1990). Transition. *Topics in Early Childhood Special Education, 9*(4).

Simner, M. L. (1983). The warning signs of school failure: An updated profile of the at-risk kindergarten child. *Topics in Early Childhood Special Education, 3,* 17–27.

BEST PRACTICE SUMMARY CHECKLIST

Chapter 9

Can Professionals Forecast and Plan for Kindergarten Success?

[ ] 1. Meet with your supervisor, building principal, and curriculum team to advocate for administrative changes in the procedures for kindergarten screening.

[ ] 2. Take the lead with your school district to draft a plan for broader, more creative early childhood education options for at-risk children that includes relationships with community agencies and regular daycare, preschool, and learning centers.

[ ] 3. Ensure that your team emphasizes competencies that are most predictive of kindergarten success in their assessments.

[ ] 4. Foster collaboration between special-needs preschool and kindergarten transition teams.

[ ] 5. Embed transition skills/goals in the preschool kindergarten curricula.

[ ] 6. Stress the need for curriculum coordinators to blend aspects of both preschool and kindergarten goals and environments.

[ ] 7. Develop a timeline and sequence of events for transition that involve the parents as partners.

[ ] 8. Select only technically superior screening instruments to identify suspected developmental deficits.

[ ] 9. Always use a Convergent Assessment Battery to confirm or refute the screening results.

[ ] 10. Use criterion- or curriculum-based systems to link assessment, intervention, and progress evaluation.

10

How Can the Team
Evaluate the Program's Impact?

ISSUES IN PRACTICE

- Why is program evaluation not really competitive or threatening?
- What three program aspects should be evaluated?
- If not already in use, one of the first duties of the psychologist is to persuade program staff to adopt a working curriculum. Why?
- What is convergent program evaluation?
- What practical metrics are available for summarizing program-related change?

Professionals who believe in and operate early intervention programs must document change. Parents and professionals continually evaluate. They make judgments about how well a child is doing, the quality of teaching or parenting, the utility of assessment, staff morale, and other program aspects. Indeed, program evaluation of some sort goes on implicitly if not explicitly, and informally if not formally.

At its worst, formal program evaluation is sometimes regarded as a perfunctory task. When the evaluation procedures and outcomes have little utility for the staff or parents and are disconnected from program content, it is easy to understand the view of evaluation as a bureaucratic routine. Unfortunately, many evaluative efforts and materials do fail to provide any constructive information and are useless for subsequent decision-making. At its best, however, evaluation is an integral part of the program and is valued for the information it provides regarding the status and change of enrolled children, families, staff, and the quality of program operations. When the appropriate instruments and procedures are used, program evaluation documents the hard work of the staff, progress of the children, satisfaction of the parents, and the overall quality of effort. Doing a program evaluation is much like having a physical examination: perhaps it's a little anxiety producing, but it is intended to offer a check-up and suggestions for improvement. Likewise, a program "check-up" should yield a status report and suggestions for improvement. Evaluation need not be arduous, complicated, or abound with statistics. This chapter offers several suggestions for making program evaluation sensible, useful, and positive; it illustrates strategies for the psychologist to help preschool staff to document changes and their own effectiveness.

GUIDEPOINTS

- Plan for program evaluation prior to or at the start of a new program year.
- Design the evaluation so that the findings will be helpful in improving the program.
- Plan to examine both program outcomes (product) and procedures (process).

WHAT PROGRAM EVALUATION IS *NOT*

Because of some confusion regarding what program evaluation involves, it may be helpful to dispel a few misconceptions and concerns.

Not a Useless Routine

As mentioned above, evaluation can be of great help and value to the staff and parents. Evaluation answers real questions, helps adjust program procedures, satisfies parents, and documents the effort and success of the staff. The purposes of program evaluation depend on the questions or issues of concern. There is no Bureau of Standards for what can and should be evaluated and how it must be accomplished. There are, however, several usual aspects that are addressed in a program evaluation;

these typical concerns (to be discussed) can be supplemented with any number of other questions that parents or staff may have. We emphasize, however, that program evaluation should be tailored to the questions, interests, and concerns expressed by program participants. Evaluation should also be a vital source of feedback that helps to adjust program goals and procedures.

Not Comparative Research

Program evaluation is not comparative, but is usually program-specific. On the other hand, evaluation *research* is typically designed to discover generalities that cut across programs (Casto, 1988). Do children do better or as well in integrated programs when compared with segregated? What approaches are more effective? Are parents more satisfied with program A or B? These comparative concerns are not the purpose of program evaluation per se, any more than a physical check-up is meant to compare your health with that of someone else's. Furthermore, since program evaluation is *within* and not across programs, few or no statistics are involved. It is not the mission of program evaluation to determine if enrolled children's development is "significantly different" from a national norm or from children in another program. Of course, certain computations will be made—such as the average progress of enrolled children, or total number of therapy hours, etc., but these calculations do not involve comparisons. The fact is that programs differ so much in so many ways, that valid comparisons simply cannot be made. The enrolled children exhibit different levels of handicap across programs, family circumstances differ, staff capabilities vary, length and intensity of efforts change considerably, and a host of other variables operate to make meaningful comparisons not feasible. Emphasizing to program administrations and staff that evaluation is *not* comparative should eliminate most of the anxiety frequently associated with competitive comparisons.

Not Exclusively Child-Focused

The major missions of early intervention are, of course, to optimize children's development, to minimize handicapping circumstances, and to expand each child's functional capabilities. Contemporary empirical research as well as logic, however, shows us that child development is not simply maturational—it is the result of interactions with physical and social contexts experienced by the child. When the importance of the child's environment is recognized, assessment must be expanded to include appraisal of the "ecology" of the child, including the family/parenting circumstances and quality of the preschool environment. *Program evaluation must capture some context-based information.* Measures of changes in parent ratings of their child's development, of the acceptability of the child's program, of improved family functioning, of the team's cohesiveness, and of the program arrangements are examples of valuable ecological measures. It can be said that early intervention and assessment are focused on child progress, but within a developmental context that includes the family, home, and programmatic circumstances.

Not Based on One Type of Measure

Several types of assessment approaches and instruments are now readily available to professionals and parents (see Chapter 4). Assessment approaches such as direct observation, interviews, and informal and standardized testing can be employed. Types of instruments include those referenced to norms (Norm-based Assessment [NBA]) curricular objectives (Curriculum-based Assessment [CBA]) and parent, peer, or professional judgments (Judgment-based Assessment [JBA]). These assessment approaches and types of instruments can be useful in appraising not only the child but the family and preschool contexts. Clearly, it is not acceptable to use a single measure at the beginning and end of the year as the sole evaluation of a program; this is analogous to taking a child's temperature each year in order to evaluate the effectiveness of a health-promotion program. Such a measure is of some importance, but certainly falls short of being sensitive to critical health aspects and program effects.

We must again emphasize the several problems associated with the use of child-focused normative instruments for evaluating program efficacy. First, most norm-referenced measures (especially intelligence tests) are not sufficiently sensitive to detect many changes in child performance. For example, a child may evidence great improvement in motor and social development, but this progress may not register on an intelligence test. Even cognitive advances may not be detected by many norm-based measures, since they only employ items that are psychometrically selected to discriminate among age groups. Second, the content of normative measures seldom reflects the instructional content of a program. Again, items included in norm-referenced instruments have met certain psychometric criteria (e.g., a high percentage of children who are a certain age pass the item compared with a low percentage of children who are younger). A good psychometric item is not necessarily a good instructional item. "Stands on one foot" and "stacks three blocks" are items on norm-based developmental inventories that are not sensible instructional targets! We are not urging the abandonment of normative measures, but increasing the priority of other types of measures, especially curriculum-based, and the use of multiple companion measures.

Not Exclusively Outcome-Focused

Improvements in child and family status are certainly cardinal aspects to be evaluated. But program evaluation encompasses recording of program efforts, as well as program-related effects.* It is often quite important to know how much time and effort were involved in working with parents, to toilet train a child, to provide speech and language therapy, and to provide specified services. An accounting of the program's intensity should accompany the reported effects. What it took to bring about a goal is important information to parents, staff, and agency administrations. Sometimes evaluation of staff effort will reveal that inordinate time and work are entailed in bringing about minor changes. Often, the effort should be shifted to a more productive program aspect. In this regard, some curricula require much more work to implement than is reasonable for a busy staff. Analysis of staff activities will help to detect various time and effort "sink holes."

GUIDEPOINTS

- Focus the evaluation on the expressed concerns of parents and staff.
- Reduce staff anxiety concerning program evaluation by emphasizing that it is not competitive or comparative, but corrective.
- As feasible, include criterion-, norm-, and judgment-based evaluation measures.

A CONVERGENT PROGRAM EVALUATION MODEL

Professionals working in early intervention settings typically are very busy people. A large case load, children with diverse handicaps, long travel times, and the need to work with less-than-cooperative parents and staff can frustrate even the most dedicated professional. But, program evaluation need not be arduous, an afterthought, or an add-on to the program; it can and should be integral to a comprehensive assessment plan. *Program evaluation is the systematic appraisal of progress toward expressed program goals and of the activities involved in working toward those goals.*

---

*We use the term *program-related effects* or outcomes recognizing that seldom can definitive cause-effect connection be asserted between program variables and child-family changes.

Convergent program evaluation includes multiple instrument types, information sources, and occasions for the appraisal of program goal attainment.

Convergent program evaluation "in action" relies upon the gathering of child, family, and program ecology information from multiple sources. Program evaluation should fulfill both direct service and administrative missions. However, the most important consideration is not "what tests to choose" but rather *what questions are to be posed and answered.* Once the questions have been posed, the clinical and administrative staff can design and select program evaluation methodologies that most sensitively address the program's missions. The developmental school psychologist can offer pivotal consultation to the early intervention program staff and administrators because of expertise in research and measurement/evaluation.

A convergent program evaluation model has three major attributes: (1) it includes norm, curricular, and judgment-based measures; and (2) where feasible, the measures are the same ones employed for child or family assessment, but are summarized to provide information on group (rather than individual) progress; and (3) measures of program and family ecology and dynamics are included to yield information concerning the characteristics of the physical, social, and instructional circumstances.

Because of federal legislation, research support, and today's professional standards, program goals are typically formulated with respect to child, family, and program components. Thorough evaluation includes all three of these aspects, although child progress is almost always emphasized. After all, early intervention programs are dedicated to the early education and treatment of the child. Family and environmental concerns are included because they provide the developmental context for the child; however, they are not the object, per se, of intervention. (See Figure 10.1 for a convergent evaluation illustration.)

The Child

Most often, accountability rests on how well children fare as a result of their participation in a program. Child progress may be seen as a *product,* while program arrangements and procedures are considered *process.* Of course, program administrators and staff usually strive to use the process they believe will yield the optimal products (e.g., progress in children's development). Often, however, program activities are driven more by a theory, set of principles, or expedience than by outcome data. As an example, a program may have goals and procedures for "fostering creativity," but never evaluate this worthwhile goal. Clearly, then, *a first responsibility is to clarify child goals and objectives so that they are subject to evaluation.* Until this criterion is met, child attainment cannot be objectively assessed either through norm- or criterion-based instruments. Subjective evalua-

TABLE 10.1. Convergent Program Evaluation Model and Example

Component	Question	Component			Metric
		Type	Example		
CHILD	What is the extent of curricular gains by program children during instruction/therapy?	CBA	HELP		CEI
CHILD	Do the children show different rates of progress within and across developmental domains?	NBA	BDI/HELP		IEI
CHILD	Do program children show comparable rates of progress expected for age?	NBA	BDI		DA/DQ
FAMILY	Do parents show more positive and effective management of children after program participation?	JBA	PPS		Rating Observations
FAMILY	Do families report reduced conflict and stress at home among members?	JBA	PSI		Ratings
FAMILY	Do families report fewer needs for supportive services after program participation?	CBA	FNS IFSP goals		Ratings IFSP Criteria
FAMILY	Have parents learned more effective ways to play with and teach their children?	CBA	TSI		Ratings Observations
PROGRAM	Are there increases in the interactions among handicapped and nonhandicapped peers in the preschool?	EBA	SSRS CI		Ratings Time sampling
PROGRAM	Have program services become less intense as children have progressed?	EBA	SPECS		Ratings Frequency data
PROGRAM	Have classroom physical arrangements been changed to match the special needs of children?	EBA	ECERS		Ratings
PROGRAM	What changes exist in the interactions of team members and parents during team meetings?	EBA	SPECS CI		Ratings Frequency data

BDI, Battelle Developmental Inventory; CBA, Curriculum/Criterion-based Assessment; CEI, Curricular Efficiency Index; CI, Critical Incidents; DA, Developmental Age; DQ, Developmental Quotient; EBA, Eco-based Assessment; ECERS, Early Childhood Environment Rating Scale; FNS, Family Needs Survey; HELP, Hawaii Early Learning Profile; IEI, Intervention Efficiency Index; IFSP, Individualized Family Service Plan; JBA, Judgment-based Assessment; NBA, Norm-based Assessment; PPS, Parent Practices Scale; PSI, Parenting Stress Index; SPECS, System to Plan Early Childhood Services; SSRS, Social Skills Rating System; TSI, Teaching Skills Inventory.

tion of child status is accomplished through judgment-based measures; concurrence of these measures with the more objective measures provide a social validation of the findings. The roles of criterion-, norm-, and judgment-based evaluation of the child program component are summarized below.

Criterion/Curriculum-Referenced Assessment

Programs usually employ an organized and teachable series of (typically developmental) objectives that comprise the *curriculum*. Often a program will "sort of" have a curriculum which, upon inspection, is little more than a list of major developmental landmarks, perhaps along with some program-specific goals. Such loosely organized quasi-curricula are akin to sketchy blueprints: they do not provide much guidance and will not focus efforts toward predetermined outcomes.

Programs should be urged to adopt one or more of the quality curricula available (see Chapter 6). It may be the responsibility of the school psychologist or other professional to discuss with program staff and administrators the virtues of a structured curriculum so that criterion or curriculum-based child assessment and program evaluation can take place.

Assuming that the program is using one or more curricula, child program progress is best appraised through CBA. Indeed, it can be said with some truth that the curriculum is the heart of the program.

CBA is the most relevant, direct, and sensitive measure of the program's influence on the child's performance. Many curricula provide ways to monitor attainment of curricular objectives. For purposes of *program* evaluation, the curricular progress of enrolled children can be summarized and averaged. The average performance of children within the curriculum can be extremely helpful in gauging the general impact of the program. Sometime, program staff also wish to detect the possible *differential* impact of the program on the several domains of development included in most curricula (e.g., cognitive, motor, social, language). So, for example, the average attainment in motor skills may be compared with the average attainment in the cognitive, social, and communication areas. When great discrepancies are revealed, this has implications for strengthening program efforts in the weaker developmental domains.

Curriculum-based child program evaluation need not be complicated. Curricular evaluation consists of the steps outlined in Table 10.2. As mentioned, numerous curricula are commercially available and choice among curricula will depend on factors such as child characteristics and staff preferences (as described in Chapter 6). From the standpoint of program evaluation, age inclusiveness is an especially important curriculum characteristic. Curricula that span several years provide continuity and lend themselves to pre-posttest assessment. Contrary to this, use of one

TABLE 10.2. Procedures for Curriculum-Based Program Evaluation

---

- At Time 1, assess each child's initial level in the program's curriculum (i.e., number or percentage of total objectives achieved at program entry). Various curricula provide ways to estimate entry levels. Sometimes a few weeks into the program must elapse before good estimates can be made concerning children's curriculum levels.
- At Time 2 (mid or end of year), tally the number of curriculum objectives attained by each child. If a running record is not available, the program evaluator will have to take the time to appraise attainment (observation, test probes, and interviews with the staff through the same means are used to estimate entry levels).
- Sum number of attainment objectives for all enrolled children. Totals for the several developmental domains may be separately summed to permit inspection and comparison of group progress in each domain.
- Encourage program staff to keep records of curricular progress; again, many curricula provide means for tracking progress.
- Compute summary scores to depict group progress within developmental domains or across the entire curriculum. Several scoring or summarization procedures are available, including percentage change in mastery of objectives, change in absolute totals (and domain totals), goal attainment scaling, and the Curricular Efficiency Index (CEI). (These scoring options and others are described in the final section on Evaluation Metrics).

---

curriculum at the beginning and then another at the end of the year because a child has moved beyond the first one creates special evaluation problems. Fortunately, curriculum developers are sensitive to this issue and have produced curriculum packages that accommodate longitudinal monitoring and evaluation.

Norm-Referenced Assessment

Imbedded in the training of most clinical and school psychologists is extensive preparation in the use of norm-referenced assessment. Trait- or construct-based instruments (e.g., personality and especially intelligence tests) are viewed as primary and enduring instruments (Zigler & Balla, 1982). Normative assessment does offer a larger picture or referent to help professionals make judgments concerning a child's status with respect to age peers. Because of their norm-based and psychometric properties, however, these instruments are not program specific and thus lack the content validity required to assess achievement within the program. Further, norm-referenced assessment of preschoolers is difficult to conduct and is typically insensitive to smaller performance changes, in contrast to criterion-based measures tied to program content. Norm-referenced assessment, however, taps broader capabilities that idiosyncratic project measures may overlook. Additionally, normative devices are built on standards and procedures that permit a common basis for classification decisions. Because of their differing purposes and qualities, both NBA and CBA measures are important in program evaluation. The clear content validity of curriculum-based assessment makes it the primary measure for planning and evaluating the child's program. Norm-referenced assessment is, however, an important complementary form of assessment. Indeed, when the program's curriculum (e.g., HICOMP Preschool Curriculum) and the normative instrument (e.g., Bayley Scales of Infant Development) are both based on developmental milestones, a high correlation between these measures is evidenced (MacTurk & Neisworth, 1978). Of particular utility for program evaluation are those "hybrid" instruments that combine the important qualities of criterion and norm-referenced measures. The Battelle Developmental Inventory (BDI) is an excellent example of a developmental scale that provides curricular objectives that are norm referenced. When the program's curriculum is based on the BDI, a child's progress can be appraised within the program as well as compared with peers in the national norm group.

To summarize, substantial child gains must occur before they are registered on norm-referenced instruments, since these instruments are composed of psychometrically derived items that differentiate between (age) groups. Nevertheless, NBA is a way to compare performance with a representative or peer group; this provides a standard useful for continued decision-making concerning classification. It should also be noted that a program is more than its curriculum, and normative instruments may be a means for detecting child progress not directly addressed by the curriculum. Finally, norm-referenced instruments provide some continuity in assessment when children move to other programs that may not employ similar curricula.

Several factors must be considered in choosing norm-referenced measures for some aspects of program evaluation. Some normative instruments are better than others for purposes of program evaluation. The right choice of an instrument can speed and ease the program evaluation effort. Three qualities of norm-based instruments are especially worthwhile: program relevance, age inclusiveness, and item density.

Program relevance is a major criterion to heed. The missions of most early intervention programs usually include promoting language, social, cognitive, and motor development. In addition, other child-specific objectives are addressed, as noted on Individualized Educational Programs (IEPs) and Individualized Family Service Plans (IFSPs). Use of normative instruments that assess traits only obliquely related to the program's developmental basis makes little sense. Personality measures and tests of ego-strength or anal–oral fixation, for example, would not be relevant to most programs! Intelligence tests, while revered and psychometrically sound, are also tangential to most program content. As a rule, the most relevant normative devices are those that tap many of the same characteristics addressed by a program. *Typically, normative instruments that are developmentally based are likely to be program related.*

Age-inclusiveness refers to the developmental age range accommodated by the instrument. As with CBA, a wide range permits the instrument to be employed over several years for longitudinal use. Age-inclusiveness is especially important when children are transitioned to advanced programs (e.g., from preschool to kindergarten to first grade).

Item density is especially important for detecting the smaller increments of change often evidenced by preschoolers with more pronounced delays and handicaps. The insensitivity of normative devices noted earlier is in great part due to their item sparsity. Fewer items translates to greater improvement needed to pass an item. It is helpful to employ scales that have greater item floor-to-ceiling ranges, thus providing more items to detect smaller improvements. Scales with more items may require longer administration time, but their increased utility for program evaluation is a priority consideration.

Judgment-Based Assessment

Perceptions of child progress can compliment or even bring into question curriculum- and norm-based assessment. Program evaluation is incomplete unless it includes some means to detect judgments of child progress. Certainly, it is important that parents be able to register their impressions about program influence. Improvement in social development on the curriculum that are not noted by parents or others may be questioned as "real" improvement. Several factors may be responsible for the lack of concurrence between curriculum and judgment-based program evaluation. Often, children perform quite differently across settings. Children who show mastery of objectives in the preschool may not evidence such attainment outside these circumstances. Lack of generalization or the situational-specificity of learning can be detected through surveying the judgments of parents and professionals who work with the child in different settings and occasions. Ideally, program evaluation provides the strongest documentation of child progress when JBA corroborates normative curriculum results.

Choice of JBA instruments should be based on two major considerations: program relevance and cross-rater use. The instrument (usually a rating scale) should, of course, be program-relevant. As with NBA, scales that rate characteristics not included within the program or the child's individualized plan do not contribute much to program evaluation. It is best to select scales that survey developmental and behavioral dimensions of general and/or program concern. The Developmental Specs (D-Specs) scale (see Chapters 2 and 12) uses a 5-point scale for rating 19 child dimensions. Most of the D-Specs dimensions are congruent with curriculum content, but several scales (e.g., normalcy, temperament, health, and growth) are useful for judging other aspects of child status that are difficult to assess objectively but are nevertheless program-relevant.

The second consideration, cross-rater use, refers to utility of the scale by various professionals, staff, and parents. Discipline-specific scales cannot easily be used by related professionals. A common scale that is easy to use across professionals and by parents is optimal. Such a common instrument permits comparative ratings, is easy to summarize for program evaluation, and provides more convincing evidence than a potpourri of scales and checklists.

As with CBA and NBA information, ratings should be collected at Times 1 and 2 (e.g., beginning and end of year). Ratings can be averaged to depict group status on whatever scales are employed. Changes in overall group ratings reflect the collective judgments of raters. Of course, average ratings can be computed for separately scaled dimensions (e.g., language, cognitive). Also of interest is a profiling of the group's standing at Times 1 and 2. Visual inspection of the changes may be sufficient.

GUIDEPOINTS

- Be certain that child objectives are measurable rather than elusive.
- Assist program staff in selecting an overall curriculum for the program.
- Make curriculum-based child (group) progress the top priority for evaluation.
- Use norm-based assessment to provide a reference for child progress.
- Select one norm-based instrument to provide a reference for overall child progress and other normative measures for special concerns.
- Include judgment-based measures to assess the social perceptions and validity of changes. Parents, staff, and exam peers should be included.

THE FAMILY

Child development specialists and educators have for some time reported that early intervention effects go beyond the child (e.g., Garber & Heber, 1977; Klaus & Gray, 1968) and that family involvement is crucial for optimizing short- and long-term intervention impact (Brofenbrenner, 1975).

TABLE 10.3. Examples of Family-Related Evaluation Questions

- How many and what type of family goals and objectives were written into IFSPs?
- How many goals and objectives were attained?
- What changes occurred in family expressed needs?
- What changes occurred in support services provided?
- Did the quality of home environments change?
- Were there changes in parent–child interactions?
- Were there "spill-over" effects detected or reported with siblings or other family members?
- Did family demographic measures improve (e.g., income, education)?

As almost any educator knows, some families are easy to work with and some definitely are not! Further, children at-risk or with delays or handicaps may very well come from families that do not resemble old fashioned nuclear families. A single parent (usually the mother), or low-income foster family with several siblings is not unusual. Frequently, the grandmother or even an older sibling may be a major if not primary care-giver. High levels of stress and distress, poor nutritional practices, sporadic employment, and other difficulties often vex families with special needs preschoolers. The complexities and obstacles associated with these families can understandably produce much professional avoidance behavior. But troubled families are the very ones that need the most help to offset the debilitating circumstances that distort and delay child development. In addition to the logical arguments, public law, and continued research, professional ethics dictate that early intervention programs address the family context. Since family program participation is now a mandate, family-relevant measures must be routinely included in program evaluation (Table 10.3).

Like children, families are idiosyncratic and there is no predetermined set of evaluation questions and measures that "fits all." (Procedures and instruments described in Chapter 8 can be useful for assessing family concerns and program impact.)

Consider the following to illustrate evaluation at the family level. Perhaps the mother of a 4-year-old has asked for help to improve parenting skills, or a social worker has observed this need. The Home Observation for Measurement of the Environment (HOME) (Caldwell & Bradley, 1978) could be employed at Times 1 and 2. HOME assesses qualities of parent–child interaction and can act as a criterion-referenced tool to provide parenting objectives. Those skills apparently lacking can become IFSP objectives; attainment of the parenting skills can then be assessed and improvements included in program evaluation reports. Improvements across several families might be separately documented as well as summed.

As another illustration, many families of children with handicaps experience great stress that interferes with family life and caregiving. The Parenting Stress Index (PSI) (Abidin, 1986) has proved to be a useful gauge of family stress levels. Many PSI items (e.g., those dealing with mood, sense of competence, child activity level) can become targets for the IFSP or for counseling recommendations.

Similarly, the Family Needs Survey (Bailey & Simeonsson, 1988a–c) enables parents to report their family's priorities so that the IFSP can incorporate these. Program evaluation efforts, then, would document whether or not services had been effectively delivered over a time period to address the family's goals.

The program evaluators must first help to identify the major family questions/concerns prior to selecting instruments. Repeated use of the instruments can help to register the changed status of the family and reflect favorably on the program.

PROGRAM ECOLOGY

An early childhood education "program" is a composite of its missions, clients, staff, and physical environment, as well as its curriculum. Too often, program evaluation fails to include appraisal of those aspects of the program that can indirectly or even directly affect child and family services. The extent and quality of child integration, staff morale, child study team functioning, and the acceptability of program objectives and methods are examples of factors that can seriously influence program effectiveness.

Issues such as the breadth of program goals, the intensity and duration of services, and the detection of unintended effects (Zigler & Balla, 1982) are valuable to examine through program evaluation. Use of multiple measures and inclusion of child, family, and program ecology components can go a long way in providing a more complete picture of program effects. We remind the reader of the poor showing evidenced by Head Start programs when IQ was used as a primary evaluation criterion. When grade level advancement, reduced enrollment in special education, improved peer relations, and other dependent variables were examined, the evaluation picture was much more positive (Lazar & Darlington, 1978).

Several aspects of program ecology are briefly discussed in this section; these are selected because they are often common (but by no means the only) program concerns. Table 10.4 surveys sample evaluation questions pertinent to program ecology. For each question, a Time 1 to Time 2 measure can be taken to assess stability or change in that aspect. Sometimes program circumstances, such as availability of learning materials and space, are excellent at the beginning of the year but deteriorate after

TABLE 10.4. Examples of Program-Related Evaluation Questions

- Is the staff:child ratio satisfactory with respect to requirements?
- Is the staff:child ratio adequate to deliver the program?
- Are staff qualifications satisfactory, especially with respect to the inclusion of children with special needs?
- Are staff inservice activities scheduled and/or completed?
- Are staff inservice training helpful as judged by the staff?
- Has inservice training noticeably improved staff/program operations?
- Are IEPs/IFSPs available for all enrolled children with special needs?
- Are the IEPs/IFSPs "working documents" and useful or perfunctory?
- Does the program have an overall curriculum that meets the needs of enrolled children and staff capabilities?
- Are proper ancillary services available to the children who need them?
- Are ancillary services coordinated and delivered satisfactorily?
- Is child progress monitored and recorded?
- Are the intensities of services recorded and do they change?
- Is the child service team cohesive and collaborative in their assessment and reporting activities?
- Are program goals and procedures acceptable to parents and staff?
- Are assessment reports useful for program planning?
- Are transitional interagency services in place and effective when a child is sent to a new program?
- Are follow-up procedures and information in place for children who have left the program?

several months and full enrollment. Likewise, social intergration can certainly shift through time.

There are many evaluation questions related to program operations. Evaluation must begin with several agreed upon major questions; as the year begins, other concerns can be added. It is also important to note that available instruments can contain numerous items that cover many of the questions sampled in Table 10.4. To illustrate, the Early Childhood Environment Rating Scale (ECERS) (Harms & Clifford, 1980) includes 37 items that appraise personal care routines, furnishings and display, language reasoning experiences, fine and gross motor activities, creative activities, social development, and adult needs. The ECERS uses a 7-point rating scale, yields a profile, and can be used to suggest targets to refine and improve program circumstances. Similarly, the Teaching Skills Inventory (TSI) (Robinson & Rosenberg, 1985) is an efficient way to estimate adult teaching skills, including sensitivity to child cues, use of appropriate language levels, and provision of prompts and positive consequences. The Parent Behavior Progression (Bromwich, 1981) is especially helpful for identifying degrees or levels of skills along a hierarchy or task analysis of important caregiver skills. It also can be used to suggest a "curriculum" for the caregiver.

With respect to evaluation of social behavior and peer relations, several easily used instruments are available—some with norms to help identify social difficulties. The Preschool Behavior Questionnaire (PBQ) rates the extent of problem behaviors using 30 descriptions of disorders that have been shown to differentiate between normal and clinical behavior.

Evaluation of program service delivery typically has been limited to a simple listing or number of services provided. Stating that children received speech and language services or that occupational therapy was provided to a certain number of children is an inadequate evaluation. This is much like early research in special education when reports only stated that children were enrolled in special or regular classes—without specification of what was "special." The *intensity* of services (e.g., number of hours, sessions) is crucial information for evaluating program efficiency and impact, and for helping professionals to detect relationships between intervention variables and outcome. SPECS (Bagnato & Neisworth, 1990a,b) includes a Program Specs component that provides a relatively easy way to quantify the extent of program activities, yielding a profile of the intensity of program services. The recording and evaluation of program intensity has been urged (e.g., Zigler & Bella, 1982) and is now a requirement for reporting under Public Law 99-457.

GUIDEPOINTS

- Absolutely include family-related measures to show change in needs, resources, and capabilities.
- Have parents judge the acceptability of program goals and their child's objectives.
- Evaluate the adequacy of the program's physical facility, materials, and staff qualifications.
- Be certain to have staff plan and keep track of the intensity of service delivery for reporting purposes.
- Plan to evaluate program reports to parents by asking parents to rate or otherwise appraise the utility and clarity of the reports.

EVALUATION METRICS

Criterion-Referenced Data

Criterion-based evaluation is arguably the most relevant way to estimate child program impact. When goals, objectives, and other measurable criteria are stated, a real program for child attainment is created. We may, of course, debate the value of the program (or specific child) objectives. Assuming, however, that a program adopts a reasonable developmental curriculum or other set of agreed upon objectives, criterion-referenced evaluation has unquestioned content validity and accountability.

Several metrics and procedures are available for summarizing criterion-related progress, including (1) number of criteria mastered, (2) percent mastery of program objectives, (3) goal attainment scaling, and (4) the Curricular Efficiency Index (CEI).

Number of Objectives Achieved

A simple yet important kind of information is the total number of curricular objectives reached by each child. These totals can be summed across children to yield a group total. Totals can also be summed for each curricular domain. Many curricula (see Chapter 6) include ways to check off mastery and record totals for each and across domains.

Percent Objectives Achieved

Absolute number of achieved objectives does not include any comparative information. Most teachers wish to know where a child is in the program curriculum at entry. Again, many curricula include ways to probe approximate levels of mastery at the onset of the program. A percentage can be computed with the estimated number of objectives already attained over the total number of objectives within the curriculum appropriate to that child's age. A 4-year-old may show uneven mastery across domains or, in the case of general developmental delay, an even profile. At Time 2, a percentage can again be calculated which will reveal actual progress compared with possible progress (see section below on the Curricular Efficiency Index for similar approach). Table 10.5 illustrates the use of percentage to evaluate curricular progress.

Goal Attainment Scaling

Goal Attainment Scaling (GAS) (Kiresuk &Lund, 1976) has predominantly been used in adult programs but offers strong advantages for early intervention evaluation (Simeonsson, Huntington, & Short, 1982). Essentially, GAS techniques involve identification of individual child goals and the specification of five levels of possible attainment for each along a continuum of worst to best or minimal to maximum outcomes. This is akin to task analysis or instructional analysis procedures of describing a performance progression wherein, for example, the behavior occurs but only with maximum prompting and support, then with increasingly reduced support, until it is performed independently under typical circumstances. A progression or scale is thus constructed and attainment can be tracked

TABLE 10.5. Percent Curriculum Objectives
Mastery at Beginning and End of Year

Domain	Child	Time 1	Time 2
Communication [a]	1	20	60
	2	10	40
	3	35	80
Motor	1	25	
	2	20	
	3	30	
Social	1	50	
	2	32	
	3	60	
Cognitive	1	28	
	2	46	
	3	42	

[a] The appropriate age level of the curriculum should
be used; this might be based on chronological age or
developmental age.

along the scale. With GAS, however, progress toward individualized goals can be compared across children and programs. The technique also includes the option of differentially weighting the goals to reflect presumed importance or difficulty. The weights are determined by clinical judgment and should probably be determined in concert with parents.

GAS scores can be derived at any time during intervention. Child attainment can be compared between Time 1 and Time 2. Also, attainment might be compared with predicted outcomes (akin to aimlines used in some individual-referenced methods; see Tindal & Marston, 1990).

A standardized score is computed, with a mean of 50 and SD of 10. The GAS score is calculated by use of a formula (Kiresuk & Lund, 1976). Because they are transformed, GAS scores are comparable across children, goals, and programs. In this sense, the technique combines features of normative and curriculum-based assessment.

Consider the display of a goal attainment scale for a preschooler (Table 10.6). The attainment of the child can be compared with initial attainment level and with levels at later times. (The interested reader is referred especially to Carr, 1979; Cytrynbaum, Ginath, Bindwell, & Brandt, 1979; Romney, 1976; and Simeonsson, Huntington, & Short, 1982.)

Curricular Efficiency Index

The CEI is a convenient way to summarize the curricular progress of children relative to their time in a program, to their peers, and to curricular expectations. The CEI can be used with individual or group data. It is

TABLE 10.6. Goal Attainment Scale for Child

Scale Attainment Levels	Scale 1: Expresses, Communicates	Scale 2: Social Orientation (w2=2)	Scale 3: Attention Span (w3=3)	Scale 4: Play Behavior (w4=4)	Scale 5: Frustration Response (w5=3)
-2 Most unfavorable treatment outcome likely	Communicates needs/wants by use of upper extremities, reaches for/pushes away with hands (I)	Turns away from social approach, no response to persons present (I)	Attends to tasks for less than 30 sec (I)	Plays with toys/objects less than 30 sec, throws it when finished (I)	Gives up if only slightly frustrated, 1 or 2 attempts, cries if pushed (I)
-1 Less than expected	Will have command of 10 signs, difficult to elicit	Intermittent response to social approach and persons present less than half the time	Attends to task for 1 min if receives reward and social reinforcement	Plays with toy/object for 30 sec, puts down when finished half the time (A)	Gives up if only slightly frustrated, will try again is pushed without crying
0 Expected level of treatment success	Will have command of 10 signs and will use them when reminded	Consistently responds to social approach, shows awareness of others present less than half of time (A)	Attends to task for 1 min when receives much social reinforcement (A)	Plays with toy/object for 30 sec, puts down when finished 100% of time	Gives up only after several attempts (5–6) (A)
1 More than expected success with treatment	Will have command of 10 signs and will use them whenever appropriate (A)	Consistently responds to social approach, shows appropriate awareness of others present	Attends to task for 1 min with little or no reinforcement needed	Plays with toy/object for up to 1 min	Will persist through a good number of tries (8–10) before giving up
2 Best anticipated success with treatment	Will have command of and consistently use 15–20 signs	Consistently responds to social approach, initiates social interaction with familiar others	Attends to task for as long as is appropriate in situation, switches to new task as presented	Plays with toy/object for as long as 3 min	Will use varied and imaginative ways to achieve the end before giving up

w, Weight; I, initial performance; A, attained level.

From "Individual Differences and Goals: An Approach to the Evaluation of Child Progress" by R.J. Simeonsson, G.S. Huntington, and R.J. Short, 1982, *Topics in Early Childhood Education, 1* (4), pp.71–80. Copyright 1982 by PRO-ED, Austin, TX. Reprinted by permission.

similar to the Intervention Efficiency Index (IEI) but uses curriculum- rather than norm-referenced measures (see p. 186).

In its simplest form for summarizing group progress, the formula for CEI is

$$CEI = \frac{\text{Mean \# of curricular objectives attained}}{\text{months in program}}$$

(The numerator refers to the total number of objectives achieved by all children divided by the number of children.) Use of this simple formula will yield a value that shows the average number of objectives attained per month by a group. But in the simple form, the CEI does not compare progress with what *could* or *should* be achieved—to do this, a standard for comparison must be used. The curricular progress of special-needs preschoolers can be compared with two standards: (1) the expected normal progress as indicated in the curriculum; and (2) the progress of nonhandicapped age peers using the same curriculum and preferably enrolled in the same integrated program.

The first standard, normal expectation as structured by the curriculum, refers to the use of the number of objectives available within an age range in the curriculum employed. If there are 40 motor objectives expected of 4-year-olds within a year of development, then that figure may be used to divide into the average number of motor objectives achieved within a year by program children. Thus, if the group average for the year in motor development were 30 objectives, this divided by 40 would produce an index of .75 or a rate of 75% expected by the curriculum developers. This sort of comparison can be within each domain as well as with the total across the entire curriculum. *Use of the CEI in this way presumes full-year programming,* since the objectives included in most developmental curricula are based on a full year of development. When the program is less than a year, the normally expected number of objectives can be adjusted. A 6-month program, for example, could not expect even normally developing youngsters to master a full developmental year of objectives.

Use this CEI formula to compare the group's actual with the expected curricular attainments based on the commercial curriculum used by the program:

$$CEI = \frac{\text{Mean \# objectives attained by children in program}}{\text{\# objectives expected for full year} \times \text{\% year of actual programming}}$$

It is best to employ the above CEI formula in a summative fashion, near the end of a program cycle. The information generated can be informative to staff, parents, and related agencies. A total CEI should be calculated to summarize overall curricular progress. This total CEI is in addition to separate CEIs for each curricular domain.

Cross-domain comparison is especially important when the mission is to encourage balanced, "whole child" development. It may be true, of course, that participating children may have special difficulties with certain developmental domains (e.g., language) but a low comparative CEI should alert staff to bolster efforts in that domain.

The second CEI standard for comparison uses a kind of "local norm" and offers information on the relative progress of special needs versus other children within a program. This CEI is used for evaluation within developmentally integrated programs where group comparisons are feasible. It is often the case, for instance in Head Start, that integrated programs may include five or six special-needs youngsters within a total group of about 20 children. The in-program comparison group can then consist of five or six selected nonhandicapped peers who appear to be developmentally typical for age.

When a comparative group is available, the formula for the CEI is:

$$CEI = \dfrac{\dfrac{\text{Mean \# objectives attained by special needs children}}{\text{months in program}}}{\dfrac{\text{Mean \# objectives attained by peers}}{\text{months in program}}}$$

Comparing progress with an "in-house norm" has distinct advantages since many variables are held constant (i.e., same curriculum, room, teacher). However, the "normalcy" of the peers and other factors may limit interpretation of relative attainment (Bailey & Wolery, 1989).

GUIDEPOINTS

- Summarize curricular progress of individual children and across all children; use one or more metrics to quantify results.
- Use the CEI to summarize and compare curricular progress across children and developmental domains.

Norm-Referenced Data

When program evaluators use norm-referenced scores, they have the advantage of being able to note Time 1 – Time 2 changes in the position of enrolled children relative to a norm group. Since normative scores are corrected for chronological age, increases in a child's normative position show that he or she is more than keeping up with the norm group. Four types of comparative scores are widely used: developmental age (DA), developmental quotient (DQ), percentile (or percentile rank), and standard (or deviation) scores. (Variations on these four score types are also used, including deciles, quartiles, *t* and *z* scores and normal curve equivalents.)

Developmental Age

A DA is the average age at which 50% of children in the norm group attained a given raw score. The attraction of this score type is its ease of interpretation (e.g., a 3-year-old child's motor performance is like that of a 4-year-old in the norm group). "He's acting like a child of age ___ " is understood by parents and is much more appreciated by them than statistical statements or confidence intervals. However, for evaluation reports, the reader should be cautioned against stretching the interpretation of changes in DA, since developmental age increments are not of equal intervals and cannot be mathematically manipulated as would an equal interval scale.

Ratio Developmental Quotient

Similar to the old ratio IQ formula, DQ is obtained by dividing a child's DA by the CA and multiplying by 100. A child who is maintaining a "normal" status will obtain a DQ of 100. But as with IQ (MA divided CA × 100), there are limits to the interpretation of DQs when averaged across children or in comparing them pre-posttest.

Again, because of unequal intervals, a child who evidences a DQ of 50 cannot be said to be developing only half as much as normal. A change from a DQ of 80 to 120 cannot be interpreted as a 50% increase in rate. Nevertheless, like DA, the ratio developmental quotient is understood by most parents and should be considered for reporting except where more accurate and formal interpretations are needed.

Percentiles

Like DA, percentiles are not based on equal intervals. Movement from a 50 to 60 percentile, for example, requires a smaller raw score increase than near the end of a distribution, e.g., from the 80th to 90th percentile. Thus, like DQ, a doubling of percentile rank cannot be interpreted as "twice as good," since *interpretation is distorted by unequal interval nature of the ranks*. Again, however, percentile rankings are easily communicated and carry useful meaning.

Deviation Standard Scores

Most norm-based instruments now use the standard score to interpret performance. A standard score has a mean and standard deviation that is the same across age groups, usually, a mean of 100 and SD of 15 or 16. Score distributions and increments are adjusted to fit the properties of a normal curve; this permits comparative interpretation. A standard score of 116 (based on an SD of 16) would mean performance that is equal to or exceeded by 84% of the normally distributed scores. Evaluators should be certain to know the SD of an instrument, since tests with different SDs are not directly comparable. Because they are scores that have been transferred to normal curve equivalents, *standard scores can be compared from Time 1 to Time 2 and can be used to evaluate progress.*

Intervention Efficiency Index

The Intervention Efficiency Index (IEI) (Bagnato & Neisworth, 1980a,b) is a way to express gains with respect to time in a program. The IEI is computed as follows:

$$\frac{\text{DA gain in program (in months)}}{\text{Time in program (in months)}}$$

We emphasize that *gain* here can be expressed in months of progress (DA Time 2 − DA Time 1). Time in program is usually expressed in months, producing an index of gain per month of participation. For purposes of program evaluation, a child's absolute gain must be interpreted with respect to time in program. Obviously, the same gain evidenced in half the time would produce a higher IEI. Like other indices of changes, a number of problems are associated with the IEI if it is viewed as being a pure measure of program impact. The child's rate of development at program entry, the assumption of developmental rate constancy while in a program, and other issues limit the IEI for more exacting purposes (see Rosenberg, Robinson, Finkle, & Rose, 1987). However, *the IEI is a way to evaluate gains relative to duration of program participation.* It is a practical way to summarize children's progress while in (but not necessarily due to) an early intervention program. It should be clear, however, that one program IEI cannot be meaningfully compared with another because of, for example, differences between children enrolled in the two programs. It may be useful, however, to examine differences between IEIs *within* the same program. When children evidence quite different IEIs within the same program, it is possible that the program is differentially effective for one type of handicap than another; this may produce implications for increased service intensity or other program adjustments.

Proportional Change Index

The Proportional Change Index (PCI) (Wolery, 1983) is essentially the same as the IEI but is presumably adjusted for the child's previous rate of development. The PCI is computed as follows:

$$\frac{\text{Gain in program}}{\text{Time in program}} = \frac{\text{Program entry developmental age}}{\text{Program entry chronological age}}$$

The PCI may be a more pure gauge of program impact since it corrects for DQ at program entry. The DQ itself, however, is not without problems (see Sheehan & Keogh, 1982) and as more manipulations of scores are included within a formula, the more the intervention effects may be distorted. Both the IEI and PCI may be computed for program evaluation, and both produce summaries of performance within the program.

Qualitative Data

There are numerous observational, sociometric, and interview techniques available to the evaluators that are beyond the scope of this book. We do emphasize, however, the important role of qualitative information as indicated in the discussions of JBA and the convergent model. Specifically, we draw attention to an evaluation method that is useful both formatively and summatively and that can be conducted within and across early intervention programs: the critical incident technique. We also provide at the end of this chapter a number of suggested resources for details on techniques not focused on in this chapter.

Critical Incident Technique

Among the many kinds and variations of qualitative methods for evaluation, the *Critical Incident Technique* (CIT) (Flanagan, 1954) stands out in its relative simplicity and utility. It has been used predominantly in industry and community services for about 40 years. More recently, CIT is finding use in education and related fields (e.g., Harrison, Lynch, Rosander, & Borton, 1990). The technique is a way to collect the impressions of key individuals concerning the strengths and weaknesses of certain circumstances, procedures, or people.

Several steps are involved in using the CIT and they are usually done with relative ease in the early intervention setting. Essentially, the evaluator must select respondents who will be asked several key questions about program-related matters. The informants may be parents, teachers, professionals, children, or a combination of these. The selected respondents are asked to state the two or three most positive and negative incidents over the past month they can recall relative to the topic being investigated. For example, the evaluator may use the technique to assess social integration within a mainstreamed kindergarten. The teacher, assistant, and several parents can be chosen as respondents. Each can be instructed as follows: We are trying to discover how well the children are getting along and the positive and negative aspects of this combination of children. Try to recall two positive examples of social integration; that is, how the special needs children and the others are getting along. Be specific, what happened as best as you can recall?

After the answer, the respondent can be asked why the incident is deemed to be positive. After positive incidents are reported by a respondent, two negative incidents are then called for.

Now, can you recall two negative examples of integration; that is, two things that happened that do not favor putting these children together?

By collecting positive and negative incidents across different respondents (children may very well be included), some extremely useful qualitative information can be produced that has utility for program adjustments. Usually, the evaluator then begins to sort the reported incidents into categories through an inductive process. Through this procedure, certain factors about the children, staff, or program are identified that are related to desired outcomes. In one informal study on early integration, the example, the investigator used the CIT with children as respondents and discovered that the major negative category that was induced was the "bad odor" of some children who were not played with, and not necessarily their developmental disabilities!

A summary of the steps for conducting a critical incident survey is provided in Table 10.7; further details and related literature are available (see especially Fivars, 1980).

GUIDEPOINTS

- Evaluate developmental progress of children through one or more evaluation metrics (e.g., changes in DA, DQ).
- Use the Intervention Efficiency Index or related metric to evaluate program impact.
- Do not omit a qualitative appraisal of program functioning or impact; consider the great utility of the Critical Incident Technique.

AN ILLUSTRATION OF CONVERGENT PROGRAM EVALUATION

Table 10.8 provides an illustration of a convergent program evaluation plan. Note the emphasis on the type and array of child, family, and pro-

TABLE 10.7. Summary of Steps for Conducting the Critical Incident Technique

1. Identify major concerns or issues to be investigated.
2. Select respondents; try to include respondents who might provide different perspectives.
3. Compose questions asking for about two positive or enhancing and two negative or inhibiting incidents. Ask for recent specific incidents. (Recall by adults over a month may not be accurate.)
4. Interview respondents separately. Ask why reported incident is seen as positive or negative.
5. Collect enough incidents over sufficient time to permit a sorting into categories; a total of 100 or more incidents may be adequate.
6. The CIT survey may be conducted over the year or for several years (see Harrison, Lynch, Rosander, & Borten, 1990) to provide a continuing qualitative source of socially valid program information.

gram ecology questions posed. These vary from examining the differential rates of curricular progress within various developmental domains to concerns about reductions in parent-identified levels of family stress to changes in the "intensity" or amount of specialized effort program staff exert for special needs children. Matched with these questions are examples of relevant measures and metrics that will help to answer pertinent administrative questions and concerns to guide ongoing program review and necessary changes in program practices. *Program evaluation is an important check-and-balance, quality assurance operation.* Program evaluation answers larger questions about changes in groups of children and parents as well as general changes in the physical and social environment and procedures of the program, itself, as it attempts to address child and family needs. Well-conceived program evaluation methods can begin to answer questions about the efficacy of the program and its practices—the expertise and hard work of its staff.

This final section offers a brief illustration of the contents and results of the evaluation of an integrated preschool program. Tables 10.8–10.11 address four major direct service and administrative issues: the curricular progress of enrolled children, reductions in child social behavior problems, reductions in the stress levels of parents and families, and changes in the amount and intensity of services provided to children by the early intervention staff.

The illustrative preschool program enrolled 30 nondevelopmentally delayed (NDD) and 25 developmentally delayed (DD) children (average chronological age at program entry = 57 months) within five integrated classrooms (approximately 11 children per classroom). The program evaluation effort was conducted over a 7-month period of intervention.

TABLE 10.8. Child Curricular Progress on the BDI and HELP After Seven Months of Integrated Preschool Programming

Factor	Nondevelopmentally Delayed (NDD)					Developmentally Delayed (DD)				
	DA_1	DQ_1	DA_2	DQ_2	IEI	DA_1	DQ_1	DA_2	DQ_2	IEI
Domain	42	74	51	80	1.29	36	62	45	69	1.29
Personal/Social	49	86	59	92	1.43	43	74	51	78	1.14
Adaptive	49	86	55	86	.86	46	79	49	75	.43
Gross Motor	49	86	55	86	.86	46	79	49	75	.43
Fine Motor	46	81	56	88	1.43	41	71	51	78	1.43
Motor	48	84	55	86	1.00	42	72	50	77	1.14
Receptive Language	50	88	62	97	1.71	39	67	56	86	2.43
Expressive Language	45	79	56	88	1.29	35	60	45	69	1.43
Communication	45	39	51	80	.86	35	60	45	69	1.43
Cognitive	51	89	61	95	1.43	42	72	51	78	1.43
Total Development	47.2	56.2	82.8	88	1.26	39.8	68.6	49.2	75.4	1.33

DA, developmental age; DQ, developmental quotient or ratio; IEI, Intervention Efficiency Index.

TABLE 10.9. Reductions in Child Social Behavior Problems on the Preschool Behavior Questionnaire After Seven Months of Preschool Programming

| | NDD | | | | DD | | | |
| | Pre | | Post | | Pre | | Post | |
Factor	Teacher	Parent	Teacher	Parent	Teacher	Parent	Teacher	Parent
Hostile/ Aggressive	50	70	50	70	80	81	70	81
Anxiety	65	80	65	80	92*	87	80	88
Hyperactivity/ Distractibility	40	46	40	44	90*	75	90*	71
Total Behavior Disturbed	40	70	30	60	90*	84	80	84

*90th percentile or above = elicited cutoff for child psychopathology.

TABLE 10.10. Reductions in Parent/Family Stress Levels During Program Participation on the Parenting Stress Index

| | NDD Group Parents | | DD Group Parents | |
Factor	Pre (%ile)	Post (%ile)	Pre (%ile)	Post (%ile)
Child Stress	20	22	86	61
Parent Stress	38	31	92	62
Total Stress	30	31	84	59
Life Stress	41	38	91	60

Child, family, and program ecology components were targeted for evaluation. The program evaluation included convergent information to demonstrate that children and families benefitted substantially from program participation. Table 10.8 shows that NDD and DD children equally benefitted from the program. In fact, curricular progress data suggest that some children classified as NDD actually showed evidence of being at risk for developmental difficulties at program entry in personal–social skills and expressive language skills. The DD group showed notable gains in all domains with measurable increases in personal–social, fine motor, communication, and cognitive/conceptual skills. Both groups showed accelerated rates of progress during the 7-month intervention period (IEI rates on Total Development = 1.26 and 1.3, respectively).

Similar beneficial changes in child social behavior were evident also

TABLE 10.11. Changes in the Intensity of Needed Program Services
Over a Seven-Month Period of Intervention on the Program Specs

| | Program Intensity Levels | | | |
| | NDD | | DD | |
Service	Pre (%)	Post (%)	Pre (%)	Post (%)
Program Option	10	5	60	45
Early Education	0	0	30	25
Adaptive Services	20	15	65	45
Behavior Therapy	30	15	71	50
Speech/Language Therapy	20	10	75	50
Physical Therapy	0	0	35	20
Occupational Therapy	0	0	65	40
Vision Services	0	0	25	5
Hearing Services	5	5	45	15
Medical Services	0	0	10	5
Transition Services	5	5	70	50

(see Table 10.8). The group of NDD children showed no clinically significant behavior problems compared with age peers; some concern, however, was initially expressed by teachers and parents concerning the anxious behaviors. Preschoolers in the DD group showed reductions in
observed levels of anxiety and general behavior problems. Evidence of
hyperactive and distractible behavior remained after 7 months of intervention. This most probably reflected the continuing developmental
immaturities of the children and the need for the program to continually
emphasize prerequisite behaviors in the IEP and IFSP goals.

Parents reported significant changes in how they viewed themselves
and their family's ability to cope after participating in parent support
groups, behavior management counseling, and classroom participation
with their children. Some parents of NDD children participated also.
Stress levels for DD parents dropped substantially from 84% to 59% during the intervention period.

Finally, staff and administrators, in reviewing the 7-month intervention period and planning allocation of staff and resources for the following year, were interested in overall changes in the level of intensity of program support services. These included such factors as hours of
speech/language and occupational therapy services, the number of children transitioning into diagnostic or regular kindergarten settings, the
number of children diagnosed with specific developmental disabilities,

the type of adaptive technology (e.g., computers, communication systems, microswitch toys) needed for children, and the number of children needing medical consultation. Table 10.11 outlines the changes in program intensity on the SPECS system that incorporate the above considerations. In general, DD children show substantially fewer program intensity needs in several areas including specialized early education services, occupational therapy, hearing services, and transition services.

With these data, the psychologist can help program administrators and staff to plan for next year and to alter the program to continue its fine record of effective service delivery to children and families.

SUGGESTED READINGS

Bricker, D., & Gumerlock, S. (1988). Application of a three-level evaluation plan for monitoring child progress and program effects. *Journal of Special Education, 22*(1), 61–81.

Gabor, P. (1989). Increasing accountability in child care practice through the use of single case evaluation. *Child and Youth Care Quarterly, 18*(2), 93–109.

Garwood, G. (Ed.). (1982). *Topics in Early Childhood Special Education: Program evaluation, 1*(4).

Odom, S., & Karnes, M. (Eds.). (1988). *Early intervention for infants and children with handicaps: An empirical base.* Baltimore: Paul H. Brookes.

Sheehan, R., & Laskey, J. (1987). Program evaluation. In J. T. Neisworth & S. J. Bagnato (Eds.), *The young exceptional child: Early development and education* (pp. 433–466). New York: Macmillan.

Thurlow, M., Ysseldyke, J., & Weiss, J. (1988). Early childhood exit decisions: How are they made? How are they evaluated? *Journal of the Division for Early Childhood, 12*(3), 253-262.

BEST PRACTICE SUMMARY CHECKLIST

Chapter 10

How Can the Team Evaluate the Program's Impact?

[ ] 1. Meet with the program staff and team to plan the evaluation goals before the program year begins.

[ ] 2. With the team, select convergent measures and procedures to evaluate program efforts and outcomes.

[ ] 3. Be certain to involve parents or their advocates to help identify what outcomes are of concern to them.

[ ] 4. Urge the staff to use a curriculum that will organize instruction and become the foundation for criterion-based assessment.

[ ] 5. Choose a norm-based and judgment-based instrument to provide the outside referent and social validity needed for comprehensive child progress evaluation.

[ ] 6. Carefully identify ways to assess progress on family and program-related goals.

[ ] 7. Consider what metrics are feasible for your evaluation plan. Remember that the evaluation report must be clear and useful.

11

How Can Psychologists Solve Four Persistent Preschool Assessment Problems?

ISSUES IN PRACTICE

- What must be included in an assessment battery to ensure its utility and compliance?
- What factors should be emphasized for program eligibility determinations?
- How does an IFSP differ from an IEP and what should be included?
- Instead of test-centered reports, what are more effective formats for preschool assessment reports?

Psychologists in preschool settings face numerous practical problems regarding assessment. This chapter poses several "best practice" solutions for four of the most prominent early childhood assessment problems: (1) selecting valid convergent assessment batteries; (2) determining eligibility for services; (3) linking assessment, intervention, and progress evaluation; and (4) communicating assessment results to parents and professionals.

PROBLEM 1:
SELECTING VALID CONVERGENT ASSESSMENT BATTERIES

Effective early childhood services require tailored assessment just as much as tailored intervention. Convergent assessment batteries must be chosen based on an individual child's functional needs or disabilities (see Chapter 4). Appendix A presents sample "modal" convergent assessment batteries organized by age and disability. First, however, the psychologist must apply a framework for choosing an individualized convergent assessment battery that when constituted meets seven criteria (Table 11.1). Table 11.2 illustrates a generalized modal convergent assessment battery which meets these selection criteria for a 2–5-year-old child.

TABLE 11.1. Criteria for an Individualized Convergent Assessment Battery

Comprehensiveness	Estimates status across developmental domains and environmental and/or social circumstances.
Continuity	Includes tasks to track progress across wide age, stage, and functional levels.
Sensitivity	Contains sufficient items and skill sequences to detect change and skill improvements.
Adaptability	Task demands can be adjusted to child's response and sensory capabilities.
Treatment validity	Assessment results have direct and immediate instructional relevance.
Social validity	Professional/parent/child ratings of program goals, techniques, and results.
Technical adequacy	Depending on purpose, reliabilities, and validities may be relevant.

TABLE 11.2. A Generalized Modal Convergent Assessment Battery for 24–60-Month Age Range

Scale Type	Measure
Norm-based	Battelle Developmental Inventory
Curriculum-based	Hawaii Early Learning Profile/HELP for Special Preschoolers
Judgment-based	System to Plan Early Childhood Services (SPECS) and the Child Behavior Checklist
Ecological	Parenting Stress Index

Comprehensiveness

Broadly survey capabilities within and across numerous developmental, behavioral, and ecological domains. At a minimum, batteries must include the typical developmental curricular domains (i.e., cognitive, language, perceptual/fine motor, social–emotional, gross motor, self-care), behavioral concerns (i.e., self-regulation, motivation, attention, atypical patterns), medical concerns (i.e., seizures, medication effects, endurance), family needs (i.e., stress, needs for information, needs for support), and environmental dimensions (i.e., adequacy of home and preschool settings, grouping arrangements, need for structure, interactive qualities).

Continuity

Sample capabilities in a sequential, hierarchical manner by developmental age/stage or functional levels, across a wide age range (e.g., newborn–infant, infant–preschool, preschool–kindergarten, kindergarten–early childhood transition), and across time (e.g., beginning-of-year/end-of-year; yearly reevaluations).

Sensitivity

Choose measures, especially the curriculum, that encompass representative task analyses of skills with enough items for adequate floors, ceilings, and transitional ranges (Bracken, 1987). Detailed skill progressions enable psychologists and team members to monitor small increments of learning in a sensitive manner; for example, a skill progression for infant social competence might include this progression: visual recognition of familiar adults → smiling in response to an adult → smiling spontaneously → participating in a reciprocal ball-rolling game initiated by an adult → self-initiating a game.

Adaptability

Include adaptive measures or provisions for accommodating to the child's best response mode and the stimulus characteristics of objects and activities to make the assessment truly handicap-sensitive. Nonverbal measures for language-disordered children and response-contingent toys for children with neuromotor impairments are examples of adaptive strategies.

Treatment-Validity

Select measures that have a high relevance for planning and implementing instruction and therapy. They should sample functional behaviors that form the goals of intervention and suggest specific treatment strategies. They should not emphasize behaviors or tasks because those tasks "survived" the norming process and are effective discriminators of normal and abnormal behavior. Such tasks as "placing pegs in a pegboard" may distinguish children but would have little relevance as an instructional goal. On the contrary, "activating switches on a mechanical toy" may not discriminate well but is a behavior that has high treatment validity and predictive validity for later independent functioning.

Social Validity

Measures should sample the judgments of professionals, parents, peers, and/or the child regarding the importance and acceptability of intervention. This produces a broad ecological survey of means and ends from independent perspectives. The selection of goals, acceptability of intervention strategies, and significance of changes can be assessed through rating scales or other means to register the social validity of the child's program.

Technical Adequacy

As much as possible, psychologists should choose measures with acceptable levels of reliability and validity. However, many preschool measures do not meet established standards (Bracken, 1987). Nevertheless, a convergent assessment approach rests on the concept that multiple measures and sources of information will increase the sample of behavior and, in turn, the validity of the results; the whole battery is greater than the sum of its parts. Psychologists need to be good consumers and balance the technical versus pragmatic advantages and disadvantages of measures. Recall that measures are not inherently invalid; they are invalid for certain purposes. Recall, also, that psychometric properties are not the major concern for choosing measures that are instructionally relevant.

GUIDEPOINT

- Design a convergent assessment battery that includes the four types of measures that collectively meet the seven criteria for batteries.

PROBLEM 2: DETERMINING ELIGIBILITY FOR SERVICES

Ideally, all young children whose early history, behavior, and life circumstances display even the slightest risk factors should be afforded early intervention services. The reality, however, is that only a certain amount of money and professional resources are available even if we mainstreamed all young children in regular preschool and daycare programs. The developmental school psychologist must be an advocate who fights creatively and persistently for the young child and family by "working the system" to an advantage in the face of administrative and regulatory constraints.

Administrative constraints often force us to justify the need for services. Specific diagnostic classifications are giving way to a more general sorting of children. Public Law 99-457 uses the term *developmental delay* as the global classification for young special needs children. Each state is directed to determine its own operational definitions for what constitutes such a "delay." In effect, states can be restrictive or quite liberal in their definitions. Unfortunately, the economics of education and mental health services dictate that most state definitions will represent the former. Yet, federal guidelines allow for the provision for an "at-risk" classification; predictably, many states are ignoring this provision with its implications for "opening the flood gates" to all young children and families who need services.

Psychologists and early intervention teams need a framework that makes sense of the cacophony; they need guidelines that enable them to balance equitably ethical versus practical demands—"what's right versus what's required." To this end, we offer a framework consisting of four criterion strategies for a *child/family-centered perspective for determining program eligibility:* (1) norm-based assessment, (2) criterion-based assessment, (3) judgment-based assessment—team consensus, and (4) ecological assessment—developmental risk classification (see Table 11.3 for a summary of these criteria). We have developed these criteria, which balance conservative and liberal interpretations of "delay," after a thorough review of various state, federal, and professional resources about proposed guidelines to meet the mandates of PL 99-457 (Commonwealth of Pennsylvania, State Board of Education, 1990; Garwood & Sheehan, 1989; Smith & Schakel, 1986). Moreover, recent research demonstrates that eligibility classification procedures that focus exclusively on child deficits or adverse medical events are inadequate and lead to false positive/negative errors in diagnosis. Multivariate screening efforts that differentially weight child, family/environmental, and medical factors result in more accurate estimates (Kochanek, Kabacoff, & Lipsitt, 1990).

Norm-Based Assessment: Child Performance

This strategy is used most often by early intervention programs and is dictated by state regulations. We recommend a criterion approach that requires *corroboration of developmental delay by the congruence of at least two independent sources of diagnostic information.* One source always involves par-

TABLE 11.3. Suggested Program Eligibility Criteria Within a Child/Family-Centered Perspective

Criterion Type	Criteria	Measurement Examples
Norm-Based Assessment: Child Performance	Deviation standard score cut-off of 85 or less in, at least, 1 of 6 domains on a *developmental measure*	Battelle Developmental Inventory (BDI; Newborg al., 1984)
Norm-Based Assessment: Parent Report	Same as above on a rating or interview-based *developmental measure*	Developmental Profile II (Alpern, Boll, & Shearer, 1988)
Criterion-Based Assessment	25% delay in age functioning in, at least, 1 of 6 domains on the curricular tasks of a *developmental measure*	Hawaii Early Learning Profiles (HELP; Furuno et al., 1979, 1986)
Judgment-Based Assessment: Team Consensus	*Team Specs* consensus score of 3 or less in, at least, 1 of 6 domains or 4 or less in 2 of 6 domains **and** *Program Specs* intensity score of 30% or higher in 1 of 10 intervention areas	System to Plan Early Childhood Services (Specs; Bagnato & Neisworth, 1990)
Ecological Assessment: Developmental Risk	*Established risk*—medical condition or syndrome	Medical records
	Biological risk—pregnancy, birth, neurodevelopmental events	(Kochanek, 1990)
	Environmental risk—family, home, and SES factors	Home Observation for Measurement of the Environment (HOME; Caldwell Bradley, 1979)

ent report; the other(s), the assessment results by an early intervention team or diagnostic specialist (e.g., psychologist). *Benchmark: If the parental report of child functioning is lower than the professional estimate, determination of eligibility should weight the lower estimate.* Specific cutoff criteria for service eligibility are suggested below that could be applied with the previous benchmark in mind.

- Child performance on a norm-based developmental measure that converts to deviation standard scores (e.g., developmental quotients) of 85 or less in at least one developmental domain (e.g., language, social, cognitive, play, fine motor, gross motor, self-care, behavior). A common example of such a norm-based measure is the Battelle Developmental Inventory (Newborg, Stock, Wnek, Guidubaldi, & Svinicki, 1984).

Norm-Based Assessment: Parent Report

To determine parental estimates of developmental delay which "factor in" to the criterion formula, one could use the Developmental Profile II (Alpern, Boll, & Shearer, 1986), an interview and observational measure which reports comparative performances by developmental age levels and deviation discrepancy scores.

Criterion-Based Assessment

This strategy uses curriculum-based developmental assessment measures as a vehicle to directly link the purposes of eligibility determination, individualized goal planning, and progress evaluation. The suggested cutoff criteria are the following:

- Child performance on a criterion-based developmental measure (curriculum-referenced) that reports results by developmental ages which can be converted to ratio developmental quotients. Child performance should show at least a 25% delay in developmental age functioning in, at least, one developmental domain with an equivalent ratio developmental quotient of 75 or below. For example, a child with a chronological age of 48 months with a 25% delay would have a developmental age functioning level of 36 months which converts to a ratio quotient of 75. A common example of such a criterion-based measure is the Hawaii Early Learning Profile (Furuno et al., 1985).

Judgment-Based Assessment: Team Consensus

Federal mandates require team assessments, but do not dictate the form of those assessments. Research demonstrates that structured, multisource clinical judgment data provide a reliable and valid vehicle for team decision-making about a child's developmental and service delivery needs (Bagnato, 1984; Bagnato & Neisworth, 1985, 1990; Blacher-Dixon & Simeonsson, 1982; Mattison, Bagnato, & Strickler, 1987). The judgment-based system employed should rely on independent multisource estimates of developmental and behavioral competencies, generate scores that classify degree of functional deficits, and translate to estimates of intervention and service delivery needs. Examples of two such systems are System to Plan Early Childhood Services (SPECS) (Bagnato & Neisworth, 1990a,b) and the Social Skills Rating System (SSRS) (Gresham & Elliott, 1990).

For example, a team could employ SPECS (see Chapters 2 and 12) to structure parent and professional team decision-making; arrive at a "consensus" about child, family, and service delivery needs; determine program eligibility; establish the level and scope of "program intensity" required; and evaluate child progress and program efficacy. SPECS consists of three instruments: Developmental Specs, an individual rating profile; Team Specs, a team consensus and service delivery matrix; and Program Specs, a detailed questionnaire and profile of specific program services and their intensities.

We recommend the following cutoff criteria that must occur on both of the following two Specs components to justify program eligibility using judgment-based team decision-making:

- *Team Specs.* By rating 19 developmental dimensions, the team (which includes the parent) must converge on a consensus score that does not exceed 3 (a mild problem level) in at least 1 of 6 functional domains or does not exceed 4 (at-risk for problems) in 2 of the 6 domains (e.g., communication, sensorimotor, physical, self-regulation, cognitive, self-social).
- *Program Specs.* Concurrently, on the Program Intensity Profile, the team must rate the child on, at least, the 30% level in 1 of 10 program option intervention areas (e.g., early education, adaptive services, behavior therapy, speech/language therapy, physical therapy, occupational therapy, vision services, hearing services, medical services, transition services).

Ecological Assessment: Developmental Risk Classification

Tjossem (1976) has proposed a clinical decision-making model that allows early intervention specialists to sort young children and families into risk-status categories or combinations of categories. This model distinguishes young children and families on a "risk continuum" from definite to presumed risk for developmental disabilities. This model can be used by psychologists on teams composed of other educational, medical, and mental health professionals to determine program eligibility when other data are not available or when other eligibility criteria are not clearly fulfilled. This may be the situation when young children have no obvious current developmental delays, but have life circumstances which are highly correlated with later developmental, learning, and behavioral disorders. Again, the "child-in-the-family" is the client and the objective is to provide services to as many in need as possible.

The three developmental risk categories as described by Tjossem (1976) are

- *Established Risk.* Includes children that have medically diagnosed conditions or syndromes (e.g., Down syndrome, spina bifida, Lesch-Nyhan) which may have specific causes such as genetic and metabolic disorders.

- *Biological Risk.* Includes children whose birth and early developmental histories (e.g., head trauma, toxic insults, diseases, infections, pre and postmaturity, history of maternal drug/alcohol abuse, low Apgar scores) strongly predict the probability of later neurodevelopmental problems. Only a few medical and biological factor risk inventories are available (Kochanek et al., 1990).
- *Environmental Risk.* Includes children within unstable and impoverished physical, social, and home environments that may involve such factors as poor nutrition and health care, child abuse, lack of stimulus and response opportunities, and limited caregiver/child interactions. Professionals determine degree of environmental risk by using a combination of parental report and direct observation measures and rating scales to appraise such variables as adequacy of the home environment, family stress levels, emotional responsivity in caregiving, and opportunities for play and stimulation. Some examples include the Home Observation for Measurement of the Environment (Caldwell & Bradley, 1978) and the Parenting Stress Index (Abidin, 1986). The adequacy of the child's early environment is highly correlated with adaptive behavior and intelligence levels at 3 years of age (Elardo, Bradley, & Caldwell, 1975).

GUIDEPOINTS

- Use eligibility criteria that consider norm, criterion, and judgmental standards.
- Within reasonable administrative and economic constraints, employ as liberal criteria as feasible.

PROBLEM 3:
LINKING ASSESSMENT WITH EARLY INTERVENTION

Individualized program planning for the child and family is the ultimate, overarching mission of early childhood assessment. Simply, early childhood assessment must prescribe preschool programs. The convergent assessment battery described earlier provides the link to treatment that makes these prescriptions possible. The curriculum, of course, establishes the developmental content for the child's Individualized Education Program (IEP) goals as well as indications of the types of behavioral strategies that will be effective for instruction. The curriculum also provides a way to monitor child progress. Judgment-based and ecological scales allow the team to integrate parent perceptions, plan family goals, and broaden the assessment to cover other social and physical settings. The end result is an integrated child/family intervention plan.

PL 99-457 emphasizes the link between assessment and intervention that must exist in service delivery to infants, preschoolers, and families. The law specifies many details of the intervention plan including the type of assessment, domains to be surveyed, parent/family participation, expected outcomes, and the nature of the services. It is clear that services are no longer to be exclusively child-centered. Early intervention services are to be family-focused, with the family as the primary influence and supporting milieu during the infant-preschool years. The question is how best to translate assessment results into goals and strategies for service delivery to both the child and family. New mandates require us to help the family to collaborate with professionals in determining their own child's special needs and to "self-identify" their own family strengths and needs that may affect their capability to support the child's development. Thus, assessment/intervention linkages in early childhood must address both child and family strengths and needs (recall the provisions of PL 99-457 cited in Chapter 1).

Family Needs

The Individualized Family Service Plan (IFSP) is the vehicle or document that links child/family assessment and intervention for young at-risk and handicapped children (see Chapters 5, 7, and 8). The IFSP contains nine elements that make it a "prescriptive" instrument (Table 11.4).

It is clear that the psychologist can play a central role in developing each of these nine program elements. While the child's needs are the focus, the family context and needs are integral to the IFSP. Many newly developed family self-assessment instruments address such issues as stress, needs for information, support from family members and friends, financial matters, housing, nutrition, health care, and transportation. Chapters 7 and 8 discussed and illustrated family collaboration and the development of IFSP goals and strategies. Figure 11.1 illustrates how a simple IFSP format, "Our Family Support Plan," can both integrate family-reported needs and clearly communicate goals to be worked on by the program staff and parents collaboratively (see also Chapter 12 for IFSP).

Child Needs

While the IFSP is designed for infants and toddlers (0–30 months), many states have extended the concept to include all children less than 6 years of age. The IEP remains the primary vehicle for documenting child levels,

TABLE 11.4. Elements of the Individual Family Service Plan

- A multidisciplinary team assessment that can draw on the expertise of educational, developmental, medical, and mental health professionals.
- Parent participation or collaboration with professionals in the team assessment of the child.
- Present levels of child functioning in at least five developmental and behavioral domains: physical, cognitive, language/communication, psycho-social, and self-help.
- Family strengths and needs identified through the parent's personal "self-assessment" rather than external appraisal by professionals.
- Major family outcomes to be achieved with criteria, methods, and time lines detailed.
- Major child outcomes to be achieved with criteria, methods, and time lines detailed.
- The frequency, intensity, and methods of service delivery provided to the preschooler and parents.
- Case manager that provides ongoing coordination of services.
- A transition needs statement for moving from one setting or agency to another that identifies the behavioral requirements of the "receiving environment."

goals, and program elements and is the child portion of the IFSP. IEPs for young exceptional children differ from school-age IEPs in three ways: they are (a) based on a developmental sequence, (b) integrate objectives with contexts, and (c) match goals with strategies (see Chapter 6).

First, the objectives that comprise infant and preschool IEPs are based upon a developmental sequence of competencies in which early primitive skills are prerequisites for later advanced skills. Understandably, the developmental curriculum is the foundation for these goals; assessment and instructional tasks are similar and, thus, linked. Chapter 6 illustrated a developmental task analysis of attention/task completion behaviors and goals for a young child at kindergarten transition (see Figure 6.1). Note that in the developmental model, targeted goals are the "transitional" or emerging skills—those which the child has not completely mastered but has acquired components of the required skills.

Another way in which preschool IEPs differ from school-age is in the integration of content and context (see Chapter 6, Figure 6.2). Preschool IEPs should attempt to foster developmental skills across several natural contexts during the day both in the preschool and at home (Dunst et al., 1987). This organizational approach promotes generalization by placing the young child's learning under wider stimulus control conditions and with different adults (e.g., family members and preschool staff). For example, an infant or toddler can learn to squeeze a toy to produce a sound during preschool play activities and can also squeeze a soap container during bath time routines with a mother at home—same skill, different contextual cues and materials.

Heidi Feldman, MD, PhD
Co-Director
Developmental Support Project

Stephen Bagnato, EdD
Co-Director
Developmental Support Project

Our Family Support Plan

Child: **Lenny**　　Age: **26mo.** Date: **6/89**　Caregiver: **Foster Grandma**

Things we do well to help each other at home

- Love Lenny like our own son
- Make our life with Lenny as normal as possible
- Get care and love from each other

Things we need to help ourselves and our child more

MORE INFORMATION

- How to clean and fix his tracheostomy tube
- what to do if he has a seizure

SUPPORT FROM FAMILY

- Helping our son understand why we adopted Lenny
- Letting my sister help more with Lenny's care

SUPPORT FROM FRIENDS

- Using our church groups to help out

EXPLAINING TO OTHERS

- How to tell others why Lenny must not "rock" himself

COMMUNITY SERVICES

- Getting away with my husband alone — respite care
- Getting his therapist to give me more responsibility

Help our child needs to be his best in our family

■ Playing with toys
<u>switch toys, tapes</u>

■ Playing with others
<u>starting play himself</u>

☐ Moving about

☐ Using eyes/hands together

■ Letting us know things
<u>by sounds & gestures</u>

■ Having energy to do his best
<u>Keeping him off ventilator</u>

FIGURE 11.1. Example of a simple, practical IFSP or Family Support Plan. From *Developmental Support for Special Medically Handicapped Children and Families,* by H. Feldman and S. J. Bagnato, 1988, Washington, DC: US Office of Education and Rehabilitation Services, Handicapped Children's Early Education Programs, Grant H024F 80014. Reprinted by permission,

Finally, preschool IEPs should match developmental goals with instructional and therapeutic strategies. The plan must indicate the frequency, intensity, and method of service delivery and treatment. It is not enough to set short- and long-term goals. Psychologists and other team members must collaborate and implement the most effective strategies for a particular goal. Examples include shaping procedures for cooperative play skills or peer-pairing to foster gradual integration and adjustment in larger groups. Figure 11.2 illustrates a simple, easily understood IEP that emphasizes overarching, interdisciplinary goals for a young medically handicapped toddler. Note how "My Developmental Support Plan" is written from the child's viewpoint and integrates ecological features in the plan also—"In My World" (i.e., "things that help me; things that hurt me").

GUIDEPOINT

- Select measures that directly address the IEP and IFSP requirements to identify child and family needs and goals.

PROBLEM 4: COMMUNICATING ASSESSMENT RESULTS TO PARENTS AND PROFESSIONALS

Psychologists and other professionals rarely write assessment reports that are parent "friendly." Indeed, reports are often not even understandable or useful to teachers or the agencies that request the reports! Surveys of parents and teachers indicate that psychological reports are often laden with jargon, and are test-centered, obtuse, unrelated to referral concerns, and useless for individualized program planning. Much of the difficulty with reports is that traditional formats are foreign to the content and purpose of early intervention services. Traditional psychological reports have several major limitations: they are organized by the tests administered, do not integrate information from diverse sources, focus on psychometric content and scores rather than program content, dwell on the child's diagnoses and comparative deficits, fail to offer intervention guidelines that are applicable to preschool programming, and do not explain results in "parent-friendly" terms.

Four features of effective report writing are used increasingly to solve the problems of communicating assessment results in ways that are treatment-specific, clear, and practical to parents and other interdisciplinary team members: developmentally based reports, graphic performance displays, and question-based reports.

Heidi Feldman, MD, PhD
Co-Director
Developmental Support Project

Stephen Bagnato, EdD
Co-Director
Developmental Support Project

My Developmental Support Plan

Child: __Lenny__   Age: __26 mo.__   Date: __6|27|89__

Things I am good at even though I am sick

- Smile when I hear sounds I like — Michael Jackson tape
- Smile to show I know Rose or grandma
- Finding how to turn on my tape even though I can't see

Things I need help with

WITH PEOPLE (Interactive)

- Moving toward familiar people's voices
- Exploring people's faces with my hands

WITH TOYS/OBJECTS (Adaptive)

- Finding toys I drop around me
- Using a paddle-switch to turn-on tapes and toys

FOR MYSELF (Self-Regulatory)

- Use a walker to move toward people & sound toys
- Help me to get used to food on my lips

IN MY WORLD (Ecological)

Things that help me
- ☐ Quiet times
- ☐ Mobiles I can see
- ■ Sitting upright in my chair
- ☐ Lying prone on my roll
- ■ Toys that sound, move & feel
- ■ Special toys with switches
- ■ Just holding me
- ☐ Peek-a-boo games
- ☐ Getting close to mom/friends
- ■ Having my lips rubbed
- ☐ Finding my body's "safe spot"
- ☐ Watch when I need "time out"
- ☐ Going slow with me

Things that hurt me
- ■ Too much TV/radio noise
- ☐ Too many people at once
- ☐ Playing with me too long
- ■ Always lying on my back
- ☐ Too much light
- ■ Not changing my position
- ■ Too many toys at once
- ☐ Working/playing too fast
- ☐
- ■ _Leaving me alone to "rock"_
- ☐ _____
- ☐ _____
- ☐ _____

FIGURE 11.2. Example of a simple, practical IEP or Develpmental Support Plan. From *Developmental Support for Special Medically Handicapped Children and Families,* by H. Feldman and S. J. Bagnato, 1988, Washington, DC: US Office of Education and Rehabilitation Services, Handicapped Children's Early Education Programs, Grant H024F 80014. Reprinted by permission,

Developmentally Based Reports

The results of applied field research demonstrate that developmentally based assessment reports are significantly more effective than traditional psychological reports with young exceptional children in four ways: (1) they identify a greater number of curriculum-entry points for individualized programming; (2) increase the agreement among team members about targeted goals; (3) are more clear in conveying diagnostic information to parents; and (4) offer a greater number of relevant instructional and behavioral strategies that match the preschool program's missions (Bagnato, 1981; Prus & Prus, 1988). Developmentally based reports are organized by headings that match with the developmental or curricular domains emphasized in most programs (e.g., cognitive, language, perceptual/fine motor, social–emotional, behavioral, gross motor, self-care, preacademic learning, and family needs). Information is not confined to test results but rather allows the diagnostician to integrate information from various sources that clarify the child's and family's status and needs in each area. A synopsis section offers an "advance organizer" or clear, to-the-point summary of the general results for the assessment and the implications of those results for programming and progress monitoring. A specific analysis section describes the child's developmental skills and deficits and the family's judgments with specific examples of behavior and perceptions. Functioning is described by developmental age ranges. Finally, the report concludes with recommendations presented as practical "guidelines for intervention." These guidelines are also organized by headings including instructional arrangements, behavior management, medical follow-up, child and family therapy, and other relevant dimensions specific to the child and family. Most importantly, included in this section are a list of "transitional or emerging skills" that can serve as curriculum-entry points for developmental programming. (See Appendix 11.1 for a sample of portions of a developmentally based report.) Refer to other resources for more detailed examples of alternative report styles (Bagnato, 1981; Bagnato, Neisworth, & Munson, 1989).

Question-Based Reports

Assessment reports are more "friendly" and family-centered when they directly address the concrete concerns of the parents rather than abstract program or psychometric elements. Question-based reports focus the content specifically on the chief questions or concerns presented by the parents (see Appendix 11.2). Such reports are written in colloquial terms that directly answer questions that parents have posed previously in an interview. Common concerns are—

- Why hasn't my child started talking yet?
- Is my child hyperactive?
- Is there a medical reason why my child has tantrums?
- What can we do to help our child catch up with his friends?
- Should we hold our child back from kindergarten?
- Why doesn't punishment seem to work with our child?
- Will my child always be behind in school?

The family interview should explore the parent's perceptions of what is causing a problem and how they have handled it previously. The psychologist should guide the family in posing several central questions that they want answered as a result of the team's evaluation by clarifying and rephrasing their concerns into concrete behavioral terms. In general, parents want three types of questions answered: What's wrong with my child? What will my child be like later? What can be done to help? Of course, the mission of early intervention is to implement interventions that work. Helping parents focus upon the role of intervention in promoting developmental progress is an important outcome in communicating results effectively.

GUIDEPOINTS

- Write reports that are understandable and useful to the intended recipients, and parallel the program's goals.
- Write a separate report or include a question-based section that directly responds to parent questions or "presenting problems."

Graphic Performance Displays

With the use of computers, psychologists and teams are discovering that they can tailor the presentation of assessment results to the family's level of understanding. Simple colored or shaded histograms or *developmental profiles* that illustrate the discrepancy between current developmental age functioning and chronological age within each functional domain can be quickly printed by computer. In addition, these graphic profiles can show learning curves through side-by-side comparisons of program-entry and end-of-year developmental progress levels. This visual display provides a clear and quick overall picture of child functioning; with this point of reference, the psychologist can organize a discussion of the child's skills and deficits with the parents supported by specific behavioral examples.

Developmental continuums are another type of graphic performance display that shows the developmental task analysis of skills within various

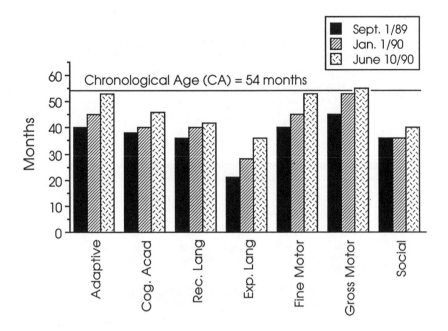

FIGURE 11.3. Example of a Developmental Profile Display. From *The Instrument for Measuring Progress (IMP)* by J. McAllister, 1988, Pittsburgh, PA: Prince George's Co., Maryland Public Schools. Reprinted by permission.

domains for a handicapped preschool child. The psychologist can show parents what skills the child has fully acquired (+), what skills are emerging (±), what skills are absent (−) in the child's repertoire, and under what conditions the child could complete tasks (verbal and manual prompts). The use of linear displays like these simply and clearly conveys the expectations of progress, the developmental "building blocks" of learning, next-step goals, and direct agreement between assessment results and program goals and methods. Figures 11.3 and 11.4 present examples of the developmental profile and developmental continuum methods of graphic performance displays for a sample preschool child.

Both types of developmental profile and developmental continuum performance displays presented in this chapter are taken from a unique developmentally based preschool curriculum-based assessment system entitled Instrument for Measuring Progress (IMP) (McAllister, 1990).

The Instrument for Measuring Progress (IMP) provides an integrated system for curriculum-based assessment, program evaluation, ongoing parent–school communication (i.e., behavioral report cards), and generation of computer assisted IEPs. The IMP uses developmentally sequenced

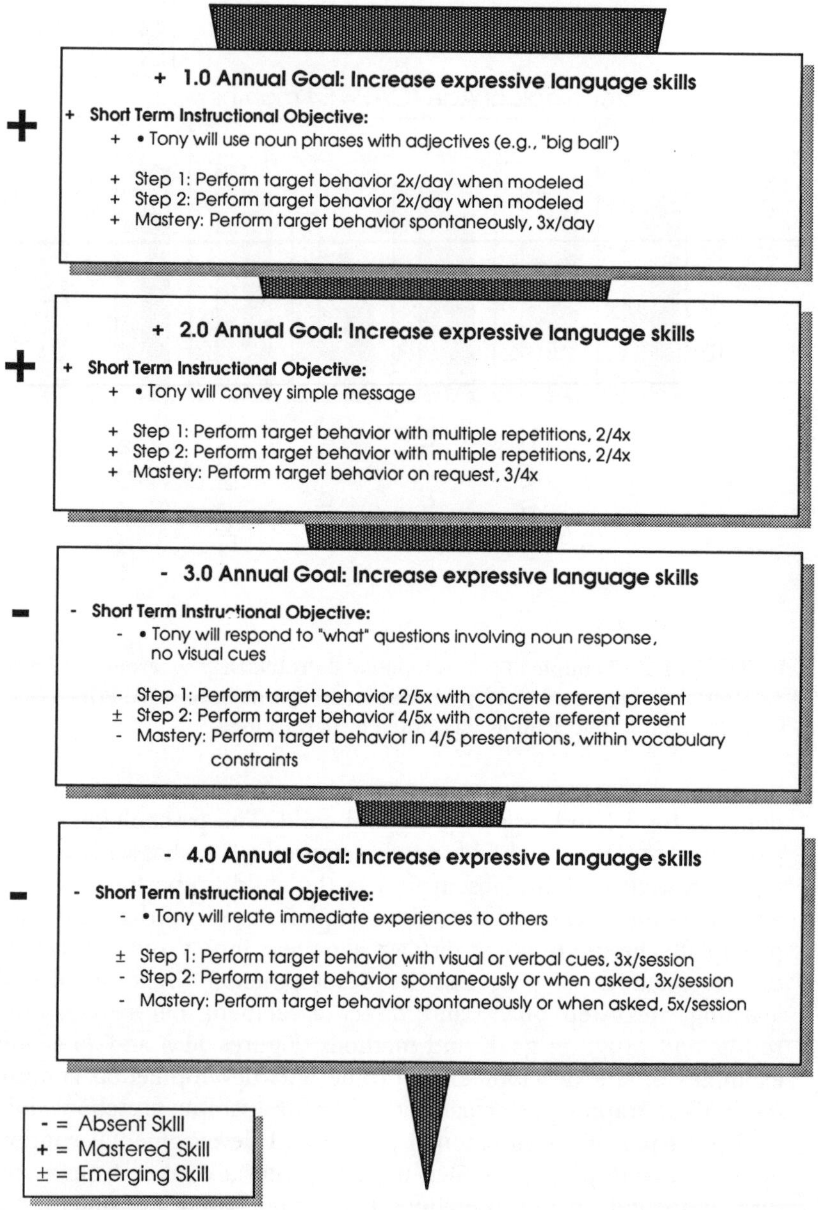

FIGURE 11.4. Example of a Developmental Continuum Display. From *The Instrument for Measuring Progress (IMP)* by J. McAllister, 1988, Pittsburgh, PA: Prince George's Co., Maryland Public Schools. Reprinted by permission.

banks of over 800 educational objectives spanning the birth to 8-year-old range. As objectives are chosen for a child, the computer program automatically calculates developmental levels for the child based on the items selected for the IEP. Scores are stored automatically, can be displayed graphically, and can be aggregated to monitor program effectiveness. The rate of change can be easily determined for an individual child, a classroom, or an entire program.

Each objective includes three steps toward mastery, with the final step representing the mastery criterion for that objective. The use of multiple steps allows for extremely sensitive monitoring of progress in each academic quarter. The report card format of the IMP allows the teacher to quickly check off mastered steps and inform the parents of progress during the reporting period.

The IMP promotes congruity between assessment and instruction. In the process of identifying a student with special needs, the child's educational program is designed and, concurrently, the appropriate measure of progress for that student is specified.

SUGGESTED READINGS

Bagnato, S. J. (1981). Developmental diagnostic reports: Reliable and effective alternatives to guide individualized intervention. *Journal of Special Education, 15*(1), 65–76.

Bagnato, S. J., Neisworth, J. T., & Munson, S. M. (1989). *Linking developmental assessment and early intervention: Curriculum-based prescriptions* (2nd ed.). Rockville, MD: Aspen.

Bricker, D. (1987). *Early intervention with at-risk and handicapped infants and young children.* Palo Alto, CA: VORT.

Kochanek, T. T., Kabacoff, R. I., & Lipsitt, L. P. (1990). Early identification of developmentally disabled and at-risk preschool children. *Exceptional Children, 56*(6), 528–538.

Odom, S. L., & Kannes, M. B. (1988). *Early intervention for infants and children with handicaps: An empirical base.* Baltimore, MD: Paul Brookes.

Smith, B., & Schakel, J. (1986). Noncategorical identification of preschool handicapped children: Policy issues and options. *Journal of the Division for Early Childhood, 11*(1), 78–86.

APPENDIX 11.1
Partial Example of a Developmentally Based Preschool Assessment Report

DIAGNOSTIC DEVELOPMENTAL ASSESSMENT

Referral Reason

TB, age 34 months, was referred for a diagnostic assessment for the purpose of more comprehensively defining her developmental and behavioral deficits and determining her instructional and therapeutic needs within the preschool setting.

Diagnostic Assessment Summary

TB was evaluated in several different situations with Mrs. B. present at the preschool diagnostic center. A previous conference was conducted with both Mr. and Mrs. B at home in order to obtain a developmental history and to initially observe TB's behavior. TB is a young, hearing-impaired child who has been enrolled in the preschool program since September, 1986.

The following battery of developmental diagnostic measures was employed in the current comprehensive evaluation:

Bayley Scales of Infant Development (BSID)
Early Intervention Developmental Profile (EIDP)
Carolina Record of Individual Behavior (CRIB)
Baby Atypical Behavior Index (BABI)

General Analysis

Assessment and observation of TB's skills, deficits, and behavioral style across home, classroom, and clinic settings provided a comprehensive and representative sample of her capabilities and needs. The results of this evaluation are clear in describing TB most accurately as a multihandicapped preschooler. In this regard, she demonstrates a severe bilateral hearing loss for which aides have been fitted; also, TB demonstrates significant deficits in important cognitive, language, social/emotional, and perceptual/fine motor areas that define a severe degree of developmental retardation. Finally, while she reveals many atypical stereotyped behavior patterns, TB does not appear functionally as an autistic child, although her self-involved and repetitive patterns are frequently observed in young children with multiple sensory and developmental deficits. While TB's level of disability is clear, the original cause is not so evident. However, it is probable that her apparent post-maturity contributed to her developmental dysfunctions, as clinical research shows that this is frequently the case with such children. The results of this evaluation will guide the design of a more individualized intervention plan for TB, which will emphasize such areas as play skills, social communication, prerequisite behaviors, behavior management, increased instructional time, and more frequent progress evaluations.

Specific Analysis

It is important to recognize that TB's multiple disabilities interact to compound her deficits in several interrelated functional areas. For example, her severe bilateral hearing loss limits her social communication with other children and adults; her repetitive play behaviors and lack of goal-directed skills also hinder her ability to understand that gestures or sounds have a communicative function. Furthermore, her self-involved and often detached ("tuning out") behavior pattern prevents her from attending to important aspects of toys or to other people's responses to her. Nevertheless, she is beginning to show several important emerging skills, such as imitation, reciprocal give-and-take play, and more pleasant, "aware" emotional reactions to toys and situations, which signal the potential for important functional changes. A clearer definition of her potential for progress hinges on her more intensive involvement in the preschool program and her development of social communication skills and prerequisite behaviors such as attending and waiting.

Cognitive, Social, and Communication Skills

At the present time, TB displays a widely scattered range of cognitive developmental, language, and social skills that span the age range 4–12 months. Her most stable capabilities are similar to those expected of an 8-month-old infant. Thus, her current rate of development is progressing only at 25% of that expected for nonhandicapped preschoolers of her age. This significant deficit in functioning signals the existence of a severe level of developmental retardation (DQ = 24). The table below presents TB's current developmental ages (DA) and developmental rates (DQ) in each major functional area.

Developmental Area	DA (mo.)	DQ
Cognitive	8	24
Language	8	24
Perceptual/Fine Motor	7	22
Social/Emotional	8	23

TB's patterns of play with toys are predominantly repetitive, consisting mostly of fleeting visual inspection, brief manipulation of parts, and banging and throwing characteristic of infant and toddler play styles. Her lack of eye contact and brief attention to only the most stimulating sights and sounds inhibit more mature play. Similarly, TB's communication skills are currently limited to the beginnings of reciprocal play and consist of activities such as rolling a ball and engaging in give-and-take peek-a-boo games with a cloth uncovering her face and that of dolls. Her high activity level also forces her play style to be disorganized and brief, as she flits from toy to toy with little purposeful interaction.

It is encouraging that since joining the preschool, TB has acquired some emerging capabilities that will be important for developing more purposeful problem-solving and social communication skills. She has demonstrated increased vocal and fine motor imitation particularly in small group activities despite her attention deficits. Also, she is responding more consistently to sounds and to her name. The use of response-contingent toys which require her to touch a switch to activate the toy have resulted in greater attention and more appropriate purposeful play with laughing, smiling, and the incentive to try the toy again. Finally, she is beginning to show greater efforts to search for hidden objects in a problem-solving task, although her attention and activity level make this very difficult.

Emotional and Behavioral Characteristics

Because of her sensory and cognitive developmental deficits, TB displays many of the emotional and behavioral characteristics often observed in autistic children, although she does not appear to be primarily an autistic child. However, her detached style of attention and interaction and her rhythmic habit patterns, such as flipping book pages, screaming, making guttural throat noises, and being in constant motion, need to be reduced in frequency and substituted with more purposeful behaviors if progress is to continue. TB has little sense of the value of verbal communication in interacting with others as a way of expressing her wants and needs. Currently, screaming and withdrawal from some activities are her primary methods of communication. Similarly, she shows little distinct variation in her emotional responses and interactions with toys or people. However, once again, the use of response-sensitive toys or toys that stimulate all the senses simultaneously are necessary to encourage greater attending skills and a wider range of smiling, laughing, and purposeful play. Behaviorally, increases must also be promoted in her attention and endurance on tasks, her orientation to objects, her goal-directed play, and her capability to accept another child in face-to-face, more individualized play with a teacher as facilitator.

APPENDIX 11.2
Partial Example of a Question-Based Preschool Assessment Report

• *Are Sally's aggressive and overactive behavior and signs of anxiety significantly different from those of the average girl her age?*
• *Will these specific behaviors prevent her placement in first grade?*

Sally's behavioral adjustment was assessed with the Preschool Behavior Questionnaire and structured classroom observation. Although she shows many irritating and inappropriate classroom behaviors, her overall pattern of behavior, given the responses on the Preschool Behavior Questionnaire, does not deviate significantly from that of the average child.

Sally is a child who does not initially trust strange adults and becomes extremely anxious in situations where she must accompany or be in the presence of strange adults. Her initial reaction is one of anxiety and fearfulness, characterized by crying and noncompliance. This continues until the adult establishes him/herself as comforting and nonthreatening. Once this occurs, her approach to adults is characterized by attention-seeking behaviors and noncompliance. During the classroom observation, she was engaged in task-related behavior for 60% of the 20-minute observation period. This compares favorably with a class average of 75%. However, her off-task behaviors were quite intrusive and disrupting. These behaviors consisted of verbal disruptions, such as interrupting the teacher, or motor disruptions, such as moving her chair around and slapping her hands on the desk. She would hide classroom materials and then refuse to give them to the teacher, making comments such as, "I wanna take this home." She would frankly state her contention not to comply with classroom limits (example: *Teacher:* "Okay, class, it's work time." *Sally:* "No it isn't," in a sing-song voice). These behaviors would certainly place her at risk for school success.

• *Why does Sally have so much difficulty following classroom directions and rules?*
• *Is it because of poor language understanding, poor attention, or just stubbornness?*

Test data and observation indicate that although Sally has a limited expressive vocabulary, her difficulty in comprehending language and complying with requests is primarily associated with inattention to directions or noncompliance. She tests the limits of social rules and engages in negative, attention-seeking behaviors. This is significantly reduced in a one-to-one situation; however, in a larger group situation where she must compete for attention with other children, her behavior deteriorates.

BEST PRACTICE SUMMARY CHECKLIST

Chapter 11

How Can Psychologists Solve Persistent Preschool Assessment Problems?

[ ] 1. Contact your state education/special education bureau and lobby to be a member of the Interagency Coordinating Council (ICC) to influence legislative and regulatory decisions about preschool program eligibility, compliance with PL 99-457, school psychological services, and other matters.

[ ] 2. Work jointly with your state psychology and special education associations to lobby for liberal criteria for program eligibility that stress curriculum-based data, team-based judgments and classifications, and definitions of at-risk status that emphasize family considerations also.

[ ] 3. Take the lead in your program to develop or purchase a computerized curriculum-based developmental assessment/monitoring system that can efficiently perform the functions of comprehensive assessment, goal-planning, and progress evaluation as well as program efficacy studies.

[ ] 4. Devise guidelines and creative ways of reporting assessment/evaluation results to parents in your program. Consider also the parents' readiness to be confronted with bad news and include graphs, computer displays, curriculum goal attainment scaling, and classification by functional level or need for different intensities of service.

12

Assessment for Early Intervention: A Preschool Case Close-up

Paul seemed always to need a little extra time, attention, and help than other children his age. He was born 2 months early (32 weeks gestation) weighing 4 lb, 2 oz. He was delivered by C-section because of an irregular heart beat. At delivery, Paul experienced breathing difficulties and elevated bilirubin levels; he remained in the NICU for $1^1/2$ months. Early on, Paul seemed unable to become accustomed to sleeping, waking, and feeding. His mother described him as irritable, not easily consoled, and "twitchy." His arms and legs seemed in constant motion as he had been in the womb. The first year with Paul was very stressful; he lost weight, could not coordinate sucking and swallowing, and was rehospitalized twice for dehydration and failure to gain weight. In addition, the father left the family causing additional stress for Mrs. Ober.

At about one year of age, Paul's health and development seemed finally to stabilize. He walked at 14 months of age, said his first word at 18 months, and began to play with toys rather than bang, mouth, and throw them. Yet, once he started to walk, he was constantly moving and climbing. Mrs. Ober seemed to be forever chasing after him and spanking him. At about 2 years of age, she became very concerned because he did not seem to say as many words as other preschoolers his age and had not begun to use two-word phrases. He communicated mostly through pointing, pulling, pushing, whining, and the tantrums which were becoming a frequent occurrence. In addition, he would rarely keep playing with a toy for long, quickly losing interest in one and trying another. When Paul was 2 years old, Mrs. Ober sought help for both his behavior and a reason for why he was not talking in sentences. He was given a developmental screening test by the local ARC child-find program. They determined that Paul seemed very capable of using his eyes and hands to match shapes, build with blocks, and to assemble Legos. However, they had difficulty keeping him in a chair; his expressive language skills were most like those of a 15-month-old while his understanding of objects in play seemed nearly age-appropriate. With Mrs. Ober's permission, Paul was enrolled in an early intervention program two half-days per week; he received individual speech/language therapy once a week for 30 minutes. This arrangement continued until he was $3^1/2$ years old when he was enrolled in a Head Start program. Although Paul progressed, Mrs. Ober became increasingly frustrated by his tantrums, lack of attention, poor memory for directions, and problems interacting with peers. His continuing speech problems made this situation worse; moreover, Mrs. Ober was greatly stressed by her role as a single mother and her financial difficulties. With the Head Start teacher's help, Mrs. Ober contacted the diagnostic clinic operated by her local school district now that he was 4 years, 11 months of age to have an in-depth evaluation of Paul. She was greatly worried that without more help, he would never be able to attend kindergarten on time.

SCREEN/IDENTIFY

Needs Assessment

The social worker received Mrs. Ober's call and arranged a meeting and observation within the home. Mrs. Ober presented concerns about Paul's development and behavior as well as her own ability to cope. The social worker interviewed Mrs. Ober and observed Paul's behavior.

While Paul's needs were important in the discussion, Mrs. Ober used the time to talk about her own frustrations as a single mother who received little support from family members. In addition, she was very unsure about her ability to cope in many ways: managing finances, balancing her work with Paul's demanding behavior, and controlling her anxious and lonely feelings. As Mrs. Ober talked, Paul constantly ran about the house, yelled loudly, whined, pulled at her, and tried to sit in her lap to gain her attention. In many ways, his immature behavior was much like that of a $2^1/2$-year-old child's.

The social worker decided to observe Paul's behavior interacting with Mrs. Ober on a few brief game activities that required following rules and cooperating. She decided as well to work with Paul in a more structured manner. Both the social worker and Mrs. Ober independently completed the Preschool Behavior Questionnaire (see Figure 12.1) to compare their independent judgments of the severity of Paul's behavior problems. In addition, Mrs. Ober provided her judgments of Paul's developmental capabilities on the Developmental Specs (D-Specs) (see Figure 12.2).

During the home observation, Paul's behavior varied little. He appeared quite overactive, inattentive, and easily frustrated with tasks that required following rules. Mrs. Ober had much difficulty keeping him in a chair and seemed powerless to manage his yelling, throwing toys, and crying; Paul even slapped her arms with no consequences when he became frustrated. When Paul worked and played with the social worker, he ini-

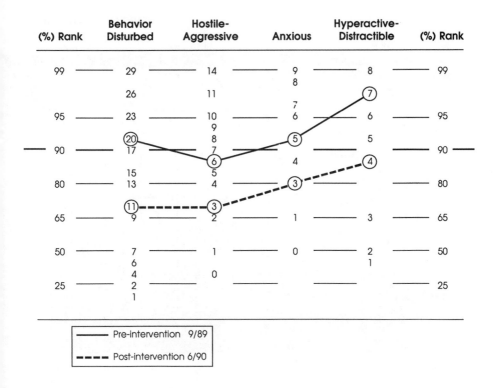

(%) Rank	Behavior Disturbed	Hostile-Aggressive	Anxious	Hyperactive-Distractible	(%) Rank
99	29	14	9 / 8	8	99
	26	11		⑦	
			7		
95	23	10	6	6	95
		9			
	㉑ / 17	8 / 7	⑤	5	
90		⑥		④	90
	15	5	4		
80	13	4	③		80
	⑪	③			
65	9	2	1	3	65
50	7 / 6 / 4	1	0	2 / 1	50
		0			
25	2 / 1				25

———— Pre-intervention 9/89

– – – – Post-intervention 6/90

FIGURE 12.1. Pre/post intervention ratings of Paul's behavior problems on the Preschool Behavior Questionnaire.

tially seemed wary and more self-controlled. However, he eventually resorted to the same behaviors shown with his mother; this time, the social worker followed some warnings with a brief time-out procedure and restraint in a chair. After 5 minutes of crying, Paul calmed and came back to the table to work more calmly.

Comparing ratings, Mrs. Ober and the social worker agreed that Paul's behavior was a problem in several areas and that such misbehavior would likely prevent him from adjusting to kindergarten without help. In addition to his inattention and overactivity, Paul is easily frustrated and can become aggressive with both adults and other children; also, he seems anxious, easily frustrated, and at times, sad (see Figure 12.1). The results of his performance in the Head Start program and Mrs. Ober's judgments show further that Paul has problems in several developmental areas also. In addition to the problems in self-regulation, Paul has trouble using language to express his feelings and needs, following directions, understanding certain concepts, and solving problems that require reasoning with words; his poor self-care skills are a problem also. Mrs. Ober and the social worker agreed that

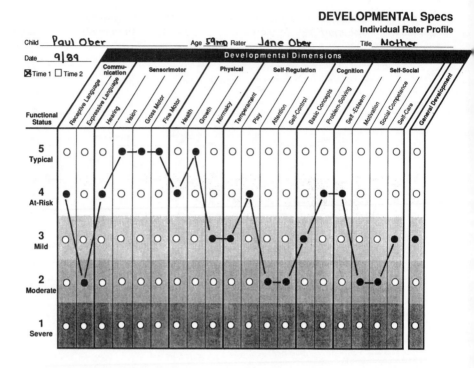

FIGURE 12.2. Mrs. Ober's ratings of Paul's development on the D-Specs.

these results would be presented to the entire assessment team at the Early Childhood Diagnostic Center at the school. The team and Mrs. Ober would then decide how to proceed to determine Paul's eligibility for their program and what needs and services to emphasize.

Team Feedback

The social worker met with the other team members including the developmental school psychologist, speech/language specialist, master kindergarten transition teacher, and occupational therapist. She presented her observations and the developmental and behavioral ratings completed by Mrs. Ober. The team discussed Paul's needs and reviewed his progress within the Head Start program. They concluded that the less-structured Head Start setting may not have effectively addressed prerequisite behavioral needs; the initial impression of the team was that Paul was probably a candidate for their program and was probably at-risk. They decided upon an initial plan to more comprehensively assess Paul. First, they would conduct a collaborative observation and team assessment pairing different clinicians. Paul would be assessed in situ in their own preschool program to observe his trial adjustment to their routines and demands. This would involve a sampling of behavior in individual and group work. The team decided that their curriculum, Help for Special Preschoolers, portions of the Battelle Developmental Inventory, and D-Specs would be used to structure their observations and assessments. Next, they would meet to discuss their initial results and broaden their convergent assessment battery as needed.

ASSESS/PRESCRIBE

Initial Preschool Observations

At first, Paul appeared afraid and reserved when he entered the preschool holding closely to his mother's side. The teacher brought them both to a small table near the game area. Another child approached Paul and gave him a toy; Paul relaxed slightly and left his mother's side to sit at the table with his new friend. However, when the friend reached for the toy to show Paul how it worked, Paul pulled back and pushed the child's hand away with a slap. Mrs. Ober stated to the teacher that this was typical for him when he was with other children; the teacher intervened and explained to Paul that they could both play with the toy, but Paul had to know "how it worked first before they could play together." Paul took the direction and began playing more cooperatively with the new child.

The teacher and the psychologist (with the mother observing) now began to work with Paul together using tasks from the Battelle and HELP to structure their classroom-based assessment. Using pictures, it was clear that Paul knew color, shape, position, and agent–action concepts. However, knowledge of numbers and letters was limited; despite his understanding of some concepts, Paul was very impulsive and distractible. Typically, he did not scan and compare among the four pictures presented but would point to the first one that he observed; frequently, the teacher had to remind him to "look with your eyes before you point with your finger" and "go slow." These verbal directions helped but frequently Paul needed a light touch on the hand to restrain his impulsive pointing. At times, Paul was obviously frustrated by his "wrong answers" and the teacher's holding his hands down as he whined, squirmed, and pushed her hand away, saying "I don't want to do this anymore!" In contrast, on fine motor and perceptual activities, Paul smiled and was motivated as he completed complex shape, animal puzzles, and Lego building games. On drawing tasks, Paul held the pencil awkwardly, drew a simple human form with disjointed lines, and could not write his name or any letters.

During free play activities, Paul chose toys randomly and within a few seconds lost interest and selected another toy briefly; he rarely played cooperatively with other children unless guided by adults. Within a 10-minute period, Paul had three instances in which he yelled or shoved other children who wanted to play with him.

During group circle time, Paul sat and attended well when the games required clapping and imitating movements to songs; yet, when a story was played on the record player, Paul constantly rose to roam the room, talked aloud, and had to be guided back to the group by the aide.

Interim Team Meeting

After the classroom observational assessment, the team (including Mrs. Ober) met to discuss their initial impressions. The mother agreed, in general, with the team that Paul's behavior today was typical of what she experienced at home as well as how he behaved in the Head Start program. His inattentive and impulsive behavioral style coupled with his frustration on language-related tasks would make his classroom adjustment and progress difficult.

At this point, the team selected a Convergent Assessment Battery that targeted Paul's behavioral and learning needs, the requirements of a kindergarten curriculum, and Mrs. Ober's concerns about herself and her family. Table 12.1 presents the individual battery chosen for Paul. The team decided to balance the focus between sampling developmental and more preacademic/academic learning skills. Thus, in addition to the Battelle and HELP measures, they selected the Kaufmann Assessment Battery for Children (K-ABC) to sample reasoning skills that did not require exclusive use of expressive language. A reinforcement system using tokens and verbal and manual prompts would be used to structure the assess-

TABLE 12.1. Convergent Assessment Battery for Paul

Type	Scale	Source
Norm-based	• Kaufmann Assessment Battery for Children	Performance
	• Battelle Developmental Inventory	Performance
Curriculum-based	• Help for Special Preschoolers	Performance
	• Instrument for Measuring Progress	Performance
Judgment-based	• Developmental Specs	Ratings
	• Preschool Behavior Questionnaire	Ratings
Eco-based	• Social Skills Rating System	Observations
	• Parenting Stress Index	Self-Report
	• Family Needs Survey	Self-Report

ment and facilitate and maintain Paul's best attention, effort, and success. The team would use several judgment-based and ecological scales to collect their individual observations and impressions across situations about development, social competence, and the impact of the environment on his performance. Mrs. Ober's family concerns, particularly levels of stress at home, would be reported on the Parenting Stress Index and the Family Needs Survey.

The day following the classroom observation, the team worked with Paul and his mother over a 3-hour period. At times, the speech/language therapist and the psychologist worked together with Paul—one guiding his behavior and maintaining him in his seat, the other presenting assessment tasks. This strategy proved successful and allowed maximum attention to reduce the impact of Paul's inattentive and impulsive behavior on performance. In another session, the psychologist worked alone with Paul using both free play and structured play activities to observe differences in his behavior. Finally, the team observed and recorded the interaction between Mrs. Ober and Paul much as the social worker had in the home. The same difficulties in managing behavior were evident again.

Collaborative Team Decisions for Program Eligibility

After the assessment was completed, the team including Mrs. Ober as a working partner met to discuss Paul's strengths and needs and the family concerns as reported by mother. The focus of the discussion was Paul's readiness for enrollment in a regular kindergarten setting. Decisions about his readiness depended on how well Paul had acquired language, learning, behavioral, and social skills necessary for kindergarten success.

Decisions were reached by combining qualitative information from observations, interviews, and reports and quantitative information from specific scales and curricula derived from various people in various group and individual situations. Both Mrs. Ober and the teacher who worked with him first agreed that without help for his attention, overactivity, and poor interpersonal skills, Paul would never be able to adjust to the demands of a regular setting. While both mother and teacher emphasized Paul's social behavior problems, the teacher stressed his lack of important skills in visual and auditory attention, completing tasks without guidance, and his language problems. Figure 12.3 profiles Paul's mastery of social and attention/task completion skills on the curriculum objectives of Help for Special Preschoolers.

Note that his social and attention skills appear most comparable to those expected at about 36 months of age. His ability to attend and complete tasks depends on almost constant guidance and reinforcement from adults. Socially, he rarely uses words to express his feelings and thoughts and needs help to play cooperatively with peers although he sometimes

HELP FOR SPECIAL PRESCHOOLERS—ASSESSMENT CHECKLIST

CA: 59 mos   68 mos

Age	ID#	Skill/Behavior	Date 9/89	Date 6/90
		20. INTERPERSONAL RELATIONS		
2.8–3.2	20.01	Watches others play and may join in for a few minutes	+	+
2.8–3.2	20.02	Exchanges items for play	+	+
3.0–3.4	20.03	Plays with adult	+	+
3.0–3.6	20.04	Responds to and makes verbal greetings	–	+
3.1–3.6	20.05	Plays with one or 2 others	±	+
3.1–3.6	20.06	Takes turns	–	+
3.7–4.0	20.07	Cooperates with another child during play	±	+
3.7–4.0	20.08	Shows affection for familiar person	+	+
3.8–4.8	20.09	Cooperates with others in group activity	–	+
3.9–4.0	20.10	Plays with group of 3 or more	–	+
3.10–4.4	20.11	Shares toys with other children	–	+
4.0–4.7	20.12	Verbalizes feelings to another prior to physical expression	–	±
4.2–5.6	20.13	Bargains with other children	–	–
5.0–5.5	20.14	Verbalizes feeling to another without hitting	–	±
5.0–5.6	20.15	Comforts playmates in distress	–	±
5.0–5.8	20.16	Plays simple competitive table games	–	±
5.1–6.0	20.17	Cooperates in group games with loose rules		–
5.1–6.0	20.18	Protects other children and animals		–
5.6–6.0+	20.19	Offers help to others voluntarily		–
5.6–6.0+	20.20	Plays difficult games requiring knowledge of rules		–
5.6–6.0+	20.21	Behaves in a courteous manner to others		–
5.10–6.0	20.22	Apologizes without being reminded		–

Learning/Cognitive:

23. ATTENTION SPAN/TASK COMPLETION

			9/89	6/90
2.6–3.0	23.01	Completes 10% of task with some attention and reinforcing	+	+
3.6–4.0	23.02	Starts a task only when reminded	+	+
3.6–4.0	23.03	Completes 10% of task with very little attention	–	+
3.7–4.0	23.04	Attends to task without supervision for 5 minutes	–	+
3.7–4.0	23.05	Works in small group for 5–10 minutes	–	+
3.7–4.0	23.06	Remains on task for 5 minutes when distractions are present	–	±
3.10–4.2	23.07	Completes 25–50% of task with little attention or prompting	–	±
4.1–5.0	23.08	Starts task with no reminding or prompting	–	±
4.1–5.0	23.09	Attends to task without supervision for 10 minutes		–
4.1–5.0	23.10	Remains on task for 10 minutes when distractions are present		–
4.6–6.0	23.11	Works in small group for 10–25 minutes		–
5.1–5.5	23.12	Completes 50–75% of task with little prompting		–
5.4–6.0+	23.13	Attends to task without supervision for 15 minutes		–

FIGURE 12.3. Sampling of Paul's mastery of curriculum-based social and attention skills pre/post intervention. From *Help for Special Preschoolers* by Santa Cruz County Office of Education, 1987, Palo Alto, CA: VORT Corporation. Copyright 1987 by Santa Cruz County Office of Education. Reprinted by permission.

can be cooperative in simple games with adults.

Table 12.2 displays the quantitative results on all the measures used to appraise development and behavior. Note the cross-measure consistency in comparable areas of development across different team members in different situations. In general, the team assessment results converge to indicate that Paul is at-risk in several areas of functioning including language, verbal reasoning, fine motor, social competence, and overall behavior, especially attention and overactivity. Cognitive skills on the K-ABC are described by a composite standard score of 81, which represents reasoning skills typical of those expected for a 48-month-old child. These levels are consistent with Paul's performance on curriculum prerequisites on the HELP (Learning/Cognitive: 42–60 months). Mild problems are observed in various areas including understanding and responding to sequentially presented information, independently eating, dressing, and toileting, relating to peers, managing own behavior, and using language socially. In addition, Mrs. Ober clearly conveys her feelings of isolation, stress, and need for help as well as how greatly she feels the current family situation is affecting Paul's feelings and behavior.

Figures 12.4 through 12.7 portray how the team members reached collaborative decisions and consensus about Paul's instructional and therapeutic needs and services. Overall, the team is in close agreement about Paul's lack of readiness for enrollment in a regular kindergarten program. Some team members offered that he is showing the early indicators of a child who may later be classified as learning disabled and possibly attention-disordered at school-age entrance without intensive services now. Figures 12.4 and 12.5 show the team consensus and each team member's judgments about Paul's functional skills on the Team Specs. No major differences in judgment are evident except in estimates of his expressive language skills; the team agreed that this difference was due to his reluctance to use language (rather than aggressive behavior) with peers in the preschool setting. On the Program Specs (Figures 12.6 and 12.7), the team rated the specific kindergarten transition skills that Paul has not yet acquired. Note that these include the attention, task completion, peer interaction/communication as well as basic skill problems assessed previously. This leads the team to estimate that Paul will need some special services in order to learn basic preacademic and social behavioral skills most effectively (see Figure 12.7). Clearly, Paul is eligible for special support services. Thus, the team decides that the best placement for Paul would be a diagnostic or transitional kindergarten placement for one year. In this setting, the program could balance developmental and academic emphases and focus on shaping prerequisite skills in attending, listening, turn-taking, following routines, and more independent work habits.

TABLE 12.2. Comparative Results Within the Convergent Assessment Battery to Support Program Eligibility for Paul

Type/Scale	Age Level (mo.)	Rate	Outcome
Norm-based			
1. Kaufmann Assessment Battery for Children (psychologist)			
Sequential processing	44	75	Mild
Simultaneous processing	53	89	At-risk
Processing composite	48	81	At-risk
Achievement	48	82	At-risk
2. Battelle Development Inventory (team)			
Personal–social	36	61	Mild
Adaptive	44	75	Mild
Motor	60	101	Typical
Communication	39	66	Mild
Cognitive	49	83	At-risk
Total	46	78	At-risk
Curriculum-based			
3. Help for Special Preschoolers			
Self-help	38–48		Mild
Motor	55–66		Typical
Communication	36–42		Mild
Social skills	30–40		Mild
Learning/cognitive	42–60		Mild/risk
Judgment-based			
4. Developmental Specs/Team Specs (parent/team)			
Communication		3	Mild
Sensorimotor		5	Typical
Physical		5	Typical
Self-regulation		2	Moderate
Cognition		4	At-risk
Self/social		3	Mild
5. Preschool Behavior Questionnaire (parent and teacher)			
Total behavior disturbed		91st %ile	Problem
Hostile–aggressive		65th %ile	Problem
Anxious		92nd %ile	Problem
Hyperactive/distractible		98th %ile	Problem
Eco-based			
6. Social Skills Rating System (teacher)			
Social skills		60	< Average
Problem behaviors		126	> Problems
7. Parenting Stress Index (parent)			
Child domain		85th %ile	Problem
Parent domain		91st %ile	Problem
Total stress		90th %ile	Problem

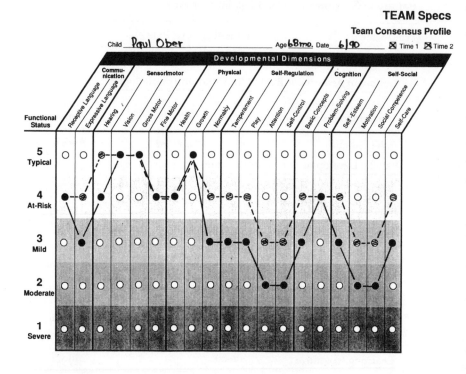

FIGURE 12.4. Pre/post intervention team consensus about changes in Paul's developmental skills on Team Specs.

PROGRAM/INTERVENE

Design the IEP/IFSP

Over the next 3 days, the team discussed the most relevant child goals that should comprise Paul's IEP or Developmental Support Plan and family goals for the IFSP or Family Support Plan (see Tables 12.3 and 12.4). The team identified goals in all major developmental and behavioral domains for Paul. For example, particular emphasis was placed on his need to acquire basic prerequisite skills in selective and sustained attention, cooperative turn-taking in activities and games, and using language instead of aggressive behavior to resolve differences with peers. The team identified a variety of instructional strategies and arrangements that were designed to accomplish these goals—some of which had already proven successful during the assessment sessions. These included verbal and manual prompts, sticker and social praise reinforcers, subvocal reminders, and simulated small group situations to model and practice appropriate behavior with adult guidance.

TEAM Specs
Team Summary

Child Paul Ober Age 59 mo. Date 9/89 ☒ Time 1 ☐ Time 2

Developmental Dimensions

Record each member's ratings Service Options, determine the range, and discuss discrepant ratings to reach a consensus.

	Communication		Sensorimotor				Physical			Self-Regulation				Cognition		Self-Social			
Team Member	Receptive Language	Expressive Language	Hearing	Vision	Gross Motor	Fine Motor	Health	Growth	Normalcy	Temperament	Play	Attention	Self-Control	Basic Concepts	Problem-Solving	Self-Esteem	Motivation	Social Competence	Self-Care
Parent	4	2	4	5	5	5	4	5	3	3	4	2	2	3	4	4	2	2	3
Early Childhood Special Educator	3	3	3	5	5	5	5	5	3	3	3	2	2	3	4	3	2	2	3
Paraprofessional Aide																			
Speech/Language Therapist	4	3	4	5	5	5	5	5	3	3	4	2	2	3	4	3	2	2	3
Developmental School Psychologist	4	3	4	5	5	4	5	5	3	3	3	2	2	3	4	3	2	2	4
Physical Therapist																			
Occupational Therapist																			
Pediatrician																			
Social Worker	4	4	4	5	5	5	4	5	3	3	3	2	3	3	4	4	2	2	3
Vision Specialist																			
Hearing Specialist																			
Preschool Program Supervisor																			
Other																			
Range	3-4	2-4	3-4	0	0	4-5	4-5	0	0	0	3-4	0	2-3	0	0	3-4	0	0	3-4
TEAM CONSENSUS	4	3	4	5	5	4	4	5	3	3	3	2	2	3	4	3	2	2	3

Team Ratings

FIGURE 12.5. Summary of individual team member Developmental Specs ratings for Paul's status on Team Specs.

The IFSP contained family goals that were contributed in collaboration with Mrs. Ober who identified her own and her family's most pressing needs. Mrs. Ober feels that she wants some information, in addition to behavior management techniques, about whether Paul has an Attention-Deficit Hyperactivity Disorder that could be treated by the use of Ritalin; she wanted more information from the psychologist and her pediatrician about this issue so that she could make the best decision since she "heard about it on the Donahue show." Mrs. Ober reports that she needs someone to talk to regularly who can help her make the best decisions, learn how to manage Paul's behavior, and cope with her feelings of loneliness, anxiety, and sadness. Having someone, family or friends, to help her share the burden is what she wants. The team decided that a combination of therapy approaches would have the greatest likelihood of success for Mrs. Ober along with her regular participation in the preschool setting. Helping her to be her own case manager would be one objective of this approach.

3.0 Transition Readiness Checklist

10.10 Which behavior/learning problems or needs listed below must be considered in team decision-making for this child at transition? (Check each that applies.)

		INTENSITY RATINGS
		Time 1 Time 2

Time 1 Time 2

Time 1	Time 2	
■	☑	Inattentive (1)
■	☑	Impulsive (1)
■	☑	Distractible (1)
■	☐	Needs adult guidance to complete tasks (1)
■	☑	Has trouble following classroom routines (1)
■	☑	Lacks self-directed behavior (1)
■	☐	Fails to follow 2- or 3-step directions (1)
■	☑	Has trouble recognizing numbers/letters (1)
■	☐	Has trouble writing numbers/letters (1)
■	☐	Lasks effective peer/adult communication skills (1)
■	☐	Has trouble interacting with peers (1)
■	☑	Lacks sharing, waiting, and turn-taking skills (1)
■	☑	Lasks listening comprehension skills (1)
■	☐	Lacks self-care skills (1)
☐	☐	Lacks mobility skills to move about independently (1)
☐	☐	Other: (1) _____

(Sum values of all options checked under 10.10)

14	8

FIGURE 12.6. Paul's readiness for transition to kindergarten rated by the team on Program Specs.

TABLE 12.3. Sample Developmental Goals from Paul's IFSP: Time 1 and Time 2

Assessed Needs	Goals	Interventions	Progress T 1 9/89	T 2 6/90
Developmental Support Plan				
1. Sustains looking and listening to task for only 30 sec w/o distraction	Completes 10% of task with sustained attention for > 1 min	Verbal reminders: "Look before you point"; pointing cues, stickers and social praise	±	+
2. Selectively looks and listens only briefly before responding impulsively	Discriminates among four pictures after >15 sec of selective comparisons	Pointing cues, verbal reminders, stickers, and social praise	–	+
3. Fails to take turns in social games	Follows simple turn-taking rule in Candyland game 3/4 turns	Simple subvocal verbal reminders: "Wait for my turn"	–	+
4. Shoves peers instead of stating feeling or wants first	Expresses feelings and wants in three consecutive incidents w/o fights	Simulated situations to model behavior first with adult guidance then natural classroom situations	±	+

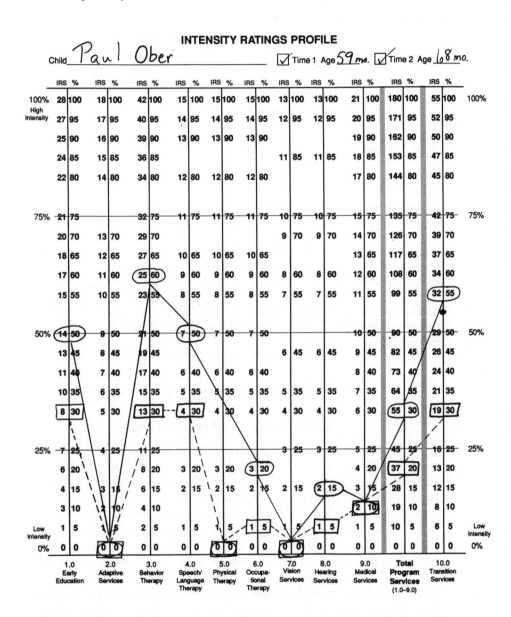

FIGURE 12.7. Intensity of instructional and therapeutic services as prescribed by the team for Paul before and after intervention on Program Specs. Time 1: solid line. Time 2: dashed line.

TABLE 12.4. Sample Family-Identified Goals from Paul's IFSP

Assessed needs	Goals	Interventions	Progress T 1 9/89	T 2 6/90
		Family Support Plan		
1. Feels powerless and anxious with Paul's misbehavior and her job demands	Reduces negative thoughts/fears; organize job tasks	Supportive counseling with social worker	−	±
2. Responds with inconsistent consequences to misbehavior	Learn and apply a plan for contingent rewards and discipline techniques	Behavior management counseling with psychologist	−	+
3. Feels alone and unsupported by family	Widen emotional and physical support from sister and friends	Problem-solving techniques with social worker	−	+
4. Wants information about the use of medication for Paul	Gain information to improve problem-solving	Meet with psychologist; readings on Ritalin	−	+

EVALUATE/MONITOR

Child, Family, and Program Data

Paul and his mother have participated in intensive early intervention services since September (Chronological Age [CA] = 59 months) until June (CA = 68 months). The team's plan emphasized both child and family services in an integrated fashion. For Paul, services stressed enrollment in a highly structured diagnostic or transitional kindergarten placement. The goal-plan targeted the shaping of prerequisite behavioral skills in attention, listening, following directions, turn-taking, peer interaction, resolving conflicts without aggressive behavior, and use of language in a social context. In addition, preacademic goals included the development of pre-reading skills in letter and number identification, listening comprehension, greater independence in self-care skills, and general knowledge of basic concepts as well as understanding and using language. For Mrs. Ober, services stressed a family-centered approach that emphasized involvement in counseling to increase her ability to manage Paul's behavior at home, to problem-solve about her personal, financial, and social situation, and to reduce her feelings of anxiousness and depression. The team used both qualitative and quantitative data to describe the substantial progress made by Paul and his mother.

TABLE 12.5. Evidence of Child's and Mother's Progress and Response to Early Intervention in Selected IFSP and IEP Curricular Areas

Goal area	Time 1		Time 2		Gain	Outcome
	Age	Rate	Age	Rate		
1. Help for Special Preschoolers						
Social	35 mos	59%	60 mos	88%	25 mos	2.0× expected
Attention	36 mos	61%	50 mos	73%	15 mos	1.3× expected
2. Social Skills Rating System						
Social		60		100		Average
Problem behaviors		126		80		< Problems
3. Parenting Stress Index						
Child stress		85%ile		62%ile		No problem
Parent stress		91%ile		55%ile		No problem
Total stress		90%ile		60%ile		No problem

Table 12.5 displays the curricular progress Paul showed over a 9-month period in many of the targeted areas. Rates of progress (ratio developmental quotients as percentages) demonstrate a 25-month gain in the development of crucial social skills—two times the expected rate of progress. Paul's general style of interacting with others is now more typical of that expected of a 5-year-old child. Similar gains are evident in the development of attention skills. Figure 12.3 shows these gains in greater detail on the activity objectives of the HELP curriculum. Paul is now beginning to be more independent in starting a task without reminders by adults and can use some rehearsal strategies on his own. Socially, he can play competitive table games with only a few instances of conflict that he generally resolves by stating his feelings rather than hitting others.

Mrs. Ober has changed dramatically in having a more positive, energetic outlook and feeling in greater control of her ability to manage Paul at home (see Table 12.5). She has joined a parent support group and has even become its leader and a state advocate for learning disabled and attention-disordered children through ACLD. Her ratings on the Parenting Stress Index show that she perceives much less stress in Paul and particularly in herself (90th vs. 60th percentile). Figure 12.1 presents results that corroborate Paul's gains across both Mrs. Ober and Paul's teacher. On the Preschool Behavior Questionnaire, ratings of behavior problems have decreased below the critical range in all areas rated. Some attention problems still persist and signal continuing needs in this area for programming next year.

Collaborative evidence of the program's impact are presented through consensus team data in Figures 12.4 through 12.7. Program intensity scores have decreased from 60% to 30% in the behavior therapy area, 50% to 25% in early education services, and 60% to 35% in transition services. The team agrees that substantial progress beyond initial expectations are evident in all major goal areas with particular gains in the general dimension of self-regulation. However, Paul also shows progress in acquiring basic concepts using language and feeling more positive about himself. On the Transition Readiness Checklist (Figure 12.6), Paul's scores have decreased significantly indicating the need for less restrictive and intensive services next year. He still lacks independence in many skills such as sharing, listening, following classroom rules, and inattention. The continuing attention problems may need to be reviewed to possibly diagnose an Attention-Deficit Hyperactivity Disorder that may respond to a double-blind placebo-controlled Ritalin trial. Continuing services are needed, but Program Intensity scores on the Program Specs (Figure 12.7) have decreased into the low intensity range for the first time in 3 years.

The team and Mrs. Ober have agreed that Paul will be mainstreamed in a regular setting for next year but will need the services of a learning disability specialist and other team members to continue to target prerequisite self-regulatory behaviors and learning skills simultaneously.

References

Abidin, R. R. (1986). *Parenting stress index* (2nd ed.). Charlottesville, VA: Pediatric Psychology Press.

Alberto, P. A., & Troutman, A. C. (1986). *Applied behavior analysis for teachers* (2nd ed.). Columbus, OH: Merrill.

Allen, K. E. (1980). *Mainstreaming in early childhood education.* Canada: Delmar.

Alpern,G., Boll, T., & Shearer, M. (1986). *Developmental Profile II, Manual.* Los Angeles, CA: Western Psychological Services.

Bagnato, S. J. (1981). Developmental diagnostic reports: Reliable and effective alternatives to guide individualized intervention. *Journal of Special Education, 15*(1), 65–76.

Bagnato, S. J. (1984). Team congruence in developmental diagnosis and intervention: Comparing clinical judgment and child performance measures. *School Psychology Review, 13,* 7–16.

Bagnato, S. J. (1990). The inappropriateness of traditional intelligence tests for preschool "diagnosis" (unpublished manuscript).

Bagnato, S. J., & Hofkosh, D. (1990). Curriculum-based developmental assessment for infants with special needs: Synchronizing the pediatric early intervention team. In E. D. Gibbs and D. M. Teti, *Interdisciplinary Assessment of Infants: A Guide for Early Intervention Professionals.* Baltimore: Paul H. Brookes.

Bagnato, S. J., Munson, S. M., & MacTurk, R. (1987). Exceptional infants and toddlers (pp. 180–205). In J. T. Neisworth and S. J. Bagnato (Eds.), *The young exceptional child: Early development and education.* New York: Macmillan.

Bagnato, S. J., & Murphy, J. P. (1989). Validity of curriculum-based scales with young neurodevelopmentally disabled children: Implications for team assessment. *Early Education and Development, 1*(1).

Bagnato, S. J., & Neisworth, J. T. (1980). The Intervention Efficiency Index: An approach to preschool program accountability. *Exceptional Children, 46*, 264–269.

Bagnato, S. J., & Neisworth, J. T. (1985). Efficacy of interdisciplinary assessment and treatment for infants and preschoolers with congenital and acquired brain injury. *Analysis and Intervention in Developmental Disabilities, 5*(1/2), 107–128.

Bagnato, S. J., & Neisworth, J. T. (1985). Assessing young handicapped children: Clinical judgment versus developmental performance scales. *International Journal of Partial Hospitalization, 3*, 13–21.

Bagnato, S. J., & Neisworth, J. T. (1990a). *System to Plan Early Childhood Services* (SPECS). Circle Pines, MN: American Guidance Service.

Bagnato, S. J., & Neisworth, J. T. (1990b). *System to Plan Early Childhood Services—Team Specs.* Circle Pines, MN: American Guidance Service.

Bagnato, S. J., Neisworth, J. T., & Capone, A. (1986). Curriculum-based assessment for the young exceptional child: Rationale and review. *Topics in Early Childhood Special Education, 6*(2), 97–110.

Bagnato, S. J., Neisworth, J. T., & Munson, S. M. (1989). *Linking developmental assessment and early intervention: Curriculum based prescriptions* (2nd ed.). Rockville, MD: Aspen.

Bagnato, S. J., Neisworth, J. T., Paget, K. D., & Kovaleski, J. (1987). The developmental school psychologist: Professional profile of an emerging early childhood specialist. *Topics in Early Childhood Special Education, 7*(3), 75–89.

Bailey, D. B., & Brochin, H. (1989). Tests and test development. In D. Bailey & M. Wolery (Eds.), *Assessing infants and preschoolers with handicaps* (pp. 22–46). Columbus, Ohio: Merrill Publishing Company.

Bailey, D. B., & Simeonsson, R. J. (1988a). *Carolina Institute on Infant Personnel Preparation.* USDE Grant, Early Childhood Research Institute, Washington, DC.

Bailey, D. B., & Simeonsson, R. J. (1988b). *Family assessment in early intervention.* Columbus, OH: Merrill Publishing Company.

Bailey, D. B., & Simeonsson, R. J. (1988c). Home-based intervention. In S. L. Odom & M. B. Karnes (Eds.), *Early intervention for infants and children with handicaps: An empirical base* (pp. 199–215). Baltimore: Paul H. Brookes.

Bailey, D. B., & Wolery, M. (1989). *Assessing infants and preschoolers with handicaps.* Columbus, OH: Merrill Publishing Company.

Blacher-Dixon, J., & Simeonsson, R. J. (1982). Consistency and correspondence of mother's and teacher's assessments of young handicapped children. *Journal of Division for Early Childhood, 3*, 64–71.

Bracken, B. (1987). Limitations of preschool instruments and standards for minimal levels of technical adequacy. *Journal of Psychoeducational Assessment, 4*, 313–326.

Bracken, B., Bagnato, S. J., Barnett, D. (1990). NASP position statement on early childhood assessment. Washington, DC: National Association of School Psychologists.

Brazelton, T. B. (1982). Assessment as a method for enhancing infant development. *Zero to Three, 2*(1), 1–8.

Brigance, A. H. (1978). *BRIGANCE Diagnostic Inventory of Early Development.* Worcester, MA: Curriculum Associates.

Brigance, A. H. (1985). *BRIGANCE Prescriptive Readiness: Strategies and practice.* North Billerica, MA: Curriculum Associates.

Bromwich, R. (1981). *Working with parents and infants: An interactional approach.* Baltimore: University Park Press.

Bronfenbrenner, U. (1975). Is early intervention effective? In B. Z. Friedlander, G. M. Sterritt, & G. E. Kirk (Eds.), *Exceptional infant* (Vol. 3, pp. 449–475). New York: Brunner/Mazel.

Bronfenbrenner, U. (1979). *The ecology of human development: Experiments by nature and design.* Cambridge, MA: Harvard University Press.

Brown, S. L., D'Eugenio, D. B., Drews, J. E., Haskin, B. S., Lynch, E. W., Moersch, M. S., & Rogers, S. J. (1981). *Preschool developmental profile.* Ann Arbor: University of Michigan Press.

Byrne, E. A., & Cunningham, C. C. (1985). The effects of mentally handicapped children on families: Conceptual review. *Journal of Child Psychology and Psychiatry, 26,* 847–864.

Caldwell, B., & Bradley, R. (1978). *Home observations for measurement of the environment.* Little Rock, AR: University of Arkansas, Human Development.

Carey, W. B., McDevitt, S. C., & Fullard, W. (1975). *Behavioral style questionnaire.* Media, PA: W. B. Carey.

Carr, R. (1979). Goal attainment scaling as a useful tool for evaluating progress in special education. *Exceptional Children, 46,* 88-95.

Casto, G. (1988). Research and program evaluation in early childhood special education. In S. Odom and M. Karnes (Eds.), *Early intervention for infants and children with handicaps: An empirical base* (pp. 51–62). Baltimore: Paul H. Brookes.

Clark, G. N., & Siefer, F. C. (1985). Assessment of parents' interactions with their developmentally delayed infants. *Infant Mental Health Journal, 6,* 214–225.

Clark, L. (1985). *SOS! Help for parents.* Bowling Green, KY: Parents Press.

Commonwealth of Pennsylvania, State Board of Education (1990). *Special Education Standards and Regulations.* Harrisburg, PA: Bureau of Special Education.

Cummings, S. T. (1976). The impact of the child's deficiency on the father: A study of fathers of mentally retarded and chronically ill children. *American Journal of Orthopsychiatry, 46,* 246–255.

Cytrynbaum, S., Ginath, Y., Bindwell, I., & Brandt, L. (1979). Goal attainment scaling: A critical review. *Evaluation Quarterly, 3,* 5–40.

Danielson, E. (1989). Expanding skills: Preparing to assess infants and preschoolers. *Preschool Interests, 4*(3), 3–9.

Dunst, C. J., Trivette, C. M., & Deal, A. G. (1988). *Enabling and empowering families: Principles and guidelines for practice.* Cambridge, MA: Brookline Books.

Dunst, C. J., Lesko, J. J., Holbert, K. A., Wilson, L. I., Sharpe, K. L., & Liles, R. F. (1987). A systemic approach to infant intervention, *Topics in Early Childhood Special Education, 7*(2), 19–37.

Elardo, R., Bradley, R., & Caldwell, B. (1975). The relation of infant's home environment to mental test performance from six to thirty-six months: A longitudinal analysis. *Child Development, 46*(1), 71–76.

Farran, D. C., Kasari, C., Comfort, M., & Jay, S. (1986). *Parent/Caregiver Involvement Scale.* Unpublished rating scale. Available from Dale Farran, Department of Child Development and Family Relations, University of North Carolina, Greensboro, NC 27412–5001.

Favell, J. E. (1982). Self-injurious behavior (special issue). *Analysis and Intervention in Developmental Disabilities, 2*(1), 1–125.

Fewell, R. R. (1983). The team approach in infant education. In S. G. Garwood & R. R. Fewell (Eds.), *Educating handicapped infants: Issues in development and intervention* (pp. 299–322). Rockville, MD: Aspen.

Fink, W. T., & Sandall, S. R. (1980). A comparison of one-to-one and small group instructional strategies with developmentally disabled preschoolers. *Mental Retardation, 18,* 34–35.

Fivars, G. (1980). *The critical incident technique: A bibliography* (2nd ed.). Palo Alto, CA: American Institute for Research.

Fotheringham, J. B. (1983). Mental retardation and developmental delay. In K. D. Paget & B. A. Bracken (Eds.), *The psychoeducational assessment of preschool children* (pp. 207–223). Orlando, FL: Grune and Stratton.

Fuchs, D. (1987). Examiner familiarity effects on test performance: Implications for training and practice. *Topics in Early Childhood Special Education, 7*(3), 90–104.

Fuchs, D., Fuchs, L. S., Benowitz, S., & Barringer, K. (1987). Norm-referenced tests: Are they valid for use with handicapped students? *Exceptional Children, 54*(3), 263–271.

Furuno, S., O'Reilly, A., Hoska, C. M., Instauka, T. T., Allman, T. L., & Zeisloft, B. (1985). *Help for Special Preschoolers.* Palo Alto, CA: VORT Corporation.

Gallagher, J. J., Beckman, P., & Cross, A. H. (1983). Families of handicapped children: Sources of stress and its amelioration. *Exceptional Children, 50,* 10–19.

Garber, H., & Heber, F. (1977). The Milwaukee Project: Implications of the effectiveness of early intervention in preventing mental retardation. In P. Mittler (Ed.), *Research to practice in mental retardation: Care and intervention* (Vol. 1). Baltimore: University Park Press.

Garwood, S. G. (1982). (Mis)use of developmental scales in program evaluation. *Topics in Early Childhood Special Education, 6*(3), 72–86.

Garwood, S. G., & Sheehan, R. (1989). *Designing a comprehensive early intervention system.* Austin, TX: PRO-ED.

Golin, A. K., & Ducanis, A. J. (1981). *The interdisciplinary team.* Rockville, MD: Aspen.

Gresham, F., & Elliott, S. (1990). *Social Skills Rating System* (SSRS). Circle Pines, MN: American Guidance Service.

Gresham, F. J., Reschly, D. J., & Carey, M. P. (1987). Teachers as "tests": Classification accuracy and concurrent validation in the identification of learning disabled children. *School Psychology Review, 16*(4), 543–553.

Haeussermann, E. (1958). *Developmental potential of preschool children.* New York: Grune & Stratton.

Hains, A. H., Fowler L. K., & Chandler, S. A. (1988). Planning school transitions: Family and professional collaboration. *Journal of the Division for Early Childhood, 12,* 108–115.

Hanson, M. J., & Lynch, E. W. (1989). *Early intervention: Implementing child and family services for infants and toddlers who are at-risk or disabled.* Austin, TX: PRO-ED.

Harms, T., & Clifford, R. (1980). *Early childhood environment rating scale.* New York: Columbia University/Teachers College Press.

Harrison, P., Lynch, E., Rosander, K., & Borton, W. (1990). Determining success in interagency collaboration: In evaluation of processes and behaviors. *Infants and Young Children, 3*(1), 69–78.

Healy, A., Keese, P., & Smith, B. (1989). *Early services for children with special needs: Transactions for family support* (2nd ed.). Baltimore: Paul H. Brookes.

Holm, V. A., & McCartin, R. E. (1978). Interdisciplinary child development team: Team issues and training in interdisciplinariness. In K. E. Allen, V. A. Holm, & R. E. Schiefelbusch (Eds.), *Early intervention: A team approach* (pp. 97–122). Baltimore: University Park Press.

Holroyd, J. (1974). *The questionnaire on resources and stress for families with a chronically ill or handicapped member: Manual.* Brandon, VT: Clinical Psychology.

Johnson, L. J., & Beauchamp, K.D. (1989). Preschool assessment measures: What are teachers using? *Journal of the Division for Early Childhood, 12*(1), 70–76.

Joiner, L. M. (1977). *A technical analysis of the variation in screening instruments and programs in New York State.* New York: New York Center for Advanced Study in Education (ERIC Document Reproduction Service No. ED 154 596).

Kabler, M. L., & Genshaft, J. L. (1983). Structuring decision-making in multidisciplinary teams. *School Psychology Review, 12*(2), 150–159.

Kaiser, S. M., & Woodman, R. W. (1985). Multidisciplinary teams and group decision-making techniques: Possible solutions to decision-making problems. *School Psychology Review, 14*(4), 457–470.

Kiresuk, T., & Lund, S. (1976). Process and measurement using goal attainment scaling. In G. V. Glass (Ed.), *Evaluation studies review manual* (Vol. 1). Beverly Hills, CA: Sage.

Klaus, R., & Gray, S. (1968). The early training project for disadvantaged children: A report after five years. *Monographs of the Society for Research in Child Development, 33* (4, serial no. 120).

Kochanek, T. T., Kabacoff, R. I., & Lipsitt, L.P. (1990). Early identification of developmentally disabled and at-risk preschool children. *Exceptional Children, 56*(6), 528–538.

Lazar, I., & Darlington, R. (Eds.). (1978). Lasting effects after preschool (final report, DHEW Grant 90C-1311 to the Education Commission to the States). Washington, DC: Department of Health, Education and Welfare.

Leigh, J. E., & Riley, N. (1982). Learning disabilities in the early years: Characteristics, assessment, and intervention. *Topics in Learning and Learning Disabilities, 2*(3), 1–15.

Le Laurin, K. (1985). The experimental analysis of the effects of early intervention with normal, at-risk, and handicapped children under three. *Analysis and Intervention in Developmental Disabilities, 5*, 129–150.

LeVan, R. (1990). Clinical sampling in the assessment of young, handicapped children: Shopping for skills, *Topics in Early Childhood Special Education, 10*(3).

Linder, T. W. (1990). *Transdisciplinary play-based assessment: A functional approach to working with young children.* Baltimore: Paul H. Brookes.

MacTurk, R., & Neisworth, J. T. (1978). Norm referenced and criterion based measures with preschoolers. *Exceptional Children, 45*(1), 34–39.

Mahoney, G., Finger, I., & Powell, A. (1985). Relationship of maternal behavior style to the development of organically impaired mentally retarded infants. *American Journal of Mental Deficiency, 90*, 296–302.

Mattison, R. M., Bagnato, S. J., & Strickler, E. (1987). Diagnostic importance of combined parent and teacher ratings on the Revised Behavior Problem Checklist. *Journal of Abnormal Child Psychology, 15*(4), 617–628.

McDonald, L., Kysela, G. M., Siebert, P., McDonald, P., & Chambers, J. (1989). Parent perspectives: Transition to preschool. *Teaching Exceptional Children, 22*, 4–8.

Meisels, S. J. (1985). *Developmental screening in early childhood: A guide* (rev. ed.). Washington, DC: National Association for Education of Young Children.

Meisels, S. J. (1987). Uses and abuses of developmental screening and school readiness testing. *Young Children, 1*, 4–8.

Meisels, S. J., & Shonkoff, J. P. (1990). *Handbook of early childhood intervention.* New York, NY: Cambridge University Press.

Meisels, S. J., & Wiske, M. S. (1988). *Early Screening Inventory.* New York: Teachers College Press.

Mercer, C. D., Algozzine, B., & Trifiletti, J. J. (1979). Early identification: Issues and considerations. *Exceptional Children,* September, 52–54.

Michigan Department of Education. (1984). *Superintendent's study group on early childhood education.* Lansing, MI: Author.

Minuchin, P. (1985). Families and individual development: Provocations from the field of family therapy. *Child Development, 56*, 289–302.

NASP/APA Preschool Interest Group. (1987). Preschool practices, problems and issues. *Preschool Interests, 2*(3), 1–11.

Neisworth, J. T., & Bagnato, S. J. (1986). Curriculum-based developmental assessment: Congruence of testing and teaching. *School Psychology Review, 15*(2), 180–199.

Neisworth, J. T., & Bagnato, S. J. (1987). *The young exceptional child: Early development and education.* New York: Macmillan.

Neisworth, J. T., & Bagnato, S. J. (1988). Assessment in early childhood special education: A typology of dependent measures. In S. L. Odom & M. L. Karnes (Eds.), *Early intervention for infants and children with handicaps* (pp. 23–49). Baltimore: Paul H. Brookes.

Newborg, J., Stock, J., Wnek, L., Guidubaldi, J., & Svinicki, J.S. (1984). *Battelle Developmental Inventory.* Allen, TX: DLM/Teaching Resources.

Paget, K. D., & Nagle, R. J. (1986). A conceptual model of preschool assessment. *School Psychology Review, 15*(2), 154–165.

Piaget, J. (1952). *The origins of intelligence in children.* New York: International Universities Press.

Pollaway, E. A. (1987). Transition services for early age individuals with mild mental retardation. In R. N. Ianacone & R. A. Stodden (Eds.), *Transition issues and directions* (pp. 11–24).

Prus, J. S., & Prus, A.S. (1988). *Early childhood assessment: Developmentally-based psychological reports,* paper presented at NASP, Conference, Chicago, IL.

Rogers, S. J., Donovan, C. M., D'Eugenio, D. B., Brown, S. L., Lunch, E. W., Moersch, M. S., & Schafer, D. S. (1981). *Early Intervention Development Profile.* Ann Arbor: University of Michigan Press.

Romney, D. (1976). Treatment progress by objective: Leikesuk's and Sherman's approach simplified. *Community Mental Health Journal, 12,* 286–290.

Rosenberg, S., Robinson, C., Finkler, D., & Rose, J. (1987). An empirical comparison of formulas evaluating early intervention program impact on development. *Exceptional Children, 54*(3), 213–219.

Rutter, M. (1972). *Maternal deprivation reassessed.* Harmondsworth, Middlesex, England: Penguin Books.

Schakel, J. (1987). NASP position statement on early intervention in the schools. *Preschool Interests,* 5–18.

Schopler, E., Reichler, R. J., & Renner, B. R. (1988). *The Childhood Autism Rating Scale* (CARS). Los Angeles: Western Psychological Services.

Sheehan, R., & Keogh, B. (1982). Design and analysis in the evaluation of early childhood special education programs. *Topics in Early Childhood Special Education, 1*(4), 81–88.

Shonkoff, J. P. (1983). The limitations of normative assessments of high–risk infants. *Topics in Early Childhood Special Education, 2*(1), 29–41.

Simeonsson, R. J. (1986). *Psychological and developmental assessment of special children.* Boston: Allyn & Bacon.

Simeonsson, R. J., Huntington, G., & Short, R. (1982). Individual differences and goals: An approach to the evaluation of child progress. *Topics in Early Childhood Special Education, 1*(4), 71–80.

Simner, M. L. (1983). The warning signs of school failure: An updated profile of the at-risk kindergarten child. *Topics in Early Childhood Special Education, 3,* 17–27.

Smith, B., & Schakel, J. (1986). Noncategorical identification of preschool handicapped children: Policy issues and options. *Journal of the Division for Early Childhood, 11*(1), 78–86.

Tavormina, J., Ball, N., Dunn, R., Luscomb, B., & Taylor, J. (1977). *Psychosocial effects of raising a physically handicapped child on the parents.* Unpublished manuscript, University of Virginia.

Thurman, S. K., & Widerstrom, A. H. (1990). *Infants and young children with special needs: A developmental and ecological approach* (2nd ed.). Baltimore: Paul H. Brookes.

Tjossem, T. D. (1976). *Intervention strategies for high risk infants and young children.* Austin, TX: PRO-ED.

Turnbull, A. P., & Turnbull, H. R. (1986). *Families, professionals, and exception-*

ality: A special partnership. Columbus, OH: Merrill.

Ulrey, G., & Rogers, S. J. (1982). *Psychological assessment of handicapped infants and young children.* New York: Thieme-Stratton.

Umansky, W. (1983). Assessment of social and emotional development. In K. D. Paget & B. A. Bracken (Eds.), *The psychoeducational assessment of preschool children* (pp. 417–441). Orlando FL: Grune and Stratton.

Vietze, P. & Coates, D. (1986). Using information processing strategies for early identification of mental retardation. *Topics in Early Childhood Special Education, 6*(3), 72–86.

Wachs, T. D., & Sheehan, R. (1988). *Assessment of young developmentally disabled children.* New York: Plenum.

Wertlieb, D. (1979, June). Applied developmental psychology: New directions? *APA Monitor,* 10–14.

Winton, P. J., & Turnbull, A. P. (1981). Parent involvement as viewed by parents of preschool handicapped children. *Topics in Early Childhood Special Education, 1,* 11–19.

Wolery, M. (1983). Proportional change index: An alternative for comparing child change data. *Exceptional Children, 50,* 167–170.

Woodruff, G., & McGonigel, M. J. (1988). Early intervention team approaches: The transdisciplinary model. In J. B. Jordan, J. J. Gallagher, P. L. Hutinger, & M. B. Karnes (Eds.), *Early childhood special education: Birth to three* (pp. 164–181). Reston, VA: The Council for Exceptional Children.

Zigler, E., & Balla, D. (1982). Selecting outcome variables in evaluation of early childhood special education programs. *Topics in Early Childhood Special Education, 1*(4), 11–22.

APPENDIX A
Modal Convergent Assessment Batteries for Young Children with Special Needs

ASSESSMENT BATTERIES BY DEVELOPMENTAL AGE

TABLE 1. Developmental Delay: At Risk and Mild Status

Assessment Type	Battery
	Newborn/Infant (0–6 mos)
Norm-based	Kent Infant Development Scale (1985) *or* Gesell Developmental Schedules (1980) *or* Uzgiris-Hunt Infant Psychological Development Scales (1980)
Curriculum-based	Carolina Curriculum (1986) *or* Infant Learning (1981)
Judgment-based	Brazelton Neonatal Behavioral Assessment Scale (1984) *and* Infant Temperament Scale (1977)
Eco-based	Nursing-Child Assessment Satellite Training (1978)
	Infant (6–12 mos)
Norm-based	Bayley Scales of Infant Development (1969)
Curriculum-based	Carolina Curriculum (1986) *or* Infant Learning (1981)
Judgment-based	Early Coping Inventory (1988) *or* Infant Temperament Scale (1977) *or* Trandisciplinary Play-based Assessment (1990)
Eco-based	Parent Behavior Progression (1979) *and* Home Observation for Measurement of the Environment—Form I (1978)

(cont'd)

TABLE 1. *(cont'd)*

Assessment Type	Battery
	Toddler (12–24 mos)
Norm-based	Griffiths Mental Development Scales (1970)
Curriculum-based	Hawaii Early Learning Profile (1979) *or* Carolina Curriculum (1986)
Judgment-based	Toddler Temperament Scale (1978)
Eco-based	Infant Daycare Rating Scale (1989) *and* Home Observation for Measurement of the Environment— Form I (1978)
	Toddler/Preschool (24–36 mos)
Norm-based	Griffiths Mental Development Scales (1970) *or* Battelle Developmental Inventory (1984)
Curriculum-based	Hawaii Early Learning Profile (1979) *or* Carolina Preschool Curriculum (1990)
Judgment-based	System to Plan Early Childhood Services (1990) *and* Child Behavior Checklist (1986) *and* Transdisciplinary Play-based Assessment (1990)
Eco-based	Family Needs Survey (1985)
	Preschool (36–48 mos)
Norm-based	Battelle Developmental Inventory (1984) *or* McCarthy Scales of Children's Abilities (1972)
Curriculum-based	Help for Special Preschoolers (1987) *or* Carolina Preschool Curriculum (1990)
Judgment-based	System to Plan Early Childhood Services (1990) *and* Child Behavior Checklist (1986) *or* Social Skills Rating System (1990)
Eco-based	Home Observation for Measurement of the Environment— Form II (1978) *and* Early Childhood Environment Rating Scale (1980)

TABLE 1. *(cont'd)*

Assessment Type	Battery
Preschool/Kindergarten Transition (48–72 mos)	
Norm-based	Kaufman Assessment Battery for Children (1984) *or* McCarthy Scales of Children's Abilities (1972) *and* Bracken Basic Concept Scale (1984)
Curriculum-based	Beginning Milestones (1986) *and* Bracken Basic Concept Curriculum (1984)
Judgment-based	System to Plan Childhood Services (1990) *and* Child Behavior Checklist (1986) *or* Social Skills Rating System (1990)
Eco-based	Parenting Stress Index (1986) *and* Early Childhood Environment Rating Scale (1980)

ASSESSMENT BATTERIES BY HANDICAP/DISORDER

TABLE 2. Developmental Delay: Adaptive-to-Handicap

Assessment Type	Battery
Communication	
Norm-based	Kaufman Assessment Battery (1984) *and/or* Leiter International Performance Scale (1948) *and* Preschool Language Scale (1979)
Curriculum-based	Developmental Communication Curriculum (1982) *or* Sequenced Inventory of Communication Development (1975)
Judgment-based	System to Plan Early Childhood Services (1990)
Eco-based	Parent Behavior Progression (1979)

(cont'd)

TABLE 2. *(cont'd)*

Assessment Type	Battery
	Developmental Retardation
Norm-based	Griffiths Mental Development Scales (1970) *or* Uniform Performance Assessment System (1981)
Curriculum-based	Carolina Curricula (1986, 1990) *or* Early Learning Accomplishment Profile (1978) *or* Developmental Programming for Infants and Young Children (1981)
Judgment-based	System to Plan Early Services (1990) *and* Carolina Record of Individual Behavior (1985)
Eco-based	Parent Behavior Progression (1979) *or* Home Observation for Measurement of the Environment— Forms I, II (1978) *and* Early Childhood Environment Rating—Special Needs Edition (1980)
	Neuromotor
Norm-based	Battelle (1984) *and/or* Pictorial Test of Intelligence (1964) *and* Peabody Developmental Motor Scales (1986)
Curriculum-based	Developmental Programming (1981)
Judgment-based	System to Plan Early Childhood Services (1990)
Eco-based	Teaching Skills Inventory (1985) *or* Parenting Stress Index (1986)

TABLE 2. *(cont'd)*

Assessment Type	Battery
	Autism
Norm-based	Battelle (1984) *or* Leiter (1948)
Curriculum-based	Individualized Assessment and Treatment (1979)
Judgment-based	System to Plan Early Childhood Services (1990) *and* Childhood Autism Rating Scale (1988) *or* Transdisciplinary Play-based Assessment (1990)
Eco-based	Parenting Stress Index (1986) *and* Family Needs Survey (1985) *and* Social Skills Rating System (1990)
	Visual
Norm-based	Reynell-Zinkin Developmental Scales (1979)
Curriculum-based	Project Oregon Curriculum for Blind and Visually Impaired Preschool Children (1979)
Judgment-based	System to Plan Early Childhood Services (1990) *and* Maxfield Scale of Social Maturity for Blind Preschool Children (1957)
Eco-based	Family Needs Survey (1985)
	Hearing
Norm-based	Hiskey-Nebraska Test of Learning Aptitude (1966) *and* Scales of Early Communication Skills (1975) *or* Bracken Basic Concept Scale (1984)
Curriculum-based	Clark Early Language Program (1981) *or* TOTAL Communication (1986)
Judgment-based	System to Plan Early Childhood Services (1990) *or* Transdisciplinary Play-based Assessment (1990)
Eco-based	Family Needs Survey (1985)

(cont'd)

TABLE 2. *(cont'd)*

Assessment Type	Battery

Multihandicap

Norm-based	Wisconsin Behavior Rating Scale (1980)
Curriculum-based	Carolina Curriculum (1986) *or* Callier-Azusa Scale for Deaf-Blind Children (1974)
Judgment-based	System to Plan Early Childhood Services (1990) *and* Carolina Record of Individual Behavior (1985)
Eco-based	Parenting Stress Index (1986) *and* Family Support Scale (1984)

Learning Disabled/Attention Disorder

Norm-based	Kaufman Assessment Battery (1984) *and* Bracken Basic Concept Scale (1984) *or* Woodcock-Johnson Psychoeducational Battery—Preschool Cluster (1977)
Curriculum-based	Beginning Milestones (1986) *and* Bracken Basic Concept Curriculum (1984)
Judgment-based	System to Plan Early Childhood Services (1990) *and* Preschool Behavior Questionnaire (1974) *or* Attention-deficit Disorders Evaluation Scale (1988) *or* Preschool Behavior Problem Checklist (1988) *or* Pictorial Scale of Perceived Competence and Social Acceptance for Young Children (1980)
Eco-based	Social Skills Rating System (1990) *and* Parenting Practices Scale (1987)

TABLE 2. *(cont'd)*

Assessment Type	Battery
	Prematurity
Norm-based	Uzgiris-Hunt (1980)
Curriculum-based	Infant Learning (1981) *or* Carolina Curricula (1986, 1990)
Judgment-based	Brazelton (1984) *and* Early Coping Inventory (1988)
Eco-based	Nursing-Child Assessment (1978) *and* Parent Behavior Progession (1979)
	Traumatic Brain Injury
Norm-based	Uzgiris-Hunt (1980) *or* Battelle (1984)
Curriculum-based	Developmental Programming (1981)
Judgment-based	Carolina Record of Individual Behavior (1985) *or* Brazelton (1984) *and* Rancho Pediatric Cognitive Recovery Scale (1986)
Eco-based	Parent Perception Inventory (1988) *or* Questionnaire on Resources and Stress (1974)
	Affective-Behaviorial Disorder
Norm-based	McCarthy Scales (1972) *or* Leiter (1948)
Curriculum-based	Individualized Assessment and Treatment (1979)
Judgment-based	System to Plan Early Childhood Services (1990) *and* Child Behavior Checklist (1986)
Eco-based	Social Skills Rating System (1990) *or* Pictorial Scale of Perceived Competence and Social Acceptance for Young Children (1980) *and* Parenting Practices Scale (1987)

APPENDIX B
Assessment Devices

Adaptive Performance Instrument (API) (1980). Gentry, D (Ed.)   Moscow, Idaho: C.A.P.E., University of Idaho.

Attention Deficit Disorders Evaluation Scale (1988). Carney, S. B.   Columbia, MO: Hawthorne Educational Services.

Battelle Developmental Inventory (BDI) (1984). Newborg, J., Stock, J., Wnek, L., Guildubaldi, J., & Svinicki, J. S. Allen, TX: DLM/Teaching Resources.

Bayley Scales of Infant Development (1969). Bayley, N. San Antonio, TX: Psychological Corporation.

Beginning Milestones (BM) (1986). Sheridan, S., Murphy, D., Black, J., Puckett, M., & Allie, E. C. Allen, TX: DLM/Teaching Resources.

Behavioral Style Questionnaire (1975). Carey, W. B., McDevitt, S. C., & Fullard, R. Media, PA: W. B. Carey.

Bracken Basic Concept Scale (1984). Bracken, B. A. San Antonio, TX: Psychological Corporation.

Brazelton Neonatal Behavioral Assessment Scale (BNBAS) (1984). Brazelton, T. B. Philadelphia, PA: J. B. Lippincott.

BRIGANCE Diagnostic Inventory of Early Development (1978). Brigance, A. H. North Billerica, MA: Curriculum Associates.

Callier-Azusa Scale: Assessment of Deaf–Blind Children (1974). Stillman, R. Reston, VA: The Council for Exceptional Children.

Carolina Curriculum for Handicapped At-risk Infants (1986). Johnson-Martin, N. M., Jens, K. G., & Attermeir, S. Baltimore, MD: Paul H. Brookes.

Carolina Curriculum for Preschoolers with Special Needs (1990). Johnson-Martin, N. M., Attermeir, S. M., & Hacker, B. Baltimore, MD: Paul H. Brookes.

Carolina Record of Individual Behavior (CRIB) (1985). Simeonsson, R. J. Chapel Hill, NC: University of North Carolina.

Child Behavior Checklist (1986). Achenbach, T. M. Burlington, VT: University of Vermont.

Childhood Autism Rating Scale (CARS) (1988). Schopler, E., Reichler, R. J., & Renner, B. R. Los Angeles, CA: Western Psychological Services.

Clark Early Language Program (1981). Clark, C. & Moore, D. Allen, TX: DLM.

Developmental Communication Curriculum (1982). Hanna, R. P., Lippert, E. A., & Harris, A. B. Columbus, OH: Charles E. Merrill Publishing Company.

Developmental Profile II (DP II) (1986). Alpern, G. D., Boll, T. J., & Shearer, M. S. Los Angeles, CA: Western Psychological Services.

Developmental Programming for Infants and Young Children (1981), Vols. 1–3 Early Intervention. Vol. 5 Preschool Development Profile (PDP). Moersch, M., & Schafer, D. S. Ann Arbor, MI: University of Michigan Press.

Developmental Specs (1990). Bagnato, S. J., & Neisworth, J. T. Circle Pines, MN: American Guidance Service.

Differential Ability Scales (1990). Elliott, C. D. San Antonio, TX: Psychological Corporation.

Early Childhood Environment Rating Scale (ECERS) (1980). Harms, T., & Clifford, R. Columbia University, NY: Teachers College Press.

Early Coping Inventory (1988). Zeitlin, S., Williamson, G., & Szczepanski, M. Bensenville, IL: Scholastic Testing Service.

Early Intervention Developmental Profile (EIDP) (1981). Rogers, S. J., D'Eugenio, D., Brown, S., Donovan, C., & Lynch, E. Ann Arbor, MI: University of Michigan Press.

Early Learning Accomplishment Profile (E-LAP) (1978). Le May, D. W., Griffin, P.M., & Sandford, A. R. Winston-Salem, NC: Kaplan School Supply.

Early Screening Inventory (ESI) (1988). Meisels , S. J., & Wiske, M. S. New York, NY: Teachers College Press.

Early Screening Profiles (ESP) (1990). Harrison, P., Kaufman, N., Bruininks, R., Rynders, J., Ilmer, S., Sparrow, S., Cicchetti, D., & McCloskey, G. Circle Pines, MN: American Guidance Service.

Fagan Test of Infant Intelligence (1987). Fagan, J. Cleveland, OH: Infantest.

Family Information Preference Inventory (1986). Turnbull, A. P., & Turnbull, H. R. Columbus, OH: Charles E. Merrill Publishing Company.

Family Needs Survey (FNS) (1985). Bailey, D. B., & Simeonsson, R. J. Chapel Hill, NC: Families Project, University of North Carolina.

Gesell Developmental Schedules (1980). Knoblock, H., & Pasamanick, B. New York: Harper & Row.

Griffiths Mental Development Scale (1970). Griffiths, R. England: Test Agency.

Haessermann Educational Evaluation: Psychoeducational Evaluation of the Preschool Child. (1972). Haessermann, E., Jedrysek, E., Pope, E., & Wortis, J. New York, NY: Grune & Stratton.

Hawaii Early Learning Profile (HELP) (1979). Furuno, S., O'Reilly, A., Hosaka, C. M., Inatsuda, T. T., Allman, T. L., & Zeisloft, B. Palo Alto, CA: VORT Corporation.

Help for Special Preschoolers (HELP-SP) (1987). Santa Cruz County Office of Education. Palo Alto, CA: VORT Corporation.

HICOMP Preschool Curriculum (1983). Willoughby-Herb, S., & Neisworth, J. T. San Antonio, TX: Psychological Corporation.

Hiskey-Nebraska Test of Learning Aptitude (1966). Hiskey, M. Lincoln, NE: Author.

Home Observation for Measurement of the Environment (HOME) (1978). Caldwell, B., & Bradley, R. Little Rock, AR: University of Arkansas, Human Development.

Individualized Assessment and Treatment for Autistic and Developmentally Disabled Children (1979). Schopler, E. & Reichler, R. Austin, TX: PRO-ED.

Infant Learning: A Cognitive–Linguistic Intervention Strategy (1981). Dunst, C. Austin: TX: PRO-ED.

Infant Temperament Scale (1977). Carey, W., & McDevitt, S. Media, PA: W.B. Carey.

Infant/Toddler Daycare Rating Scale (1989). Harms, T. New York: Teachers College Press.

Infant/Toddler Environmental Rating Scale (1989). Harms, T., Cryer, D., & Clifford, R.M. New York, NY: Teachers College Press.

Instrument for Measuring Progress (IMP) (1988). McAllister, J. Pittsburgh, PA: Prince George's County, Maryland Public Schools.

Kaufman Assessment Battery for Children (1984). Kaufman, A. S., & Kaufman, N. L. Circle Pines, MN: American Guidance Service

Kent Infant Development Scale (1985). Reuter, J., & Bickett, L. Kent, OH: Developmental Metrics.

Learning Behaviors Scale (LBS) (1988). Stott, D. H., McDermott, P. A., Green, L. F., & Francis, J. San Antonio, TX: Psychological Corporation.

Leiter International Performance Scale (LIPS) (1948). Leiter, R. G. Chicago, IL: Stoelting Company.

Maternal Behavior Rating Scale (1985). Mahoney, G. J., Finger, I., & Powell, A. Farmington, CT: University of Connecticut, School of Medicine.

Maxfield-Bucchholz Social Maturity Scale (1957). Maxfield, J., & Bucchholz, B. Louisville, KY: American Printing House for the Blind.

McCarthy Scales of Children's Abilities (1972). McCarthy, D. San Antonio, TX: Psychological Corporation.

Minneapolis Preschool Screening Inventory (MPSI) (1980). Lichtenstein, R. Minneapolis, MN: Minneapolis Public Schools.

Mullen Scales of Early Learning (1990). Mullen, R. Cranston, RI: TOTAL Child Inc.

Nursing-Child Assessment Satellite Training (NCAST): Feeding Scale and Teaching Scale (1978). Barnard, K. Seattle, WA: University of Washington, NCAST Training.

Oregon Project Curriculum for Visually Impaired & Blind Preschoolers (1979). Simmons, V., & Mehtvin, J. Medford, OR: Jackson County Education Service District.

Parent Behavior Progression (1979). Bromwhich, R. Austin, TX: PRO-ED.

Parent/Caregiver Involvement Scale (1985). Farran, D., Kasari, C., Comfort, M. & Jay, S. Greensboro, NC: University of North Carolina, Dale Farran.

Parent Perception Inventory (1988). Hymovich, D. P. Philadelphia, PA: University of Pennsylvania, Department of Nursing.

Parenting Practices Scale (1987). Strayhorn, J. Pittsburgh, PA: Allegheny General Hospital Early Intervention Research Institute.

Parenting Stress Index (1986). Abidin, R. R. Charlottville, VA: Pediatric Psychology Press.

Peabody Developmental Motor Scales (1986). Folio, M., & Fewell, R. Allen, TX: DLM.

Pictorial Scale of Perceived Competence and Social Acceptance for Young Children (1980). Harter, S. Denver, CO: University of Denver, Psychology Department.

Pictorial Test of Intelligence (1964). French, J. L. Chicago, IL: Riverside Publishing Company.

Planned Activities Check (1972). Doke, L., & Risely, T. Lawrence, KS: University of Kansas.

Preschool Behavior Problem Checklist (1988). Quay, H.C. Coral Gables, FL: University of Miami, Department of Psychology.

Preschool Behavior Questionnaire (PBQ) (1974). Behar, L., & Stringfield, S. Durham, NC: Published in U.S.A.

Preschool Developmental Profile (1981). Brown, S. L., & Donovan, C. M. Ann Arbor, MI: University of Michigan Press.

Preschool Language Scale (1979). Zimmermann, I. L., Steiner, V. G., & Pond, K. E. San Antonio, TX: Psychological Corporation.

Program Specs (1990). Bagnato, S. J., Neisworth, J. T., & Gordon, J. Circle Pines, MN: American Guidance Service.

Questionnaire on Resources and Stress (1974). Holroyd, J. Brandon, VT: Clinical Psychology Publishing.

Reynell-Zinkin Developmental Scales—Visually Impaired (1979). Reynell, J., & Zinkin, K. Chicago, IL: Stoelting Co.

Scales of Early Communication Skills (1975). Moog, J. & Geers, A. St. Louis, MO: Central Institute for the Deaf.

Sequenced Inventory of Communication Development (1975). Hedrick, J., Prather, J., & Tobin, B. Seattle, WA: University of Washington Press.

Social Interaction Scan (1988). Guralnick, M. Seattle, WA: University of Washington.

Social Skills Rating System (SSRS) (1990). Gresham, F. M., & Elliott, S. N. Circle Pines, MN: American Guidance Service.

Study of Children's Learning Behaviors (SCLB) (1988). Stott, D. H., McDermott, P. A., Green, L. F., & Francis, J. San Antonio, TX: Psychological Corporation.

System to Plan Early Childhood Services (SPECS) (1990). Bagnato, S. J., & Neisworth, J. T. Circle Pines, MN: American Guidance Service.

Teaching Skills Inventory (1985). Robinson, C. Omaha, NE: University of Nebraska.

Team Specs (1990). Neisworth, J. T., & Bagnato, S. J. Circle Pines, MN: American Guidance Service.

Toddler Temperament Scale (1978). Carey, W., McDevitt, S., & Fullard, W. Media, PA: W.B. Carey.

TOTAL Communication (1986). Witt, B., & Boose, J. Tucson, AZ: Communication Skill Builders.

Transactional Intervention Program (TRIP) (1986). Mahoney, G. J., & Powell, A. Farmington, CT: Pediatric Research and Training Center, University of Connecticut Health Center.

Transdisciplinary Play-based Assessment: A functional approach to working with young children (1990). Linder, T. Baltimore, MD: Paul H. Brookes.

Uniform Performance Assessment System (1981). Haring, N., White, D., Edgar, E., Affleck, J. & Hayden, A. San Antonio, TX: Psychological Corporation.

Uzgiris-Hunt Infant Psychological Developmental Scales (IPDS). Dunst Revision (1980). Dunst, C. J. Austin, TX: PRO-ED.

Wisconsin Behavior Rating Scale (1980). Song, A., & Jones, S. Madison, WI: Center for the Developmentally Disabled.

Woodcock-Johnson Psychoeducational Battery-Preschool Cluster (1977). Woodcock, R W., & Johnson, M. B. Allen, TX: DLM/ Teaching Resources.

Index